Heroes of the Crimea

HEROES OF THE CRIMEA

THE BATTLES OF BALACLAVA AND INKERMAN

Michael Barthorp

BLANDFORD

Blandford
An imprint of Cassell
Villiers House, 41/47 Strand, London WC2N 5JE

Copyright © 1991 Michael Barthorp

All rights reserved.
No part of this publication may be
reproduced or transmitted in any form
or by any means, electronic or mechanical,
including photocopying, recording or any
information storage or retrieval system,
without prior permission in writing
from the publishers.

First published 1991

Distributed in the United States by
Sterling Publishing Co. Inc.
387 Park Avenue South, New York, NY 10016–8810

Distributed in Australia by
Capricorn Link (Australia) Pty Ltd
PO Box 665, Lane Cove, NSW 2066

British Library Cataloguing in Publication Data
Barthorp, Michael
    Heroes of the Crimea: Balaclava and Inkerman.
    1. Crimean War
    I. Title
    947.073

ISBN 0 7137 2102 2

Typeset by Bookworm Typesetting

Printed and bound in Great Britain by the Bath Press, Avon

Contents

List of Maps

The maps are redrawings, plus additions, based on Victorian sources. On Maps 4–7 the numbers next to the symbols for military units are either British and French regimental numbers or British and Russian divisional numbers; letters refer to British artillery batteries or Guards regiments.

Preface

In the great wars against Napoleon, the Kaiser and Hitler, Britain and Russia were, for the most part, allies. Since 1945, however, the most serious military threat to Britain has been posed by the Soviet Union, while for the greater part of the nineteenth century it was the expansionist schemes of tsarist Russia that most menaced the security of the British Empire. Yet only once have the differences between the two nations had to be resolved by force of arms – in the conflict known in history as the Crimean War of 1854–56.

The British Army of that war has not, on the whole, had what might be termed 'a good press', compared with, say, Wellington's Peninsular Army, the Expeditionary Force of 1914, or the South Atlantic Task Force of 1982. Undoubtedly there had been a tendency for the Army to rest on its laurels since the defeat of Napoleon. Moreover, although the parts of the Army stationed overseas had fought numerous campaigns in India and other colonies since 1815, there had been no likelihood of its being tested in Europe, where peace had reigned for nearly 40 years. The Army that went to war in 1854 was certainly to reveal very serious command, staff and administrative failings. However these shortcomings, highlighted by such famous follies as the Light Cavalry Brigade's charge at Balaclava, have tended to overshadow the fact that much had been done, or was in hand when war broke out, to modernize the Army after 'the long peace'. The performance of British officers and men of the lower ranks, when confronting a European enemy for the first time since Waterloo, would show another side to the coin of well-documented inefficiency. The Light Brigade's charge itself –

with its command and staff muddle redeemed by the discipline and gallantry of the regiments which made it – is a good example of the antithesis within the Army at the time.

The Battle of Balaclava, of which this charge formed but one phase, heralded the first major Russian effort to eject the invaders from the Crimea. This counter-offensive culminated 11 days later in the Battle of Inkerman, a struggle of far greater consequence than Balaclava, yet which has received far less attention. Those autumn days of 1854 presented the British soldier with the severest test of his fortitude he had faced since Waterloo, or would face for many years to come. The purpose of this book is to examine how he coped with it.

In his book *The Weary Road*, about his experiences in the Great War, Charles Dowie wrote: 'The very atmosphere of a battle defies description and eludes the imagination. Words cannot convey even a suggestion of the sounds heard and the emotions felt, when every faculty is heightened, when every nerve is tense'. If Dowie felt this when writing of what he himself had undergone, how much more difficult must be any attempt to reconstruct battles of nearly 140 years ago. The best that can be done is to try and explain what happened, and why, and to rely on the words of those who fought – some of them men of little education, and in some cases writing years after the event – to give some flavour of what it was really like to be in action in the Crimea at that bleak time.

The spelling of Russian names follows the practice first adopted by A.W. Kinglake and emulated by most English writers on the war: for example,

Menshikoff, rather than Menshikov; Taroutine and Katherinburg Regiments, not Tarutinsky and Ekaterinburgsky; Sebastopol, not Sevastopol; Sapouné, not Sapun.

A note on the different significance of the word 'regiment' in the opposing infantry may be helpful. The British infantry, less the Foot Guards and Rifle Brigade, comprised a quantity of numbered regiments, all having one battalion (the basic infantry unit), each of eight companies. Guards regiments and the Rifle Brigade had two or more battalions, each also of eight companies, but the battalions of such regiments did not fight together. Russian infantry regiments had numbers and names (only the latter being used herein), but they consisted of four battalions, each of four companies, each regiment being a tactical entity. The French practice was comparable to the Russian, but with regiments of two battalions, each of eight companies. The approximate war establishment of British and French battalions was 1,000 all ranks, of Russian 950, although by the autumn of 1854 the actual fighting strength of all three types of battalion was more of the order of 600.

The sources used herein are listed at the end of the book. But anyone attempting to write of the Crimean War would be failing in gratitude if he did not acknowledge a special debt to the memory of A.W. Kinglake for his examination of so many eyewitnesses to produce his massive and masterly *The Invasion of the Crimea*. Dr Hew Strachan's two books on military reform and developments between 1815–54 (see Sources) have been invaluable for a picture of the Army of the period. The works of John Shelton Curtiss and Colonel Albert Seaton have been most useful for the Russian viewpoint. John Keegan's *The Face of Battle*, though not dealing with the Crimea, has provided much food for thought, both about how to contend with Charles Dowie's above-quoted observation, and what motivates men in battle.

Thanks are also due to many individuals and institutions for suggestions, the loan of texts, assistance with illustrations or help in other ways. In alphabetical order these are: Colonel Paul Adair, Mr David Cliff, Major Peter Cutler, Lieutenant-Colonel M.J. Evetts, Major Michael Farrow, Mr Nicholas Fitzherbert, Mr Peter Harrington, Mr Philip Haythornthwaite, the Right Reverend Michael Mann, Major Patrick Mercer, Major P.J.R. Mileham, Mr Alan Mitchell, Mr John Mollo, Major Frederick Myatt, Major John Peters, Mr David Rowlands, Brigadier K.A. Timbers, Lieutenant-Colonel Philip Trousdell, Brigadier Hugh Tyler, Colonel R.C. Walker, Major Hugo White, Mr D. Whybrow; the Army Museums Ogilby Trust, Imperial War Museum, London Library, National Army Museum, Parker Gallery, Paul Mellon Centre for British Art, Science Museum; the Royal Scots Dragoon Guards, Queen's Royal Irish Hussars, Royal Hussars, Royal Artillery Institution, Grenadier Guards, Coldstream Guards, Guards Museum, Royal Highland Fusiliers, Royal Regiment of Wales, Worcestershire and Sherwood Foresters Regiment, Queen's Lancashire Regiment, Duke of Edinburgh's Royal Regiment, Middlesex Regiment Museum, Argyll and Sutherland Highlanders, Rifle Brigade Museum Trust, the Staff College.

Special debts of gratitude are owed to General Sir John Akehurst for reading the text in typescript and for making many useful suggestions, as well as other assistance, to Mrs Sheila Watson for her support and encouragement, and to Alix Baker for her four skilfully drawn maps (Maps 4-7) of the operations around Inkerman.

MJB
Jersey, CI

PART

I

TO THWART THE RUSSIAN BEAR

Come all you gallant British hearts
Who love the red and blue.
Come drink a health to those brave lads,
Who made the Russians rue.
Fill up your glass and let it pass,
Three cheers and one cheer more,
For the fourteenth of September,
Eighteenhundred fifty four.

CORPORAL JOHN BROWN
GRENADIER GUARDS

1

Cheer, Boys, Cheer!

I

Reveille was sounded in London at three o'clock that chill February morning in 1854. In the crowded and fetid rooms of St George's Barracks, then just behind the National Gallery, sergeants called the roll by the flickering light of lanterns. The Guardsmen of the Grenadiers' 3rd Battalion had had little sleep that night as, contrary to all precedent, the barracks had been thronged with women – wives, sweethearts, even whores from the nearby Haymarket and Leicester Square. The Adjutant, Captain George Higginson, returning late from a farewell dinner, had been astonished by this alarming break with the Guards' strict discipline, and had spent the night trying to maintain order. However, when the NCOs reported, not a man was missing.

Shortly before five, now clad in their bearskin caps and swallow-tailed red coatees and laden with heavy marching order, the Guardsmen filed out from the National Gallery to fall in by companies in Trafalgar Square. Despite the early hour, a huge crowd had gathered and greeted the troops with an enthusiasm which Higginson 'never saw equalled'.[1] Throughout the march to Waterloo Station, the cheering crowds increased, people in night clothes waved from windows along the Strand, and the police lining the still gaslit streets had difficulty restraining the populace from breaking into the ranks to shake the men's hands. At the station the farewell cries rose above the band playing 'The British Grenadiers' as the train steamed out for Southampton docks.

Similar scenes had accompanied the 1st Coldstream Guards' departure a week before. Rumours of war with Russia had been rife since the previous July and war fever had intensified since November. As will be seen, a bellicose Russophobia gripped most of the nation, but the government led by Lord Aberdeen still held out against a declaration of war and the departure of the Guards was only a precaution, their destination being no further than Malta.

A week after the Grenadiers left, it was the turn of the 1st Scots Fusilier Guards.* As befitted their alleged reputation as the Queen's favourites, they marched from Wellington Barracks to parade at Buckingham Palace before Queen Victoria, the Prince Consort and four royal children. That evening Victoria wrote to her Uncle Leopold:

The last battalion of the Guards passed through the courtyard at seven o'clock this morning. We stood on the balcony to see them – the morning fine, the sun rising over the towers of old Westminster Abbey – and an immense crowd collected to see these fine men, cheering them immensely. They formed line, presented arms, and cheered us *very heartily*, and went off cheering. It was a touching and beautiful sight . . . . My best wishes and prayers will be with them all.[2]

As the battalion marched out of the forecourt the band played 'O where and O where has my Highland laddie gone', changing to 'Annie Laurie' in which the accompanying crowds joined.

Throughout February, March and into April, all over the United Kingdom, bands, drums and fifes, or pipers were playing their regiments to stations

---

* Scots Guards from 1877.

and docksides, chiefly to the 'Tipperary' of the day, the lively, if sentimental:

Cheer, boys, Cheer!
No more of idle sorrow.
Courage, true hearts, shall bear us on our way.
Hope points before, and shows the bright tomorrow,
Let us forget the darkness of today

These were ironical words, as events would show. Through the streets of Portsmouth, crowded with Easter holidaymakers, clattered the 17th Lancers, their lance-pennons fluttering above their leather caps, their dark-blue jackets contrasting with the sombre mass of dark green and black leather of the 2nd Rifle Brigade. Among the Riflemen marched a woman, her hair cut, armed, and dressed in uniform, one of the wives not 'on the strength' but determined not to be left behind. Soldiers' wives who had failed the ballot for the lucky four per company permitted to accompany their husbands became the responsibility of their parish, but the Rifles, having not long since returned from Cana-

The 3rd Grenadier Guards marching through Trafalgar Square on the morning of 22 February 1854, *en route* for the East. An engraving by Pound after Kunsley.

da, had many wives from that country who had no parish and consequently became a problem for the Portsmouth authorities. In contrast, and officially aboard the SS *Medway*, was a Winchester woman, 25-year-old Mrs Nell Butler, wife of a private in the 95th (Derbyshire) Regiment. Seven months later she would earn the praises of the doctors as she tended the Inkerman wounded.

Woolwich dockyard was a hive of activity in mid-March as the guns, limbers, wagons and horses of the Royal Artillery's field batteries were hoisted on to transports. A day later the men of C Troop, Royal Horse Artillery, some of the smartest and most professional soldiers in the Army in their dark-blue, hussar-style uniforms, loaded their lighter guns, unaware of the important part they would play in the defence of a small harbour none of them could have heard of – Balaclava.

The 1st Scots Fusilier Guards cheering the Royal Family at Buckingham Palace before leaving for the East on 2 March. After G.H. Thomas.

In Ireland, the 11th Hussars prepared for embarkation, their officers sending their unique cherry-coloured trousers to the tailors to be reinforced with black leather. The regiment's well-publicized appearance owed much to its rich colonel, Lord Cardigan, recently appointed to command the Light Cavalry Brigade. The 11th's spectacular turn-out was ridiculed by *The Times* of 22 April 'as utterly unfit for war service as the garb of the female hussars in the ballet of Gustavus', thereby impelling the irascible Cardigan to accuse the paper of 'petty and paltry slander'.[3]

Quartered nearby were the brass-helmeted, red-jacketed 4th Dragoon Guards, also under orders to sail. Their colonel, Edward Hodge, had watched the 11th practising pitching tents. 'We have much to learn', he noted drily in his diary. A few days later he complained he was 'quite hoarse with shouting at the stupid officers I have'.[4] His regiment's departure from Dublin was painted by

an artist, G. Quinton. Outside some hostelry a senior NCO, probably of the rear party, sits among some bibulous Dubliners being accosted by a horsey-looking individual, perhaps a creditor. A red-plumed trumpeter, already mounted, accepts a last drink from the publican. Baggage lies around. Some men are riding off to fall in; one bids a pensive farewell to his wife or sweetheart accompanied by her mother. A disinterested-looking officer is being pestered by an elderly woman brandishing a letter at him, while pointing accusingly at her sobbing daughter. Perhaps a promise about to be breached? Such scenes must have been common in the spring of 1854.

The majority of regiments marching to trains and transports were from the Infantry of the Line, each known chiefly by its number but most also having another title, like the 1st (Royal), 21st (Royal North British Fusiliers), 33rd (Duke of Wellington's), 68th (Durham Light Infantry), 77th (East Middlesex) and many more. All were in red coatees of coarse serge with different-coloured facings – blue, yellow, green, buff – above near-black trousers, and on their heads a curious black felt shako with brass fitments and peaks to front and rear, allegedly the design of the well-intentioned Prince Consort. As the red ranks tramped behind their bands through the shouting crowds, each regiment with its pair of Colours flying above the heads of the youthful ensigns,* they made a fine, brave show, but the elegant and colourful finery in which they paraded was the same clothing in which they would have to fight. Not all the regiments came from the British Isles. Also assembling in the Mediterranean were the 30th (Cambridge), 41st (Welch), 47th (Lancashire), 49th (Hertfordshire) and 55th (Westmoreland) from the garrisons of Gibraltar, Malta and the Ionian Islands. Yet despite the difference in the Mediterranean climate, these regiments were clad exactly the same as those coming from an English winter. In the mid-1850s, the authorities considered – if they thought about it at all – that the soldiers needed but one uniform, for peace and war, for sun and snow.

II

So, from the home garrisons and the Mediterranean, the regiments assembled to form the 'Army of the East', as it was grandly known. It included ten cavalry regiments, two horse artillery troops, eight field batteries and a siege train, 300 sappers, and 30 infantry battalions (including three of Guards and two of Rifles).[†] Yet it was an army in name only, for the British Army of the day was not a cohesive whole, but rather a collection of very individualistic regiments. Certainly when they moved on from Malta to Turkey, their ultimate destination, they would be grouped into brigades and divisions to facilitate command and control, but neither components nor commanders had any practice in working together. The staffs, with a few exceptions, were quite extempore and inexperienced, being merely 'regimental officers be-plumed and on horseback',[5] who owed their positions to interest or influential connections with the commanders. The latter, good men though many had been in their day, were not in their first youth, were unused to handling large bodies of troops, and some had never heard a shot fired in anger; others not since the Napoleonic War.

The youngest by many years at 35 was the Queen's cousin, the Duke of Cambridge, commanding the 1st Division; he had never been on active service. Sir George Brown of the Light Division[‡] was 64, a martinet, and he had seen no action since 1814. Sir George De Lacy Evans, 2nd Division, was an intelligent officer who had commanded a sizeable force in the First Carlist War (1836–38) but he was 67. Sir Richard England, relatively youthful at 60, had the 3rd Division; he had served at the Cape and in Afghanistan and, as a regimental commander, had been thought 'most zealous, ardent and intelligent';[6] in the Crimea an officer would find him 'a terrible fool'.[7] Only the 4th Division had a commander with a recent campaign behind him in Sir George Cathcart, also 60, who had just terminated the Eighth Kaffir War. He was irritable and short-sighted, but his chief staff officer valued his strategic grasp and thought he was ill-placed as a divisional commander, being 'a man more fitted to be first than second'.[8] The clash of personalities in the Cavalry Division between its commander, Lord Lucan, 54, who had had first-hand experience of both Russian and Turkish Armies, and his combative and arrogant brother-in-law, Lord Cardigan, aged 57 with no active service, is too well known to need repeating. Finally, there was the 66-year-old Commander-in-Chief, Lord Raglan, a man so self-effacing as to be almost invisible, of great courtesy yet with little understanding of the men under his command. He had spent his entire service life in the shadow of the Duke of Wellington, thereby acquiring much staff experience at a high level, but without having commanded so much as a company in the field; 'a good "red-tapist" but no General'.[9]

The brigade commanders' average age was 51 and most, though not all, had had recent command experience of some sort in the field. The notable ones will be met in person later.

In the two decades before 1854, the Army had fought three campaigns in South Africa, seven in India, Burma and Afghanistan, and one each in China, Canada and New Zealand. There was, therefore, considerable campaigning experience about but, except against the Sikhs in India, it had

---

* The most junior commissioned rank – cornet in the cavalry.

† See Appendix A.

‡ The term 'Light' had no tactical or organizational significance, its battalions being ordinary infantry, though perhaps some of the best-trained in the army.

been largely irregular skirmishing in bush, jungle and mountain, not conventional warfare against a European enemy of a kind last encountered by the Army in 1815. Furthermore, of the 30 battalions sailing East, only five had been in action in the campaigns of the 1840s, and only the 1st Rifle Brigade had seen service in the previous five years, in South Africa; of the Cavalry, only the 4th Light Dragoons had been in action since Waterloo, in the Afghan War of 1839–42.

Since Waterloo the Army, like Raglan himself, had existed in the shade of the Duke of Wellington, particularly in the period 1842–52 when, in his late seventies, he had been Commander-in-Chief. Great commander though he had undoubtedly been in the Napoleonic War, his still immense prestige and influence, added to his rooted aversion to changing an instrument that had defeated Napoleon, all conspired to delay the reforms and modernization many voices within and outside the Army were demanding. In all areas his elderly hand applied the brake on progress. Far from pressing the government of the day for the larger budget much-needed reform required, he maintained that the public debate aroused by increased expenditure would eventually be harmful either to the nation's interest or the Army's; both were best served by the strictest economy. When it was proposed to replace the percussion musket with the far superior Minié rifle, Wellington approved but insisted it be called a rifled musket, not a rifle, otherwise 'the soldiers will become conceited, and be wanting next to be dressed in green, or some other jack-a-dandy uniform'.[10]

In 1852 Wellington died and would-be reformers took heart from the appointment of his successor, not, as some anticipated, Raglan, but Lord Hardinge, whom the *United Service Magazine* described as 'a friend to improvement . . . we may expect to see alterations, but they will be neither hazardous nor ill-considered'.[11] Hardinge had earlier held high appointments: as Secretary at War he had instituted measures to benefit the ordinary soldier and as Master-General of the Ordnance he had begun the increase, improvement and modernization of the hitherto-neglected artillery. The need for change was further heightened by fears of possible invasion as a result of the revived Bonaparte dynasty in France under Louis Napoleon, who proclaimed himself Emperor in 1852 as Napoleon III. In the event, Russia would prove the enemy and France the ally. But before war broke out, Hardinge oversaw the re-arming of the infantry with the Minié, a weapon that was to have decisive effects later, the establishment of a School of Musketry to ensure that the Minié's greatly improved range and accuracy was properly applied to the infantry's shooting, and instituted measures to advance the military education of staff and junior regimental officers.

Regimental training hitherto had been largely a matter for individual commanding officers, usually within very limited manoeuvre areas. Though many achieved a high standard within their own units, there were no field exercises with other regiments and other branches of the Army. To overcome this, and to accustom senior officers to handling large bodies of troops, Hardinge organized a Camp of Exercise at Chobham in 1853. This, the first of its kind, attracted much public attention and revealed many training defects. The Russian general Ogaroff visited the manoeuvres with a military mission and, when one mock-attack went wrong, George Higginson, who was present and overheard the Russians' comments, found that 'it was with difficulty that I affected not to notice this expression of ridicule so marked as to be offensive'.[12] He later wondered whether Ogaroff's report had caused the Tsar to discount the effectiveness of British intervention on his expansionist schemes.

Like all large-scale manoeuvres, the Chobham experience proved of greater value to the senior ranks than their juniors, one of whom wrote with hindsight gained in the war, 'it taught us regimental officers nothing in the way of practical soldiering'.[13] Though it was to be the forerunner of the great camp at Aldershot, it was not repeated, for the following year all Hardinge's reforms were overtaken by war. He had, however, achieved much in a short time and felt justified in telling Palmerston, 'We have done more in two years than during the last century'.[14] As the war would show, there was much that was still inefficient, chiefly in the fields of logistics, administration and manpower provision, but at least, as the historian of the British Army, Sir John Fortescue, has judiciously pronounced, the Army of the East was 'probably as fine a lot of men, for their numbers, as were ever put into the field'.[15]

14

III

The upper echelons of political power in the 1850s were still largely the preserve of the aristocracy, but increasingly it was the influence and prosperity of an ever-growing middle class which set the tone of the age. Powerful though this class was in the country, particularly its mercantile element, it was little represented in the Army, whose regiments were manned by 'the horny-handed sons of toil' and commanded by 'the children of luxury'.[16] The middle class tended to despise the former and disapprove of, but also to envy and ape, the latter.

Taking one infantry battalion in 1854 as an example: its men before enlistment had been 76 per cent agricultural labourers, a type preferred by officers and NCOs for their fitness and docility; 11 per cent from manufacturing industries; 9 per cent from trades favouring physical development, such as masons; 1 per cent shopmen and clerks; the remaining 3 per cent having no previous occupation.[17] Scotland had been much favoured as a recruiting area for the Army as a whole, and particularly for potential NCOs, because of the greater literacy north of the border; the percentage of Scotsmen in the Army in 1830 was nearly one and a half times their percentage of the United Kingdom population. Thereafter, however, many Scotsmen preferred work on the growing railway network, and even some Highland regiments had to revert to English and Irish to complete their establishment. In contrast the 93rd (Sutherland)

An 11th Hussar's last days with his family in Ireland before the war. A watercolour by M.A. Hayes.

had so many Gaelic speakers in 1850–51 that four NCOs received extra-duty pay as interpreters of the English words of command.

It may seem curious that, in 1854, 41 per cent of the 23rd Royal Welch Fusiliers were Irish, a race which 20 years earlier had provided just over that percentage of the entire Army. The Irish famines and emigrations of the 1840s had markedly reduced Irish recruitment by the mid-1850s, though the proportion of Irish in the Army was still higher than their proportion of the United Kingdom population. There were, of course, regiments which were predominantly, if not entirely, Irish, like the 88th (Connaught Rangers), and references to Irish soldiers crop up in most regimental accounts of the time. But it was in the English countryside, or from countrymen increasingly drifting to towns and cities to find work, that the recruiting parties had to look for men to take the shilling. Using one fairly typical English regiment, which will reappear frequently, as an example, the men of the 95th (Derbyshire) just before landing in the Crimea were 62 per cent English, 37 per cent Irish and 1 per cent Scottish. The proportions among its 33 officers were 19, 10 and 4 respectively.[18]

Very few enlisted for adventure or the glamour of the uniform. In 1846 an infantry NCO calculated that 67 per cent of recruits were 'labourers and mechanics out of employ, who merely seek for support'. Some 13 per cent joined because they considered 'a soldier's life an easy one', 7 per cent were 'discontented and restless' with civilian life, and another 7 per cent were bad characters. Actual criminals were less than 1 per cent, equalling those who were 'ambitious'. The balance were 'perverse sons', 'respectable' but unfortunate, or 'others'.[19] Alexander Somerville joined the 2nd Dragoons (Greys) when without money and in 'a black prison of despair'.[20] Sergeant Taffs of the 4th (King's Own) had been 18 and starving in London when he determined to walk to Chatham and enlist. A Yorkshire miller's son, Henry Franks, enlisted in the 5th Dragoon Guards when, as 'a young simpleton', he thought a soldier's life all 'beer and skittles'.[21] In contrast, Joseph Grigg, a soldier's son, had 'always wanted to see a battlefield'[22] and joined the 4th Light Dragoons on his eighteenth birthday; he would see his boyhood desire amply fulfilled at Balaclava.

Enlisting in 1843, Grigg joined for unlimited service, in practice about 21 years. From 1847, however, in an attempt to attract a better type of recruit, the engagement was reduced to ten years for the infantry, 12 for cavalry, artillery and engineers, with the option of re-engaging for a further 11 or 12 years. Men already in the Army remained on unlimited service. The average age of the rank and file* in the Army of the East was 26 and their average length of service seven years.

Though a recruit might express a preference for one branch of the Army, the regiment in which he found himself was usually, but not always, dictated by whatever recruiting sergeant picked him up. John Fisher, the son of a 7th Hussar veteran of Waterloo, naturally asked for the cavalry when recruited by a sergeant of the 41st (Welch), but found himself in the Rifle Brigade which he 'never had occasion to regret and would do the same thing again tomorrow if I were starting life again'.[23] Most infantry regiments had nominal county affiliations, but these had little significance and recruiting was not localized. Furthermore, a man might, if he so volunteered, serve in more than one regiment. Richard Ellis (who will reappear at Inkerman in the 21st Fusiliers) was an Irishman from County Wexford who originally enlisted in the 57th (West Middlesex), went to India in 1841, but volunteered for the 21st to remain in India when the 57th went home in 1846. The 95th was brought up to war establishment before embarkation with volunteers from the 6th, 36th, 48th and 82nd.

Once enlisted, the cavalryman received a basic rate of 1s. 3d. per day, the infantryman 1s,† to which might be added good conduct pay, beer money of 1d. per day, and certain extra-duty pay, but from which was deducted stoppages for messing (1 lb bread, ¾ lb meat per day), laundry, hair-cutting, barrack damages and maintenance of 'necessaries',‡ leaving the soldier with as little as 2½d. a day. He lived in usually cramped, badly ventilated barrack rooms with a third less cubic feet of air than a convict was allowed; at least by 1854 he had his own bed instead of sharing a four-man

---

* Corporals and privates.

† About £1.55 at today's prices.

‡ A soldier's kit consisted of clothing and accoutrements, issued free, and necessaries, such as underclothing and cleaning materials, provided and maintained at his expense.

Fitzroy James Henry Somerset, 1st Baron Raglan, Commander-in-Chief, the Army of the East. 'A good red-tapist but no General'. A painting by Sir Francis Grant.

crib as formerly. Washing, cooking and lavatory facilities were of the most basic kind and frequently a health hazard. If married, with his wife 'on the strength', the couple and their children were permitted to live in the barrack room, screened from the other soldiers by a flimsy curtain. His main recreation was the raucous drunkenness of the wet canteen, resulting in much indiscipline, for which the chief punishments were imprisonment and flogging. The maximum number of lashes any court could award had been reduced since 1847 to 50, but to this could be added a term of imprisonment, if the offence merited it. In 1848, for example, a drummer of the 58th, found guilty of drunkenness when on guard on active service, was sentenced to 50 lashes and 12 months' imprisonment. Breaches of discipline by NCOs were usually punished by loss of rank.

Despite the harshness of barrack life, it was often

no worse and frequently better than what the soldier was escaping from by enlisting. By the 1850s measures were being taken to improve the soldiers' lives, such as the provision of regimental libraries, savings banks and the education of their children. Instead of deterring men from evil – a policy deemed essential by the Duke of Wellington – a growing number of officers believed that, notwithstanding the appalling circumstances from which many soldiers came, more fruitful results than those produced by the lash could be achieved by encouraging men to be good, a policy first tried half a century before by Sir John Moore. Its success depended on the example, humanity, interest and, where material improvements were concerned, the pockets of the regimental officers, from the lieutenant-colonel commanding down to the ensigns or cornets.

Above all else, the criterion for British Army officers was that they should be, as the Adjutant-General declared in 1840, 'gentlemen by education, manners and habits'.[24] Just over a third came from titled or landed families, the remainder being sons of Service families, or with fathers in the other gentlemanly professions of those days, the Church, the Bar, the magistracy and the upper echelons of the Civil Service. As Kinglake wrote, 'when they fall in battle, it is the once merry country-house, the vicarage, or the wayside cottage of some old Peninsular officer, that becomes the house of mourning'. Such were the likely homes of Line officers, but Guards' officers came from what he called 'the central body of English Society'.[25] Status, education, standards of behaviour were not the only gentlemanly characteristics required; not every man who counted himself a gentleman possessed the less tangible qualities of probity, honour, courage and unselfishness expected of an officer. A young man of the right stuff should also have the ability to become a competent officer, but it had long been felt that the acquisition of military knowledge would come after he was commissioned.

Some had been educated privately, others at the public schools. Measures to reform the savagery, corruption and chaos formerly prevalent in such schools had begun in the 1830s, following the example of Dr Arnold at Rugby with his aim of educating boys to become 'Christian gentlemen'. This ideal will be returned to presently but, notwithstanding the reforms, these schools still

Chobham Camp. Officers in undress and a sentry, 13th Light Dragoons. After H. Alken.

offered a rigorous regime which could make or break a boy in his formative years from about 12 upwards. Thus a young officer, despite his gently nurtured childhood and comfortable home, could have had as tough an upbringing, though in a different way, as his men.

The term 'children of luxury' quoted earlier was in fact hyperbolical as most officers, particularly in the infantry and artillery, were neither rich men nor pampered youngsters. The wealthier cavalry and Guards certainly had some, but when a cavalry regiment left home for, say, India, its complement of officers was often quite different, the rich ones having 'sold out' or exchanged with poorer men in other regiments remaining at home. The dissent that might occur between both categories, particularly under an aristocratic commanding officer, has been well portrayed in Cecil Woodham-Smith's

description of the 11th Hussars under Cardigan.[26] One reason for having officers of similar backgrounds was that it promoted social harmony and *esprit de corps* within the officers' mess, which had a beneficial effect downwards throughout the regiment.

Though the Army was held in low esteem by the rising middle class, to some of its newly prosperous members a son with a commission may have offered the social cachet which their money had been unable to buy. Such sons may have made perfectly good officers, but a feeling existed among traditional elements that the offspring of a small village squire would have a better understanding of, and thoughtfulness towards, the rural peasantry in the ranks than an industrialist's son. Sir Charles Napier, an officer of surprisingly radical sympathies, with experience of the industrial North, preferred 'an ancient lineage with an empty purse' to 'the son of a millionaire who hardly speaks to a soldier'.[27] Moreover, the social differences of such a young man could incur the antipathy of his brother officers, while his original background might be little different from the better-educated NCOs, who would see his position over them as based on no more than the new wealth which had acquired his commission. Shortly before sailing for the East, the officers of the 46th Regiment attracted the fury of the Press and the citizens of Windsor, where they were stationed, for their bullying of Lieutenant Perry, a tradesman's son, whose two court martials for striking an officer and perjury were alleged to have stemmed from his refusal to join in their raffish off-duty pursuits.

The complexities of the purchase system, by which most, though not all, first commissions and subsequent promotions to lieutenant-colonel were obtained, have been dealt with extensively elsewhere.* With hindsight, the iniquities and injustices of the system are obvious, as they were to many reformers at the time, but to most serving officers it was simply the existing system which they had to accept. At best, their commission in any rank represented an investment against retirement – no pensions being available then. This, in turn, gave an incentive to 'sell out' for less enthusiastic officers, thereby creating promotion vacancies down the rank structure from which others could benefit. War, with a likely increase in establishments, not to mention death or disablement, would create vacancies up the structure into which the next senior would be promoted without purchase, thereby accelerating promotion and giving the lucky ones the increased value of their new ranks. In the Royal Artillery and the Royal Engineers, where purchase did not exist and promotion was by seniority, officers spent far longer in each rank than their cavalry and infantry counterparts.

The increased value of a commission was a greater asset to a financially acquisitive officer – if indeed there were any – since his higher rate of pay was hardly riches. An ensign's 4s. 6d. per day rose to £1 per day for a lieutenant-colonel,† and daily outgoings for messing, servants and band fund almost always exceeded income. On top of that, the officer had to pay for and keep up his expensive uniform, plus accoutrements and sword, which served for peace and war. An officer of the 88th

Infantrymen outside the guardroom of a barracks in County Tipperary in 1853. A photograph by Fox Talbot.

recorded that he spent his first night in the Crimea in a rainstorm without shelter, wearing a coatee costing 20 guineas‡ which he had once worn to a ball in Paris. Some private income was therefore essential; another reason, besides social differences, why commissioning of deserving cases from the ranks was so rare. The mid-nineteenth century officer served not for pay but for the privilege of doing so, and for a congenial life among like-minded fellows.

He had to learn his drill alongside the recruits and the complexities of its manuals but, apart from attending the daily orderly room where disciplinary cases were disposed of, he was not over-worked, much of the daily barrack routine being left to the regimental staff and the NCOs. At home stations, he had little contact with the men. The difficulties, discomforts and dangers of foreign, and more especially active, service, despite their unpleasantness, forged a much closer bond between commissioned and non-commissioned ranks within a regiment, which now became home and family for all.

---

* See Sources: Anglesey, Spiers, Strachan, Woodham-Smith.
† About £7 and £31 today. Although the colonel's pay was only just over four times the ensign's, the value of his commission was ten times greater.

‡ About £650 today.

Frederick Short, a sergeant of the 4th Light Dragoons, enlisted in March 1846. He was promoted to troop-sergeant major and awarded the DCM after Balaclava.

In the decade before the Crimean War, despite reactionary obstruction, steps were taken to educate officers, whether commissioned by purchase or as cadets from Sandhurst or Woolwich, so that the Army would become more of a profession than an occupation. These steps included entrance examinations, revision of syllabuses at the cadet colleges (whose products had often been found less satisfactory than those commissioned straight from public schools) and, from 1850, a scheme for promotion examinations. War broke out before much of these had taken effect, but the realization of a need for greater professionalism had taken root.

Furthermore, changes in society's values became mirrored in the officer's gentlemanly code. The precepts of Dr Arnold had spread to other public schools, affecting their products' outlook. Thus the old type of gentleman-officer, with his 'Regency buck' attitude, was giving way to one who had more humanitarian feelings, not perhaps to brother officers of different social origins, but to those less fortunate than himself – his men – with a sense of *noblesse oblige* and an awareness of Christian principles.

Private James Orr of the 5th Dragoon Guards wrote of his troop commander, Hon. Grey Neville, a son of Lord Braybrooke of Audley End, that 'to the men of his troop he was indulgent, kind and courteous – popular with all'.[28] Neville's elder brother, Henry, in the Grenadiers, was 'always cheerful, always ready to help and set a good example'. Another Grenadier, Edward Pakenham, a grandson of the Earl of Longford, whom Higginson thought 'one of our best officers and in the truest sense a leader of men', had been elected MP for County Antrim shortly before the Grenadiers left England. When asked why he had not resigned his commission before sailing, he replied: 'I could not look at my father's picture in the old house at home and think of the honour he had won in the Peninsula, without feeling I ought to do something to maintain the family tradition'.[29] He was to fall at Inkerman.

Philanthropic officers of the Guards, concerned at the appalling conditions in the London barracks for married soldiers and their families, and refused any money for improvements by the War Office, established a fund to build a lodging house for 54 families in 1852. They later organized an institute for Guardsmen and refurbished the interior of the Guards Chapel in Wellington Barracks.

Officers in Line regiments were seldom rich enough for such undertakings, but a greater care for their men's welfare, especially the spiritual kind, was apparent. Captain Hedley Vicars of the 97th incurred some scorn for introducing Bible study and prayer meetings among his men, but they would deeply mourn his gallant death in the Crimea. Major John Champion of the 95th, who will be mentioned again, had been destined for the Church until he decided he could better support his widowed mother on an officer's pay than a curate's; he was known in his regiment as much for his piety as for his gallantry. He was described by a brother officer as 'gentle and forbearing, a true, good Christian man, a thorough gentleman and a most brave soldier'.[30] Not all the officers of the Army of the East merited such an encomium, but it was a standard many strove to attain.

Above Officers and men of an infantry regiment's Grenadier company on guard at the Castle, Dublin, before the war. A photograph by Fox Talbot.

Below Guards and Line officers. Left: Hon. William Amherst, Coldstream Guards, son of Earl Amherst, commissioned 1853, later severely wounded at Inkerman. Right: Anthony Morgan, Grenadier Company, 95th Regiment, commissioned 1847, fought in the Crimea until invalided in December 1854.

IV

And so, under their gentlemanly officers, the regiments of 'strong, hardy, well-intentioned fellows whom no nation on earth could match'[31] marched or rode away to the waiting transports. Little did the crowds who cheered their departure realize they were seeing the last of the old Army, the like of which would not come again. A decade later, when the Army was no longer recruited chiefly from the rural areas, but from the slums of the big cities, a romantically minded Irish officer mourned the passing of the pre-Crimean soldier, 'men of splendid physique and well-chiselled feature, keen, steady eyes, resolute jaws...those old Greek gods, gone as the buffalo are gone from the prairies'.[32]

As events would prove, they were a remarkable breed and it was fitting that the people of England should rise early from their beds to shout farewell above the thudding drums and shrilling fifes. It had not been ever thus. The England they were leaving – the country and people described by Dickens and Thackeray, Trollope and Surtees, painted by Frith or caricatured by John Leach – that England had little regard for, and considerable prejudice against, her soldiers. Much was held against the Army, chiefly by the middle and 'respectable' working classes: its closed nature, its role in aid of the Civil Power as in the Chartist riots, the social exclusiveness of its officers and incidents like the Perry case, its savage discipline. To most civilians it offered poor material prospects as a career, while for many families a son who became a soldier seemed likely to be lost to them forever.

Aspects of all these criticisms were undeniable but, until the troops were seen *en masse* marching away in their glory in the spring of 1854, many civilians had scarcely seen a soldier. Much of Hampshire and Surrey had seen the troops at Chobham, the Guards were evident in London, but the rest of the Army, hidden away in widely dispersed small garrisons and much of it overseas in India and elsewhere, was almost invisible. The Duke of Wellington had done his best to keep the Army out of the public domain, but what is unknown is distrusted and consequently disliked.

In 1854, however, the English people, proud, self-confident, and with nearly 40 years of peace behind them, felt the time had come to settle with the Tsar. Thus they were willing to turn out and

Cavalry officers. From the left: 1st Royal Dragoons, 13th Light Dragoons (mounted), 6th Inniskilling Dragoons, 11th Hussars. After G.H. Thomas.

cheer the men whom they, as taxpayers, expected to do the work for them – as long as it did not cost too much. Since the 1820s animosity towards Russia had been growing. Radicals deplored its autocratic tyranny. In 1831 a Polish insurrection had been brutally suppressed. In 1848 Russia had restored order in the nominally Turkish Danubian principalities of Moldavia and Wallachia (as by treaty it was, in fact, entitled to do). The following year Russian troops had assisted the Habsburg emperor to stamp out Kossuth's independence movement in Hungary. All this aroused Liberal opinion, while Tories were increasingly concerned at Russian expansionism with its possible threat to India and the communications thereto. However, political and national animosity was one thing, war quite another. How it came about must now be explained.

2

A Blow at Sebastopol

For most of the nineteenth century the Great Powers were preoccupied with the 'Eastern Question'. This concerned the potential for disintegration of the vast Ottoman (or Turkish) Empire which sprawled across the junction of Europe, Asia and Africa. From its centre of authority at the Sublime Porte, at Constantinople, its possessions reached north-westwards through the Balkans to the Danube, eastwards to the Caucasus, the Persian Gulf and Arabia, southwards through the Levant to Egypt, and westwards across North Africa to Tunis. Its position astride the lands between the eastern Mediterranean and the Indian Ocean made it strategically important, but its dominion over its many races owing allegiance to Islam, Christianity and Judaism was, inevitably, unpredictable.

To its north lay the Tsar's great empire. Despite its huge land mass, Russia's only outlets to the seas were in the Far East, through the narrow, often frozen Baltic, and the even more frozen White Sea, and from the Black Sea, through the narrows of the Dardenelles under the Turkish guns at Constantinople, to the Mediterranean. Consequently, Russian eyes were fixed enviously on those straits, while Turkish eyes looked apprehensively to their Balkan frontier and eastwards to where Russia was expanding through the Caucasus into Persia. The Russian bear seemed in danger of encircling the Sultan's ramshackle empire within its embrace. Not only did Tsar Nicholas I look longingly at the distant Mediterranean, but he also saw himself as the protector, and eventual liberator, of the Sultan's 13 million Greek Orthodox subjects. Living mostly in the Balkans, they had grown increasingly restive under their Muslim overlords following Greece's independence from Turkey in 1829. That same year the Tsar, assuming his role as liberator, had gone to war with Turkey and had almost taken Constantinople, thereby extracting a favourable eight-year treaty and much influence at the Sublime Porte.

Britain's foreign policy was to preserve the balance of power in Europe, thus preventing any nation becoming so over-mighty as to threaten the great empire which sustained her. Although the Turks' treatment of Christian minorities offended many in Britain, the Ottoman Empire's position across the overland route to the East, and its value as a counterweight to Russia (whose potential threat to India via Persia or Afghanistan had caused the First Afghan War) required the British to support the Sultan. In 1844 the Tsar paid a state visit to Britain, hoping for a favourable response to his ideas for a possible dismemberment of the Ottoman Empire. However, no British government could tolerate the prospect of Russians in Constantinople, so the response was more lukewarm than Nicholas had expected, being merely an agreement which affirmed both governments' interest in the stability of the Ottoman Empire but that, if it started to collapse, they would consult on how best to replace it.

The nearest and most powerful neighbour of both Turkey and Russia was the Austro-Hungarian Empire. Austria could not view with equanimity the prospect of any Russian expansion across the lower Danube and into the Balkans, but her young Emperor owed the Tsar a debt for restoring his

Hungarian kingdom to him, so opposition from that quarter seemed to Nicholas unlikely.

Prussia, not yet the power it would become, had no direct interest in the Eastern Question and in any case its king was related to the Tsar by marriage. There remained France. In addition to consolidating its North African Empire, contiguous with Turkish territory, France had long had interest and influence in the Levant and Egypt. Having become Prince-President of the republic - after the 1848 revolution, Louis Napoleon's primary aim was to strengthen his own position by restoring France's international prestige. His assumption of near-dictatorial powers after a military *coup d'état* in 1851 raised fears of a revived Bonapartist imperialism. Britain was alarmed, as was Russia – for reasons that would precipitate the descent into war.

Even now, nearly 140 years later, it is sobering to recall that so many of the men met in the last chapter, their French allies and Russian enemies, all at least nominal Christians, were to lose their lives because of an interdenominational Christian quarrel which could only be resolved by a Muslim. Perhaps war would have come anyway, but this provided the actual spark that ignited the Powers' latent bellicosity, just as a Balkan student's pistol shot was to do in 1914. In 1850, Roman Catholic and Greek Orthodox monks clashed over small matters of precedence in the holy places of Bethlehem and Jerusalem, both within the Ottoman Empire. The former looked to Louis Napoleon, the French ruler being traditionally the protector of Catholics in the East, to plead their cause with the Sultan. This he was not slow to do, sensing an opportunity to aggrandize himself and placate clerical elements in France. The Greek Orthodox monks naturally appealed to the Tsar. After lengthy manoeuvrings, the Sultan succumbed to French blandishments and found in favour of the Catholics in December 1852.

In January 1853, furious at the intervention by one he considered an upstart and a revolutionary, Nicholas made overtures to London, believing that Britain must be wary of the new Bonapartism. He reminded the prime minister, Lord Aberdeen, of their joint 1844 agreement, suggesting, in short, that so corrupt had the Porte now become, the time had arrived for a partition of the Ottoman Empire between them; Britain's portion to be Egypt and

Crete. The British reply was non-committal, but views hardened on receiving dispatches from the influential ambassador at Constantinople, Lord Stratford De Redcliffe.

Having, as he thought, guarded his flank with Britain, the Tsar had sent a threatening emissary, Prince Menshikoff, to demand of the Sultan not only restoration of the Orthodox monks' privileges, but also a Russian protectorate over all Christians in the Ottoman Empire. The quarrelsome monks were, in due course, placated but the Sultan, stiffened by Redcliffe, refused the protectorate. An incensed Menshikoff returned to St Petersburg to report to his Tsar, who was now more than ever determined to bring the Turks to heel.

In London, Lord Aberdeen remained convinced that Russian bullying would stop short of war but, harried by an increasingly bellicose press campaign and pestered by his ministers, reluctantly agreed to dispatch warships to the Dardenelles, where a French squadron was already lying. Discounting this mild show of force, the Tsar threatened to reoccupy the Danubian principalities if the Porte did not change its attitude. Reassured by the Allied fleets, the Turks remained obdurate and on 3 July Russian troops entered the principalities.

Concerned for its Danube trade, Austria hurriedly convened a conference at Vienna, attended by British, French and Russian representatives. A compromise 'Note' acceptable to all seemed to have been achieved, but the Turks, who had not been consulted, found insufficient guarantees in it against further Russian interference and demanded modifications. The Tsar would not agree to these, whereupon, after issuing an ultimatum requiring the Russians to leave the principalities – which was ignored – the Porte declared war on Russia on 5 October.

Diplomatic activity between the Powers now intensified. By late November, with his armies making little progress on the Danube and in the Caucasus, the Tsar seemed willing to accept mediation by the other Powers. In Britain the Cabinet, a coalition, was divided: at one extreme Palmerston, deeply distrustful of Russia, at the other Gladstone and Aberdeen himself, anxious for peace. All they could agree was to maintain the fleet off Constantinople. However, if the Cabinet was uncertain, the public was increasingly vocal in its demands for assistance to Turkey. On 12 Decem-

Left: Tsar Nicholas I, Emperor of Russia, 1826–55. Right: Prince Menshikoff, tsarist envoy to Constantinople in 1853 and later Commander-in-Chief in the Crimea.

ber its voice became deafening, no longer for mere support, but for revenge. Twelve days earlier the Russian Black Sea Fleet had attacked and destroyed a Turkish squadron at anchor off Sinope, killing 4,000 Turkish seamen, some allegedly while swimming helplessly in the water.

The outrage provoked by the so-called Sinope Massacre (a legitimate act of naval warfare) in Britain, and to a lesser extent in France, ensured that the Cabinet's procrastination could not be protracted much longer. Aberdeen still thought joint Anglo-French diplomacy might avert war, but had to agree to a French plan for a combined naval deployment in the Black Sea, and other contingency planning to decide how and where British arms could best be deployed if hostilities became unavoidable. While opportunities for other naval action existed in the Baltic and Far East, the most helpful military contribution seemed to be a force for the defence of Constantinople.

Though lights must have burned late in the War Office and Admiralty through that January and into February of 1854, a curious air of drift seemed to have settled on the Government. In Paris, Napoleon III's belligerence wavered, but the opportunity to avenge his uncle's Russian disaster

of 1812 beckoned. Diplomats still talked in Vienna. A Quaker deputation went and returned from St Petersburg with little result but the Tsar's expression of his regard for Queen Victoria. The day before they reached Dover, the Grenadier Guards had left London as part of the first contingent for Malta. Anglo-French warships in the Black Sea were ordered to require Russian warships to return to base. As the Scots Fusilier Guards packed their kits, an Anglo-French ultimatum was on its way to St Petersburg, demanding evacuation of the Danube principalities. No reply was received, so on 27/28 March France and Britain declared war on Russia.

Many greeted the ending of the long peace with enthusiasm – as they would again in 1914. Tennyson welcomed 'the blood-red blossom of war' as a healthy antidote to Britain's 'lust for gold'.[1] Others, perhaps distracted by the passing bands from their reading of another indictment of British society in Dickens' recently published *Bleak*

1 The Theatre of Operations

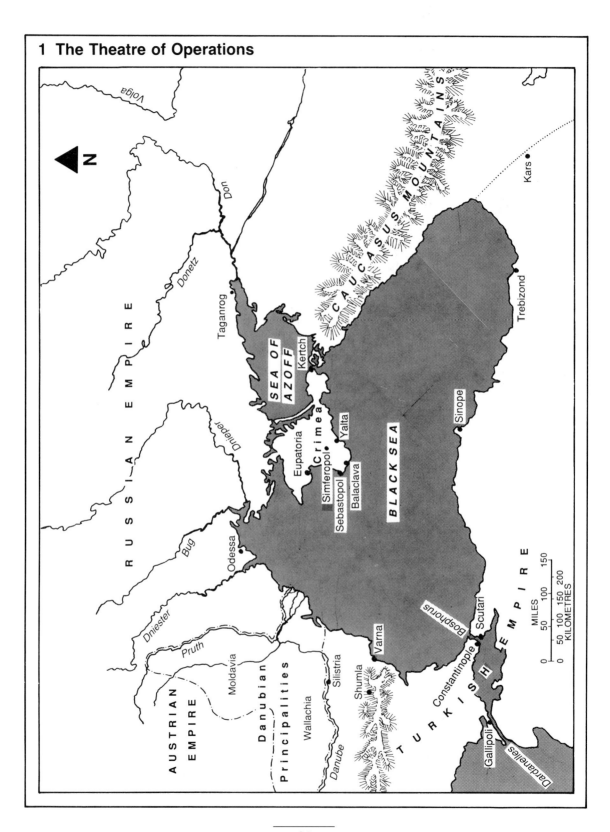

House, deplored it. The Radical MP, John Bright, believed Turkish despotism a rotten cause in which to kill fellow Christians. The Quaker, Joseph Sturge, justifiably pronounced that 'the Government was far less to blame than the people of England'.[2] With little cause to love either, the soldiers sailed away to earn their meagre pay.

'I must let him go'. Lord Aberdeen's inability to restrain the British lion's pursuit of the Russian bear. *Punch*, vol. XXVI, 1854.

II

By May the Russians, who had remained on the defensive all winter, had concentrated sufficient forces in the Danube principalities to take the offensive by besieging the Turkish frontier fortresses of Silistria on the Danube and Shumla. By now the British and French forces had landed in Turkey, many at a place where, 61 years later, their descendants would land, in alliance with Russia, to fight the Turks – Gallipoli. From there a further move was made in June to Varna in Bulgaria, the better to support the Turks now fighting successfully on the Danube.

Meanwhile, to the Tsar's astonishment, the Austrian Emperor, alarmed for his Danubian communications, massed 50,000 troops on his eastern frontiers and required the Russian evacuation of the principalities. With the Turks holding out at Silistria, and unable to risk an Austrian army across his troops' communications with Russia, the Tsar abandoned operations. By 2 August the Russian forces had recrossed their frontier. The *casus belli* thus removed, the war seemed over.

The Royal Navy had been active in the Baltic and the Pacific and had bombarded Odessa, but the Army of the East had not yet fired a shot. Furthermore, it was in little condition to do so. Varna was hot and unhealthy; commanders and staffs pestered their regiments with either unnecessary orders or those with which they could not comply, not having been provided by the staff with the wherewithal. The men, with nothing to do but drill or make friends with their new French allies (the Zouaves being particularly popular), became

Above An imperfect but rare daguerreotype by Robertson of the 1st Rifle Brigade encamped near Constantinople.

Below James Brudenell, 7th Earl of Cardigan, in 11th Hussars' uniform.

bored and drunken. Then cholera, dysentery and fever swept through the camps. George Higginson was distressed to find 'our magnificent Brigade had already undergone severe loss, four hundred men dying or being invalided through this fell disease. The company officers nursed their men with much devotion in the tents'.[3] Wilson of the Coldstream noticed that the seasoned regiments from the Mediterranean garrisons 'enjoyed comparatively robust health' in contrast to his own 'poor men, lounging about, pallid, gloomy and depressed'.[4] The 5th Dragoon Guards were not only severely afflicted by cholera, which carried off their much-loved senior captain, but were shamingly 'deserted in a mean and cowardly manner' by their disliked and despised colonel, Le Marchant, who 'never seemed to take the slightest interest from the day he joined', and chose this moment to return home on half-pay. Pronounced unfit for any duty by Lucan, the men's spirits sank lower until 'a stalwart specimen of a Dragoon', Sergeant Shegog, stood up in the mess tent and rallied them with some 'homely and simple words which had a salutary effect'.[5]

The Light Cavalry Brigade had to contend with both the appalling conditions and Lord Cardigan, at odds with everyone and particularly his brother-in-law, whom he steadfastly refused to recognize as

his divisional commander. On 25 June he set off with part of the 8th Hussars and 13th Light Dragoons on the army's first warlike operation, to see whether Russians were still on the south bank of the Danube. Sixteen days later he returned, smugly self-satisfied but revealing his total ignorance of active service by bringing back no information of any military consequence, after getting lost, exhausting his men and, through stupid orders, rendering nearly 100 of the patrol's 196 horses dead, dying or incapable.

After this fiasco, on top of the heat, dust and squalor, Captain Lysons of the 23rd might have been speaking for the whole army when he wrote home: 'I am heartily sick of such blundering. A magnificent army is sent out here to be sacrificed and die of cholera and fever without striking a blow'. [6]

Indeed throughout August and into September the question was: what was to be done with this great force of men, guns and horses, shipped out at great expense, now that the Turks, with some help from the Austrians, had finished the business? However, minds were reaching back to more important issues than a group of bickering monks or who should control some benighted Danubian provinces. British and French interests were threatened by the Russian bear's long arms reaching out to warm-water ports. Eyes of governments and generals became fixed on the Crimean

Sebastopol, the objective of the Allied armies. Beyond the triangular mast, the inner harbour, guarded, on the left, by Fort Nicholas and, on the right, by Fort Paul (demolished); the roadstead is beyond.

Peninsula, at the north of the Black Sea. Here, at its southerly tip, lay the Tsar's great naval base of Sebastopol, from which one day his fleet might sail into the Mediterranean. Here too was the lair of the perpetrators of the Sinope Massacre. Months before, Rear-Admiral Lyons had told the First Lord of the Admiralty: 'To me the bare idea of our not striking a successful blow at Sebastopol is painful'. *The Times* in June had urged that 'the taking of Sebastopol . . . would permanently settle in our favour the principal questions of the day'. [7] Britain and France conferred and agreed that, subject to any representations by their national commanders, the Allied armies would land in the Crimea and capture Sebastopol.

On learning the Government's intentions, Raglan asked Sir George Brown what the Great Duke would have done, considering that the army was reduced by disease to 27,000,* grievously lacked logistic support, and had little intelligence about the Crimea, its defences and Russian strengths. Brown's unenthusiastic reply probably reflected exactly Wellington's cautious nature, as Raglan

---

* The French would contribute 30,000, the Turks 7,000.

must have known; yet in obedience to another Wellingtonian precept, he felt that, notwithstanding the many imponderables such an operation presented, he must accept the Government's wishes as commands.[8] The French commander, St Arnaud, concurred. Out went the necessary orders to the ships and stricken camps.

So yet again the long-suffering soldiery embarked, their once-splendid uniforms soiled and shabby, their faces and frames gaunt from sickness. They would land without tents or transport, and with no more kit than each officer and man could carry rolled up in a blanket, as they were thought to be too enfeebled by disease to shoulder their knapsacks. They had no ambulances nor hospitals, only the regimental surgeons and the bandsmen, their instruments set aside, to act as untrained medical orderlies. Yet their arms were bright and serviceable, each cavalryman's sword or lance an extension of himself through years of drill, the infantry well practised with their lethal Miniés, superior to any Russian weapon, while the artillerymen treasured their guns and howitzers as much as infantrymen venerated their consecrated Colours. The horrors of Bulgaria were over, and officers and men had drawn closer in adversity within the comradeship of their regiments. Moreover, it was the medical opinion that the sickly state of the army must benefit from 'the animating presence of the enemy' [9] and the clean air of a voyage across the Black Sea.

III

On 14 September the Allied armies landed unopposed on the western shore of the Crimea at the depressingly named Calamita Bay. As the captain of the *Pyrenees* watched the fine men of the 95th's Grenadier Company going over the side, he wept to think how few of them would survive. Private Edward Hyde of the 49th thought 'the scene a very lively one, the weather mild and fine, but at night we had rain till morning',[10] which drenched generals and privates alike. After time for the British to requisition some local transport, the two armies advanced on 19 September, with the French on the right nearest the sea, the British alongside inland. Sebastopol lay some 35 miles (56 km) southwards along the coast, with three rivers intervening.

First to encounter the Russians was the Light

The British landing at Calamita Bay, near Eupatoria. An eyewitness sketch by Captain H.H. Clifford.

Cavalry Brigade in a skirmish on the River Bulganak, notable chiefly for Raglan's over-polite advice, instead of orders, which boded ill for the future; another fracas between Lucan and Cardigan; and ending with their unfortunate squadrons retiring to Russian jeers. At least the cavalry's discomfiture afforded some sardonic amusement to the sweating, footsore infantry, whose prevailing feelings were expressed by Private Williams of the 41st: 'Serve them right, silly peacock bastards'.[11]

The next day it was the infantry's turn. Across the River Alma the Russian Crimean army (33,000 infantry, 3,400 cavalry and 28 guns in redoubts) held the heights under the command of that failed emissary, Prince Menshikoff. After some delay, and much of what Raglan called 'the infernal toot-toot-tooting' of their bugles,[12] the French attacked vigorously on the right, but soon stalled. Then the British Light and 2nd Divisions, after stoically enduring an hour and a half's bombardment, attacked. Sergeant Gowing of the 7th Royal Fusiliers felt 'horribly sick, a cold shivering running through my veins – the sights were sickening'.[13] They advanced in the standard British attack formation, little changed since Waterloo: each battalion, its eight companies in line abreast,★ aligned with the other two of its brigade, the two brigades of each division also in line, the whole division covering nearly a mile wide, but only two

---

★ Or seven if one was in front, extended as skirmishers. Traditionally, this was the task of the left flank, or Light Infantry Company, the right flank being the Grenadiers, but by 1854 all eight companies were trained to skirmish if necessary.

Battle of the Alma. General view of the British attack from the left of the 1st Division. After W. Simpson.

ranks deep, thus permitting the maximum fire effect. An astonished enemy captain, Hodasevich, seeing this for the first time, had not thought it possible 'for men to be found with sufficient firmness of morale to attack, in this apparently weak formation, our massive columns'.[14] Another Russian officer, Captain Enisherloff, watching the English infantry's advance, was struck by 'the extraordinary leisureliness in their gait'.[15]

Further astonishment awaited them as the Light Division, its line disordered by the river and vineyards, actually attacked and captured its objective as a horde of skirmishers, 'a knotted chain',[16] most men firing at will instead of the regulation volleys or file-firing; each man letting off two or three rounds every minute: cartridge from pouch – bite off its end – powder and ball into barrel – draw ramrod – ram down – return ramrod – percussion cap from pouch on to nipple – cock hammer – set sights – present – aim – fire! In the Peninsular War, with the flintlock musket, only one round out of 459 fired took effect; in the Crimea, with the Minié, it was one in 16, while at 400 yards (366 m) range, against closely-packed Russian columns, one ball might pass through three, if not four men, one behind the other. The Minié was consistently accurate up to 800 yards (732 m) and could hit targets at double that distance; in contrast, the smooth-bore musket's effective range was between 150–200 yards (137–183 m).

The Light Division's men, firing as they advanced in this loose formation, took their objective, but were then too disordered to meet the ensuing Russian counter-attack which drove them back. The supporting 1st Division, hesitantly led by the inexperienced Cambridge, was too far back to consolidate the Light's success. Trying to assist, the Scots Fusilier Guards attacked prematurely and also had to fall back. But then the Grenadiers and Coldstream, advancing in perfect order as majestically as though parading in Hyde Park, drove the Russians back with their volleys, while the Highland Brigade on their left, perfectly handled by Sir Colin Campbell, completed the overthrow of the Russian right. Meanwhile the 2nd Division, whose advance had been impeded by the Russians firing a village in their path, had cleared the heights on the Guards' right.

In an hour and a half, the battle had been won and the enemy were in full retreat. It was a victory in which the regimental officers and men could take pride for, as Captain Clifford, a Rifleman on the

Staff, wrote a week later, 'no generalship was made use of, nothing but Bull-dog courage and go-ahead bravery gained the battle'.[17]

Few of the troops had been under fire before. Captain Henry Neville of the Grenadiers wrote:

It was certainly the most awful moment of my life – shot, shell, and musket balls falling in every direction; it seems a miracle how anyone escaped. I had no idea that the excitement could be so great; as long as one was quiet, the buzzing of shot and shell made one feel nervous; but when we commenced advancing and firing, one lost all feelings of the kind.[18]

Private Hyde was uncertain afterwards how he had felt: 'Whether it was fear or excitement I don't know, but I seemed dazed, and went wherever the others went, and did what they did; there was nothing to be gained by hanging back'.[19] Lieutenant Macdonald of the 95th heard of Russian prisoners saying 'we were not men but red devils'.[20]

The Army of the East had lost 362 killed and 1,621 wounded, but it had reduced the Russians by some 6,000. Many, like Sergeant McMillan of the Coldstream, were shocked by the slaughter:

It was [an] awful sight, to see some with their brains blown out, others shot through the body and in the agonies of death. Some wounded in the limbs and crying for mercy, some fainted through pain and dying quietly. And to hear the groans indeed it was most awful.[21]

For men unused to war, who not long before had been near-demoralized by disease and inactivity, from an army most subsequent critics have condemned as atrophied,* the storming of the Alma Heights by the British infantry seems no mean military achievement, reflecting credit on the regimental officers and NCOs for their leadership and peacetime training.

Lucan had been itching to pursue with his unused cavalry, but Raglan would only permit him to escort the horse artillery, which had engaged the retreating Russians, for a short distance until the fresh 3rd Division came up to form an all-arms force to pursue in conjunction with the French. However, the now-ailing St Arnaud refused to continue, thus allowing the defeated Russians to escape.

Not until 23 September could the French be induced to move. By the time the Allies approached Sebastopol, it was thought too late to launch an immediate assault from the north, supported by the fleets, as Raglan had wished. In any case, the French favoured attacking from the south, so Raglan, anxious to preserve the alliance, concurred. Thus a great chance was lost, which might have avoided all that followed.

So it was decided to circle round Sebastopol, heading for the Chersonese Plateau, south of the city, from where the armies could be supplied from two harbours: Kamiesch for the French, and Balaclava to the east for the British. Meanwhile, Menshikoff, finding an immediate attack unlikely, decided to leave a garrison of 18,000, mostly sailors, within Sebastopol, and withdraw with his field army to the interior.

In the oak woods east of Sebastopol his rearguard was spotted by I Troop, Royal Horse Artillery, accompanied by a troop of 2nd Dragoons (Greys).[†] The 6-pounders opened fire and the Greys, quickly dismounting, skirmished forward through the oaks with their carbines. Cardigan's Light Cavalry, which had been leading but had got lost, now appeared and prepared to charge, but again Raglan called them off. The Russians got clear, leaving a quantity of loot, including 'French books and novels of an improper kind'.[22] On 26 September, Balaclava was secured.

Leaving the Cavalry Division near to Balaclava, where the rest of the Heavy Brigade began landing on 4 October, the five infantry divisions moved up to the Chersonese Plateau. The land enclosing Sebastopol and the plateau was shaped similarly to, but rather less than half the size of, the Isle of Wight. The northern side, which included Sebastopol, was bounded by the sea and the Careenage creek, Sebastopol's outer harbour or roadstead, which culminated in the east at the mouth of the River Tchernaya, flowing from the south-east; Kamiesch lay near the western end. The south-west side fell to the sea. The south-east side was a steep escarpment, the Sapouné Ridge, overlooking the ground, 600 feet (183 m) below, between the Tchernaya and Balaclava on the coast.

From Sebastopol and its roadstead, a number of

---

* But see Sources: Strachan.

† The first regiment of the Heavy Brigade to land, on 24 September.

Balaclava harbour, looking towards the sea.

ravines ran up to the plateau. The largest, which ascended south-eastwards from Sebastopol's inner harbour, divided the French lines to its west from the British on their right. East of this ravine were established the lines of the 3rd and 4th Divisions, the Light Division continuing beyond to the Careenage ravine, issuing up from the roadstead. On its other side was posted the 2nd Division, facing the north-east tip of the plateau, known to the British as the Inkerman Heights, from a ruined village on the far side of the Tchernaya. Southwards was the 1st Division, with its right on the Sapouné Ridge. Further south along the ridge were two French divisions under General Bosquet, watching the rear of the Allied armies.

With the numbers available, this deployment and the nature of the ground did not permit the Allies to seal off Sebastopol from the interior, which was reached via a road alongside the Careenage creek below the plateau, or across the roadstead. By 9 October Sebastopol's garrison had increased to 25,000. Meanwhile, the commander, Admiral Korniloff, and the engineer, Todleben, had mobilized garrison and inhabitants to create defences south of the city where practically none had existed prior to the Allies' encircling march. After a fortnight's intensive labour, a 4-mile (6-km), semi-circular defence line, linking six

bastions manned with heavy guns, guarded the approaches from the Allied lines.

Confronted by these defences, the new French commander, Canrobert,[*] refused to countenance any assault without a preliminary bombardment. What might have fallen earlier to a quick assault had now to be besieged. Heavy guns, both of the Royal Navy and Royal Artillery, were landed at Balaclava and trundled up to the heights, 7 miles (11 km) away. From 9 October infantrymen, instructed by sappers, began digging batteries, entrenchments and parallels. The digging was hard; the Russian defences grew visibly stronger daily, and much-needed stores and supplies, though unloaded at Balaclava, were not reaching the camps. The soldiers subsisted on a diet of salt beef and biscuits, with no fruit or vegetables; to wash it down, 'a copper-coloured fluid about as stimulating as dirty warm water',[23] the pathetic result of much roasting, grinding and boiling over a camp fire – for which there was little fuel – of raw, green coffee beans. Diarrhoea and dysentery were rife, cholera was reappearing, and the nights were

_____

[*] St Arnaud had died on 29 September.

33

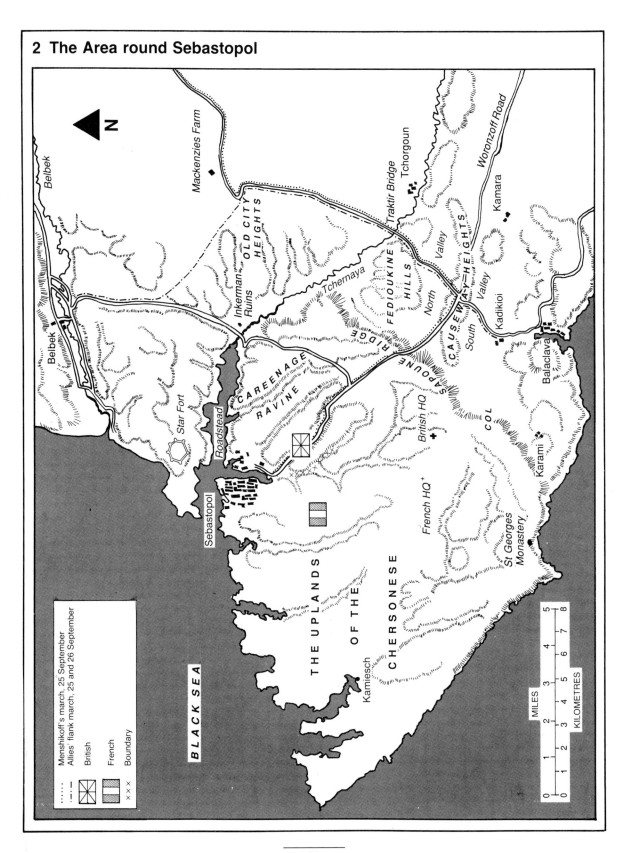

2 The Area round Sebastopol

N

Belbek

Belbek

Mackenzies Farm

OLD CITY HEIGHTS

Inkerman Ruins

Star Fort

Roadstead

Sebastopol

CAREENAGE RAVINE

Tchernaya

Traktir Bridge

Tchorgoun

Woronzoff Road

Kamara

FEDIOUKINE HILLS

North Valley

CAUSEWAY HEIGHTS

South Valley

Kadikioi

Balaclava

SAPOUNE RIDGE

COL

British HQ

French HQ

St Georges Monastery

Karami

THE UPLANDS OF THE CHERSONESE

Kamiesch

BLACK SEA

Menshikoff's march, 25 September
Allies' flank march, 25 and 26 September

British
French
Boundary

MILES

KILOMETRES

5
8

4
6
7

3
5

2
3
4

1
2

0
1
0

getting colder. As the days of toil and nights on watch passed, the high spirits after the Alma victory began to evaporate. A Coldstream officer felt his 'heart yearn towards the unflinching "common soldier", so sternly superior to privation, so proudly reckless of his life'.[24]

Hope was renewed on 17 October when the long-awaited bombardment of Sebastopol erupted from 73 British and 53 French guns ashore, followed later by the combined fleets off shore. This was to be followed by a French assault, their lines being closer to the defences, which the British would support. The naval bombardment proved ineffective and was costly in ships and men. The landward guns, particularly the British batteries, were more destructive. By mid-afternoon Korniloff was mortally wounded, and the defences around the Malakoff and Redan bastions were crumbling. Raglan was ready to assault, but the French, more heavily shelled and their firepower seriously diminished by the explosion of two magazines, could not continue. At dusk the British ceased fire and during the night the Russians repaired their earthworks. The British guns continued the next day; the French two days later.

So it went on for a week; death and destruction

Panoramic view of the area round Sebastopol, looking north-west. Balaclava is in the left foreground. Compare this with Map 2. The foreground terrain is somewhat distorted and some features – for example the Balaclava railway – did not exist in 1854.

rending Sebastopol by day, but all repaired, even improved, each night. Despite the fury of the guns and the devoted efforts of the gunners, the opportunity for an assault receded daily. The frustrated men's conditions in the camps worsened; officers scorned their generals; the generals quarrelled. Every night brought a foretaste of the approaching winter with its 'bleak winds, heavy rains, sleet, snow and bitter cold'.[25]

By 24 October Raglan had realized that his force was simply not strong enough to prosecute his share of the siege effectively and guard his rear on the Chersonese, as well as his Balaclava base, from the looming Russian field army in the interior. Recently there had been reports of a force of 25,000 concentrating beyond the Tchernaya. That night, one of the coldest yet, an urgent message was brought up from Balaclava and handed to General Airey, the Quartermaster-General, at the farm-house serving as Raglan's headquarters. A Turkish

The farmhouse on the Chersonese serving as Raglan's headquarters. After W. Simpson.

spy had reported that the Russian field army was about to attack Balaclava. As the rising wind moaned among the trees outside, Raglan and Airey assessed this information. The use of spies, in Raglan's view, was really not quite the thing, and in any case there had been other false alarms from that quarter recently. Raglan scribbled on the report. The messenger, Lord Bingham, Lucan's son and ADC, rode off into the blustery darkness, back down the escarpment to Balaclava, with nothing to show for his hurried ride but Raglan's endorsement of the message: 'Very well'.[26]

II

THE BEAR STRIKES BACK

But they rode like Victors and Lords
Through the forest of lances and swords
In the heart of the Russian hordes,
They rode, or they stood at bay.

ALFRED, LORD TENNYSON

The Trumpet, the Gallop, the Charge[1]

I

In peacetime Balaclava had been no more than a fishing village at the head of a deep but narrow inlet, three-quarters of a mile (1 km) long, which twisted in from the sea between steep, dark-red cliffs, one crowned by an old fort. By late October the harbour was a tangle of masts, rigging and wooden hulls, its muddy quayside alive with curious Tartars, harassed commissaries, busy sailors and sick soldiers, picking their way between the piles of stores overflowing from a few requisitioned sheds. Away from the green-tiled cottages, the one road meandered uphill for a mile (1.6 km) between hills to the little village of Kadikioi. Just short of it, a track bore off westwards to ascend the escarpment by what was known as the Col. A little way to the north-east rose an isolated low ridge. Two miles (3 km) further north lay the Fedioukine Hills, on the south bank of the Tchernaya, but the open ground between was enclosed by hills to the east, from which a ridge ran westwards for 4 miles (6 km) to the Sapouné escarpment, known as the Causeway Heights. Along it ran the Woronzoff road, linking Sebastopol with Baidar and Yalta. The open ground bisected by the Causeway Heights became known as the North and South Valleys.

All this was visible to General Bosquet's divisions up on the Sapouné Ridge, but the entrance to the Balaclava gorge was out of his guns' range. In any case, his task was the rearwards protection of the siege lines, not Balaclava, which was a British responsibility; in particular that of Sir Colin Campbell, temporarily detached from his command of the Highland Brigade. Aged 62, he was probably the most experienced and capable formation commander in the Army of the East, having been a regimental officer in the Peninsular War, a brigade commander in the First China War, and a divisional commander in the Sikh War. For his task he had been allotted 1,200 Royal Marines, with 26 guns emplaced in redoubts on the hills above the eastern side of the Balaclava gorge; at its entrance, near Kadikioi, were encamped the 93rd Highlanders with a Turkish battalion and W Battery, Royal Artillery (four 9-pounders, two 24-pounder howitzers). These were the inner defence troops. An outer line of six redoubts, little more than rough earthworks, had been hurriedly thrown up along the Causeway Heights: the easternmost, No. 1, being on an eminence known as Canrobert's Hill, 2 miles (3 km) from Kadikioi, with No. 6 in the west, between a quarter and half a mile from the foot of the Sapouné Ridge. These redoubts averaged about half a mile apart and were manned by Turks (mostly Tunisians), with a battalion and three 12-pounders in No. 1, half-battalions with two guns in Nos. 2, 3 and 4, each also having a Royal Artillery NCO; Nos. 5 and 6 were unoccupied.

Finally, encamped half a mile south of No. 6, from where it could attack the right flank of any advance on Balaclava, was the Cavalry Division, with I Troop, Royal Horse Artillery, under Lucan's, not Campbell's, command. Fortunately the two men had evolved a sensible relationship – hence the decision to send Bingham up to Raglan on the night of the 24th, both aware that their nearest infantry support was at least two hours' march away up on the plateau. Lucan camped with his division but Cardigan, with Raglan's approval,

Left: Sir Colin Campbell, commanding the Balaclava defences.
Right: George Bingham, 3rd Earl of Lucan, commanding the Cavalry Division.

slept each night aboard his comfortable yacht in Balaclava harbour, seldom appearing before mid-morning, leaving the Light Brigade temporarily commanded by Lord George Paget of the 4th Light Dragoons.

Whatever Lucan's faults, he was conscientious, and the daily reports of probing Russian patrols from north and east had made him doubly so, almost to the point of agitation, so that his division's morale suffered from the frequent but fruitless turn-outs. Though Raglan had seemingly discounted his latest warning, he nevertheless rode out the following morning with Paget and his staff for his usual reconnaissance of the Causeway

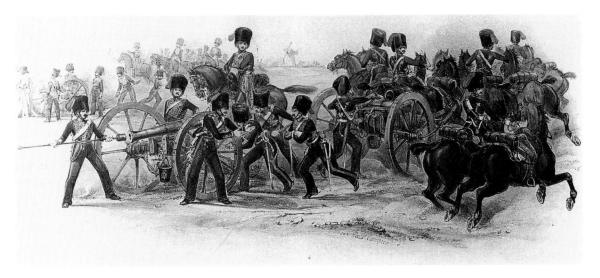

Royal Horse Artillery preparing to open fire on the command, 'Halt, Action Front!' After G.B. Campion.

redoubts as soon as the cavalry had paraded for its daily stand-to an hour before dawn.

It was misty and just growing light as the party approached No. 1 Redoubt. Looking up, they saw two flags flying against the dawn-streaked sky: the signal that enemy were advancing. Almost at once the redoubt's guns opened fire, answered by a cannonade from the east. Lucan immediately sent off an officer to appraise Raglan, while Paget galloped back to the cavalry camps to bring forward the two brigades. They were already alerted, as Sergeant Maughan of the Inniskillings recalled: 'We had picquetted our horses after watering when a shout went up, "The Videttes are circling", and they were making the figure eight, showing infantry and cavalry approaching'.[2]

The earlier reported estimates of 25,000 Russians were indeed correct. Having gained from patrols a clear picture of Balaclava's slender defences and the two to three hours it would take reinforcements to arrive from the plateau, Menshikoff was launching the recently arrived General Liprandi with 25 battalions, 35 squadrons and 78 guns against the British base. Three columns, comprising two-thirds of the infantry, supported by artillery, were to roll up the Turkish redoubts from the east; the main body of cavalry, also with guns, under General Ryjoff was to await further orders in the North Valley; while a third, smaller

force of all.arms under General Jabokritsky was to position itself on the Fedioukine Hills.

The cannonade heard by Lucan at about 6 am had signalled the opening of the attack against No. 1. First to support the embattled Turks, now fighting doggedly against six battalions covered by riflemen and 30 guns, was Captain Maude's I Troop, Royal Horse Artillery which, galloping eastwards along the South Valley, went into action on the Causeway between Nos. 2 and 3 Redoubts. Because of the dim light, as Maude wrote later, 'nothing could be distinctly seen but the flashes of the Russian guns on which accordingly our guns were laid'.[3]

Typical of the troop's 6-pounders was the left gun commanded by Sergeant Lethbridge and served by a spongeman and a loader, standing in front of the wheels, a ventsman and firer behind them, and Lethbridge himself at the trail. At the rear were two servers, bringing ammunition from the limber, drawn by six horses, each pair with its own driver, and three mounted men holding the dismounted gunners' horses. Normally such a gun detachment would have had with it another team drawing a limber and wagon carrying more ammunition, but all I's wagons had gone to Balaclava to transport ammunition to the siege lines, so the troop only had what was in the gun limbers. This was quickly expended and, since the troop was outgunned and outranged by the Russian 18-pounders, it sustained casualties in men, horses and guns, including Maude himself. Though supported by W Battery, Royal Artillery, sent up by

Campbell, I Troop, out of ammunition, had to withdraw behind the crestline.

Meanwhile, the Heavy Brigade had advanced to escort the guns and also came under artillery fire. According to Corporal Gough of the 5th Dragoon Guards: 'We could see the balls coming with such force against the ground that they would rise and go for half a mile before they would touch the ground again'.[4] Among the Inniskillings, Sergeant Maughan saw how 'Sergeant Bolton had his leg knocked off. The shot hit my horse first, came between us and doubled my sword up like a hoop and grazed my leg'.[5] It was an unnerving experience for men sitting on their horses knee-to-knee, kept by their discipline in two ranks and following the example of their officers who, motionless in front, were as conscious of their men's eyes upon them as of the oncoming balls. The Heavies could only offer a front to the slowly advancing Russian infantry, while retiring by alternate squadrons.

The 6th Inniskilling Dragoons before the war. Reading a report is Dalrymple White, then a captain, who commanded the regiment at Balaclava. A watercolour by M.A. Hayes.

For well over an hour, the gallant Turks in No. 1 Redoubt fought off their attackers but, with their 12-pounders knocked out, they could no longer prevail against the overwhelming numbers. At 7.30 their remnants abandoned the redoubt. Seeing them go, and with no help coming from their Allies, the garrisons of Nos. 2, 3 and 4, less resolute than those of No. 1, made off towards Balaclava. The Royal Artillery NCOs had no choice but to follow, though not before spiking the guns. Sergeant Mitchell of the 13th Light Dragoons encountered one who 'complained bitterly of the Turks. He had the greatest difficulty in persuading them to fight the guns at all and, after a few rounds, and seeing the enemy drawing near, they one and all bolted, leaving him alone'.[6] With the Russians now swarming into all four redoubts and mounting their own guns, Campbell advised Lucan to withdraw the cavalry westwards out of the line of fire, so as to be ready to take any advance on Balaclava in flank.

About half an hour before, while No. 1 had been making its stand, Raglan had received Lucan's first report and had ridden to the edge of the escarpment from where, the mist having cleared, he had a perfect view of the scene below, illumined by the rising autumn sun. He sent out orders for the 1st and 4th Divisions to march immediately down the escarpment. Cambridge got moving but Cathcart, still simmering about having been sent down two days before, made difficulties about turning out his men who were tired from the trenches. He was also dubious about Raglan's decisions, in which he had an especial interest, having been nominated his successor, should anything befall him. Cathcart's procrastination lost 40 minutes valuable time. Eventually, however, both divisions were on the march, though by the lengthier route down the Col to Kadikioi, instead of the more direct Woronzoff road.

Raglan, ever mindful of preserving his cavalry and not wishing them to engage before the two infantry divisions could arrive, also sent his first order to Lucan, requiring him to withdraw to the south of No. 6 Redoubt, where they could be covered by guns on the escarpment.

Once this order, ill received by the cavalry, was completed, the way across the South Valley to the Balaclava gorge must have yawned invitingly open to the Russians, now in strength on the Causeway

The 93rd Highlanders repelling Russian hussars at Balaclava. A watercolour by Orlando Norie, who shows them in two ranks, not the four stated by Leith Hay.

Heights. Only a thin dash of red, crowning the small green ridge north of Kadikioi a mile (1.6 km) away, seemed to bar the way. Perhaps suspecting a trap, the Russians paused but, at the same time, invisible to Lucan and Campbell, Ryjoff's cavalry were concentrating in the North Valley.

Meanwhile Raglan, high above like a boy deploying armies of toy soldiers, had had second thoughts about the undefended South Valley and that distant red speck on which Russian guns from the Causeway soon opened fire. Another galloper rode off down the hill with the second order to Lucan: to detach eight squadrons towards Kadikioi.

II

The red speck 2 miles (3 km) from Raglan's eyrie was of course the 93rd Highlanders, ordered into position by Campbell. Only 550 strong, they had been joined by 40 convalescent Guardsmen and 60 sick of other regiments from Balaclava. In two ranks, their line covered a frontage of some 150 yards (137 m). On either side were some Turks from the redoubts who had rallied. To the left was W Battery and making its way as fast as possible down the escarpment was Brandling's C Troop, Royal Horse Artillery.*

When the enemy guns got the range to the ridge, Campbell ordered the 93rd to shelter behind the reverse slope. This, however, unsettled the Turks, most of whom joined their other compatriots making for the harbour through the 93rd's camp, belaboured as they ran by one Highlander's large wife. Soon four squadrons of Russian hussars came over the Causeway at a trot, apparently making straight for Balaclava. Campbell immediately ordered the 93rd back on to the crest. The usual formation for infantry against cavalry was in a square, four ranks deep; this would have only presented a frontage of 20 yards (18 m) and permitted a quarter of the rifles to fire forward. Most accounts claim that the 93rd were in line, two-deep, but Major Leith Hay said they 'received them in line four deep',[7] thus bringing all rifles to bear and giving the line some solidity, should the cavalry come to close quarters.

Above the sound of the guns, 'the champing of bits and clink of sabres',[8] the Highlanders heard

* Normally attached to the Light Division and consequently armed with the 9-pounders and 24-pounder howitzers of Royal Artillery field batteries.

Campbell's 'There's no retreat from here, men! You must die where you stand!' 'Aye, aye, Sir Colin', replied Private John Scott, 'and needs be we'll do that'.[9] The Russians came nearer, breaking into a canter. The remaining Turks fired a wild volley and fled. Some of the Highlanders restlessly edged forward as though to charge, checked immediately by Campbell: '93rd! 93rd! Damn all that eagerness!'[10] The hussars' speed increased. At 600 yards (550 m) the Miniés went up and the first volley rang out. Few Russians were hit and still they came on. Calmly reloading, the Highlanders again presented. At 250 yards (230 m), another volley. A Russian officer later admitted, 'few of us were killed but nearly every man and horse was wounded. A mounted man, though severely or even mortally wounded, can retain his seat long enough to ride out of danger. Our horses would not stand the fire and we sheered off'.[11] To the 93rd it seemed as though the hussars were trying to outflank them to their right. Captain Ross's Grenadier Company on that flank quickly wheeled right. A final volley, now into the enemy flank 200 yards (180 m) distant, and they circled away, riding for the Causeway. W Battery hastened their flight, as the Highlanders threw their feather bonnets in the air, cheering.

III

By now Raglan's second order had reached Lucan. He had ordered Cardigan, who had at last joined his brigade, to remain where he was just north of No. 6 Redoubt, defending that position and

Brigadier-General Sir James Scarlett in front of the Heavy Brigade, in the costume he wore at Balaclava, including a non-regulation helmet of his own design. After Sir Francis Grant.

3 Battle of Balaclava, 25 October 1854

Charge of the Heavy Brigade

N

SAPOUNÉ RIDGE

Woronzoff Road

Bosquet

FEDIOUKINE HILLS

North Valley

Cardigan

To Tchorgoun

6 Redoubt

5 Redoubt

4 Redoubt

CAUSEWAY HEIGHTS

3 Redoubt

Vineyard

2 Redoubt

B

A

South Valley

C

Scarlett

D

G

E

From Balaclava

A 4th Dragoon Guards
B The Royals
C 5th Dragoon Guards
D The Greys
E 1st Squadron Inniskillings
F 93rd Highlanders
G 2nd Squadron Inniskillings

F

British		Cavalry squadron	
French		Cavalry brigade	×
Russians		Infantry division	
Turks		Guns	
		Russian riflemen	●
		Unoccupied redoubt	
		Occupied redoubt	

0   MILES   ½
KILOMETRES   1

Charge of the Light Brigade

N

Three Squadrons of Lancers

Aqueduct

To Tchorgoun

FEDIOUKINE HILLS

Main body of the Russian Cavalry

D'Allonville

Light Brigade

11H   17L
4LD
N

Heavy Brigade

8H   13LD

4 Redoubt

Lord Lucan

Three Squadrons of Lancers

XX

3 Redoubt

Cathcart

CAUSEWAY HEIGHTS

2 Redoubt

Two Dnieper Battalions

From Balaclava

Woronzoff Road

British
French
Russian
○N Spot where Nolan fell

0   MILES   1
KILOMETRES   1

attacking anything within reach of him. He next told Sir James Scarlett, commanding the Heavy Brigade, to move off with eight squadrons towards Kadikioi.* He then rode up to the Causeway to see what the Russians were doing.

Ahead he saw the four hussar squadrons bear away towards Campbell, but closer to hand was Ryjoff's main body, 2,000 hussars and Cossacks, riding along the North Valley towards him. As it drew level with No. 5 Redoubt, it came under fire from guns up on the escarpment and wheeled left up to the Causeway. Lucan turned his horse to ride swiftly to Scarlett.

The Heavies' commander was a big, florid, short-sighted man of 55, recently Colonel of the 5th Dragoon Guards. He was popular with all ranks and, though without any active service experience, had had the foresight to provide himself with two staff officers who had both campaigned in India: his official ADC, Lieutenant Elliot, and his unofficial adviser, Colonel Beatson. On receiving Lucan's instructions, he had ordered the Inniskillings' 1st Squadron to lead off, while he followed with their 2nd Squadron and the Greys. Behind came the 5th Dragoon Guards, followed at a distance, having been impeded by a vineyard, by Hodge's 4th Dragoon Guards. The Royal Dragoons remained south of the Light Brigade. Accompanying Scarlett were Elliot and two members of his old regiment, Trumpet-Major Monks and the man who had rallied the 5th at Varna, Sergeant Shegog, now his orderly. Some way to the right rear, Brandling's C Troop had reached the foot of the escarpment and was galloping across the plain.

As Scarlett was passing to the south of the Light Brigade's camp, Elliot happened to look left and saw what Lucan had already spotted – Ryjoff's 19 squadrons coming over the Causeway and heading directly towards them. Nearest Scarlett were the Inniskillings' 2nd Squadron and the Greys' 1st, riding in column of troops. At once he ordered: 'Left wheel into line!' This brought the four troops of these two squadrons into one, two-deep line, the Greys' 2nd Squadron conforming to make a second

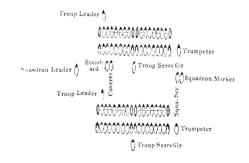

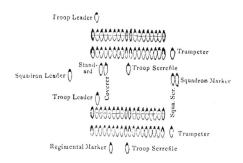

A two-squadron regiment in open column of troops, the formation of the Heavy Brigade squadrons before wheeling left into line ('Regulations for the Instruction, Formation and Movements of Cavalry', 1844).

line behind its 1st. Scarlett then saw that, owing to another vineyard, there was insufficient room for the 5th Dragoon Guards to prolong the line to the left, so he ordered the first three squadrons to wheel right by column of troops, advance a squadron's width, and wheel left again into line, thus allowing the 5th to come up on the Greys' left in the same formation.

As C Troop galloped on to some rising ground to the right rear, its officers had a perfect view of Scarlett's five squadrons now confronting the Russians: the bearskin caps of the Greys between the brass helmets of the 5th and Inniskillings, forming a first line of some 300 sabres in two ranks, about 180 yards (165 m) wide, and a second of 200 sabres behind the centre and left. The Inniskillings 1st Squadron, some 400 yards (360 m) away to the right, had halted and fronted towards the Causeway.

While these movements were happening, Lucan had galloped up in some excitement, shouting at Scarlett to charge. The 'nearly equilateral, black-looking mass' of ten Russian hussar squadrons

---

* Each cavalry regiment had two squadrons, each of two troops. Each squadron averaged three officers, 100 NCOs and men. Russian hussar regiments had eight squadrons, each officially 170 strong but in fact rather weaker; Cossack regiments had six squadrons (*sotnias*).

The Greys (2nd Dragoons) fighting in the middle of the Russian hussars. A painting by Felix Philoppoteaux.

flanked by Cossacks, all in grey greatcoats, had, on spotting the Heavies' formal manoeuvres, suddenly halted on the southern slope of the Causeway, about 500 yards (460 m) away, as if its commander was 'undecided for a moment as to how he would proceed'.[12] The hussars in the centre pulled up before the Cossacks on the flanks, so that the latter's leading ranks formed two horns to the main mass, all the while keeping up what Ryjoff irritably called 'their everlasting screaming'.[13]

Oblivious to both Lucan and the enemy, Scarlett completed his alignment, the officers calmly sitting on their horses with their backs to the Russians as the NCOs dressed the ranks. Keen to get at the Russians before they moved again, he decided to go straight into the charge from a standstill, an unusual and difficult manoeuvre, particularly up-hill. Telling Monks to sound the call, he led off with his three followers as the Russian mass lumbered forward again at a slow trot.

As all the trumpeters sounded, first away up the grassy slope was the Greys' 1st Squadron, followed quickly by the Inniskillings' 2nd, then the other three. From away on the right the Inniskillings' 1st Squadron broke into a gallop towards the enemy left. To the left rear, the 4th Dragoon Guards were advancing in column of troops, while further away still the Royal Dragoons, determined not to be left out, were riding forward.

Charging with the 5th Dragoon Guards, Lieutenant Temple Godman could see Scarlett's little party, 50 yards (46 m) in front, ride straight into the slow-moving Russian ranks, 'swords in the air in every direction, pistols going off, everyone hacking away right and left', the huge Shegog towering over all. They were quickly engulfed, but then in went the Greys, also 'surrounded and hemmed completely in, fighting back to back in the middle, the great bearskin caps high above the enemy'.[14] To watchers near and far, the fate of every Heavy could be followed by the scattering of red amid the dark mass. Seeing a Greys' officer surrounded, Sergeant-Major Grieve spurred his horse among the assailants, decapitating one and dispersing the others. Sergeant Ramage attacked seven Russians setting upon Private McPherson and saved the life of the wounded Private Gardiner.*

Conspicuous in the struggle was the tall figure and great voice of the Adjutant, Lieutenant Miller, standing in his stirrups and shouting to his men to keep together: 'Rally, the Greys, rally!'

---

* After the Victoria Cross was instituted on 5 February 1856, Grieve and Ramage were among the recipients.

The Inniskillings' 2nd Squadron drove in beside them with a wild Irish yell, their colonel, Dalrymple White, receiving a sabre stroke which almost bisected his helmet. On the left Sergeant-Major Franks of the 5th found that

after a yell of defiance, we soon became a struggling mass of half-frenzied and desperate men, doing our level best to kill each other. There was no time to look about you. Both men and horses on our side were heavier than the enemy, and we were able to cut our way through, many of them soon began to give us room for our arms.[15]

Corporal Gough had a narrow escape when his horse was shot:

He fell and got up again and I was entangled in the saddle. My head and one leg were on the ground. He tried to gallop on but fell again and I managed to get loose. A Russian lancer [Cossack] was going to run me through; Macnamara came up and nearly severed his head from his body so, thank God, I did not get a scratch.

The Russian sabre cut on the helmet of Lieutenant-Colonel Dalrymple White, 6th Dragoons.

He grabbed a riderless horse and remounted. 'A Russian rode up . . . I had seen a pistol in the holster pipe, so I shot him in the arm; he dropped his sword. I immediately ran him through the body'.[16]

Among the 5th, Grey Neville went into the charge with a presentiment of his own death which had haunted him since the outbreak of war. He became separated from his troop and saw several Russian cavalrymen ride towards him. According to a friend,

he thought it was better to attempt to ride through them and rode with all his might against the centre of the party. The concussion knocked him off his horse and knocked his antagonist, horse and all, down, and, he thought, killed him. He was then on the ground and was wounded while there. He had one large wound and three others in his back. He lay still, with his face to the ground. He heard them moving away and, thinking they were gone, raised his head to look, when a Russian dragoon [sic] dismounted and cut him with his sword over his head. His helmet saved his scalp but his right ear was cut into. Some cavalry rode over him and he felt dreadfully hurt by the horses' hooves.

Private Abbott, hearing his calls for help, dismounted and

lifted him from the ground and made him stand for a moment. He tried to walk but was so weak he could not and wanted to lie down again. The soldier would not leave him and ended finally by dragging him by bodily strength to a place of safety.[17]

Neville's worst wound had broken a rib which pierced his chest, and his foreboding was realized 19 days later.

As these five squadrons were battling in the Russian centre, the latter's horns were encircling to confine and overwhelm them by a superiority of about four to one. However, help came first from the Inniskillings' 1st Squadron which 'at a splendid pace and in good dressing, tore in on the left flank of the Russians and, catching them obliquely on the bridle arm, unhorsed whole troops of them'.[18]

Meanwhile Hodge, having brought up his 4th Dragoon Guards at a collected trot, still in column of troops, alongside the Russian right, ordered Captain Forster to wheel the leading squadron right into line and charge the enemy flank. The second squadron wheeled likewise, then both, now

Lieutenant Grylls of C Troop, Royal Horse Artillery, which completed the Heavies' victory.

in one line, dug their spurs in and almost at once crashed into the Russians, catching them on their sword arms. With their little colonel at their head,* the 4th's big dragoons carved their way across the 'hacking, jostling, pushing mêlée,'[19] from one flank to the other, where Hodge, 'panting and vehement . . . laid his commands on the first two trumpeters he could see and caused them to sound the rally'.[20] Finally, after about a mile's ride, the Royal Dragoons charged into the struggle somewhere between the 4th and 5th.

So closely had the Russians been packed that, to the observant C Troop officer watching from his vantage point, the Heavies' 'cutting and slashing was only carried on about as far as the fifth rank from the Russian front, and about as far inwards as the breadth of twelve horsemen on their flanks near the front', except where Hodge had torn through the enemy right. Though the Heavies found a head cut from above effective, a thrust with the point

was deflected by the Russians' thick clothing, and 'our men knocked and pulled them off their horses in every conceivable way'.[21] Neither side sustained many casualties as the Russian swords were equally ineffective; Elliot, with 14 cuts, was only classified as 'slightly wounded'. Nevertheless, despite the enemy's numerical superiority, the strength and savagery of the tall, red-coated dragoons achieved a moral superiority over the mass, and, once the 4th Dragoon Guards smashed in on the flank, the enemy formation began to disintegrate and break away to their left rear towards the Causeway Heights.

Only some eight minutes had elapsed since Scarlett first struck the Russian squadrons. On the Causeway their officers tried to rally the men, but Brandling, who had been keenly awaiting his opportunity, now galloped C Troop to a point where its fire would clear the Heavy Brigade and went into action at 750 yards (680 m) range, firing 49 shot and shell which broke up the rally. Ryjoff's disordered squadrons rode away out of sight into the North Valley.

The Heavy regiments had been far too intermingled to pursue immediately. But 500 yards (460 m) away, sitting on or standing by their horses watching it all, was the Light Brigade, with

---

* At Eton, aged 16, Hodge had measured only 5 ft 1 in. The minimum height for a heavy dragoon soldier was 5 ft 8 in.

Cardigan grumbling that 'those Heavies have the laugh of us this day'.[22] However, when urged to pursue the beaten enemy by Captain Morris, a veteran of the Sikh War and temporarily commanding the 17th Lancers, Cardigan refused to budge. He later blamed Lucan's last orders as an excuse for his inaction. It was not that he lacked courage: it was simply a case of a supremely self-satisfied, inexperienced and stupid officer interpreting literally orders which did not allow for his military limitations. Thus his lack of initiative, and inability to 'read' the battle, squandered Scarlett's boldness which, with the 93rd's firmness, had not only saved Balaclava and cleared the South Valley, but had also opened the possibility of a convincing rout of the enemy cavalry, which in turn might have deterred Liprandi from continuing the action. As it was, the Russians were given a breathing space, and a morning which had begun so promisingly for British arms dawdled on towards the disaster which was to follow.

IV

The Russian cavalry had retired to reform at the eastern end of the North Valley behind a 140-yard-long (130 m) screen of eight 6-pounders of the 3rd Don Cossack Battery, providing a link between Jabokritsky's troops with ten guns on the Fedioukine Hills, and the infantry with six guns then occupying Nos. 1 to 3 Redoubts and a spur which projected north-eastwards into the North Valley from No. 3. This was a defensive deployment, designed by Liprandi to cover the consolidation of the most easterly redoubts while abandoning No. 3, which the four battalions of the Odessa Regiment were ordered to demolish and dismount the captured 12-pounders.

By now two French infantry brigades of Bosquet's division had been sent down by Canrobert to the plain and the 4ème Chasseurs d'Afrique were ready to support the Cavalry Division. Raglan, still up on the Sapouné Ridge, having seen that Balaclava had been saved, was now preoccupied by the need to recapture its outer line of defence on the Causeway Heights and, with his mind harking back to another Wellingtonian precept, regain the lost guns. For this he looked to Cathcart's 4th Division, supported by Cambridge's 1st. The latter had reached the plain near No. 6 Redoubt, but Cathcart, still smarting at having been turned out,

had exhibited no urgency and, having reached the bottom of the Col, set off towards Kadikioi until turned back by a staff officer towards the redoubts. Pursuing a serpentine course between the escarpment and the cavalry camps, he ventured towards No. 6, from which he would proceed cautiously, via No. 5, to No. 4. At one point a Guards officer saw the 4th Division fallen out with arms piled!

Increasingly agitated by Cathcart's meanderings, Raglan sent down his third order to Lucan: 'Cavalry to advance and take advantage of any opportunity to recapture the Heights. They will be supported by infantry, which have been ordered to advance on two fronts'. To Lucan, then near No. 5 and without Raglan's overall view, the order seemed hopelessly imprecise as he could see no infantry and he could not conceive that Raglan, on past experience, wished the cavalry to attack alone. He decided he was meant to await the infantry, and moved his division into the 1,000-yard-wide (900 m) North Valley where he, and they, had a better view of the enemy. A mile and a quarter (2 km) away down the valley stood the Russian battery, Ryjoff's cavalry behind; around No. 3 Redoubt and its spur, the Odessa Regiment and another battery;* more cavalry, infantry and guns along the Fedioukine slopes to the left. To a cavalry officer, with an eye for country, the green turf of the valley floor invited a gallop; but it was clearly no place for a ride that morning.

So, as the minutes ticked past – half, three-quarters of an hour – they waited around their horses, the troopers smoking their pipes, the officers their cheroots. The autumn sun shone down on the red ranks of the Heavies and, in front of them, the Light Brigade's dark-blue mass, varied by the grey trousers of the 13th and 17th and brightened by the brilliant cherry ones of the 11th. Only the clink of harness and the occasional Russian shot at C Troop, up near No. 5 Redoubt, broke the silence.

High above, Raglan could hardly credit what he was seeing, despite his orders long ago received: the cavalry motionless below him; Cathcart still taking his time; even the enemy was still. Suddenly a sharp-eyed staff officer pointed out Russian artillery horses preparing to tow away the captured

---

* Out of sight to the Odessa's right rear were the Azov, Dneiper and Ukraine Regiments (12 battalions).

guns. Raglan spoke urgently to Airey who scribbled down another order, the fourth: 'Lord Raglan wishes the cavalry to advance rapidly to the front – follow the enemy and try to prevent the enemy carrying away the guns. Troop Horse Artillery may accompany. French cavalry is on your left. Immediate'. It was handed to the best horseman of the staff, the so-called 'cavalry maniac', Captain Lewis Nolan. As he rode straight down the escarpment, Raglan called, 'Tell Lord Lucan the cavalry is to attack immediately'.[23]

And so began the muddle which led to the most famous – or infamous – episode of the Crimean War. This story is more concerned with the lower ranks, and since the altercation between Lucan and Nolan which sealed the Light Brigade's doom has been so often described, it is superfluous to detail it yet again.* What ensued will be presented here through the words of the soldiers concerned, but what determined their fate can be summarized as resulting from a hasty order issued by a commander at an all-seeing viewpoint (Raglan), to an inflexible and irascible subordinate at a much more limited viewpoint (Lucan) – something seemingly not appreciated by the commander – leading to lack of clarity of purpose, and all aggravated by its bearer, an impatient and junior staff officer, intolerant of his seniors and convinced of his own expertise (Nolan); puzzlement, temper, insubordination, wild gestures – and the Light Brigade was launched, not at the redoubts' captured guns, but down that fine turf for a gallop, the North Valley, through a corridor of fire to the guns at its end.

With Cardigan leading, the Light Brigade moved off as his trumpeter, Billy Brittain of the 17th, sounded, 'Walk, March – Trot'. In the first line were the 17th Lancers with the 13th Light Dragoons on their right; behind the 17th, the 11th Hussars; 200 yards (180 m) in rear, under Lord George Paget, the 4th Light Dragoons with the 8th Hussars on their right; all with both squadrons in two-deep line, the first line covering about 145 yards (130 m) – almost exactly the frontage of the distant Russian battery. To the right rear rode the Heavy Brigade, to the left waited the Chasseurs d'Afrique. Despite the quantity of Russian artillery, no orders were issued to the division's own I

Troop, Royal Horse Artillery, nor to C Troop which, left to its own devices, engaged the redoubts whenever opportunity offered.

When the Russians opened fire, Nolan ironically was the first to fall, belatedly trying to re-direct the Light Brigade. Private James Lamb of the 13th:

I was riding close to Captain Nolan when he was mortally wounded. The next discharge tore wide gaps through our ranks and many a trooper fell. Owing to the dense smoke I lost sight of him. We still kept on at a gallop ... a crossfire from a battery on our right opened a deadly fusillade with canister and grape, causing great havoc amongst our men and horses, mowing them down in heaps. I myself was rendered insensible.[24]

Sergeant Mitchell, 13th, prayed: 'Oh Lord, protect me, and watch over my poor mother'. He heard 'oaths and imprecations between the report of the guns and the bursting shells, as the men crowded and jostled each other to close to the centre'.[25]

John Penn, 17th Lancers, Sergeant Berryman's coverer. He had served with the 3rd Light Dragoons in the Afghan and Sikh wars. Photographed after the war in the new, 1855 uniform and after being reduced to the ranks.

* See Sources: Anglesey (*A History of the British Cavalry*), Harris, Hibbert, Woodham-Smith.

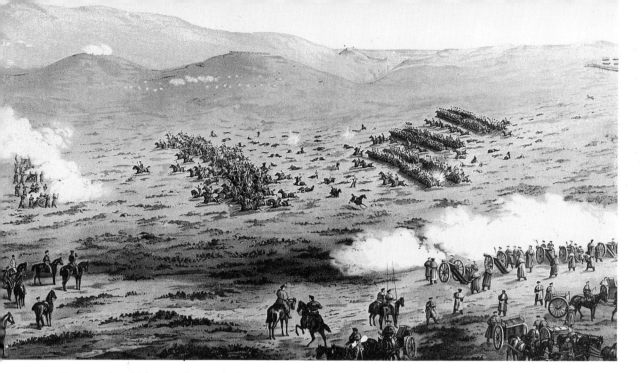

Among the 17th was Sergeant Berryman, aged 29, with eleven years' service:

'Gallop' was the order as the firing became general. A discharge from the battery to our front, whose guns were double-shotted, first with shot or shell, then with case, swept away Captain Winter and the division on my right. The gap was noticed by Captain Morris who ordered 'Right Incline' but a warning came from my coverer, Corporal John Penn, 'Keep straight on, Jack'. He saw what I did not, that we were opposite the intervals of the guns and thus we escaped. My attention was attracted by James Melrose, a Shakespearian reciter, calling out, 'What man here would ask another from England?' Poor fellow, the next round killed him and many others. This round broke my mare's off-hind leg and caused her to stop instantly.[26]

Though Cardigan and the officers tried to steady the pace, every man seemed 'convinced that the quicker we rode through the awful showers of grapeshot, musketry and shells...the better chance he would have of escaping unhurt'.[27] Inter-regimental rivalry, too, spurred them on. As he fell from his dead horse, Captain Tremayne, 13th, heard someone shout, 'Don't let those b------ of the 17th get in front, come on, come on!'[28]

A young soldier of the 17th, Private Wightman, felt a touch on his arm and heard the words, 'Domino, chum', as his right-hand man, John

The Light Brigade charging the 3rd Don Cossack Battery: the first line, 17th and 13th, suffering casualties, the 11th behind the 17th, followed by the 4th and 8th; top right, the Heavy Brigade. Anonymous watercolour.

Lees, with nine years' service, went down. To his left Peter Marsh was shouting at John Duggan for 'swearing like a blackguard when you may be knocked into eternity next minute';[29] soon after Duggan was seriously wounded. Corporal Nunnerly, 17th, saw 'a sergeant who had his head blown off but rode about thirty yards before he fell'. He felt relief as they approached the guns but

every shot now came with the most deadly accuracy. When I was within a few yards of the guns my horse was shot under me and fell on its head. I endeavoured to pull it up to dash at the gunners but found it was unable to move, its foreleg having been blown off. I left it and forced my way on foot when I was attacked by Russian cavalry through whom I cut my way, my more than ordinary height combined with a powerful frame proving most advantageous to me. I had no sooner got clear than I was knocked down and ridden over by riderless horses, together with a few Hussars.[30]

Just before the first line reached the guns, Ryjoff had ordered his hussars and Cossacks forward to protect the battery, but the latter would not face the Light Brigade and went about, firing at their own hussars to clear an escape route and throwing them into confusion. The whole force made off,

A private of the 4th Light Dragoons.

except for some officers who 'threw themselves forward against the enemy only to be cut down'.[31] These must have been the men Nunnerly encountered.

In the second line Troop-Sergeant-Major Loy Smith, with 21 years' service, rode as serrefile behind the right-hand troop of the left squadron, 11th Hussars:

We swept down the valley much nearer the Fedioukine Hills than any other regiment. The round shot passed through us and the shells burst over and amongst us, causing great havoc. The first man of my troop struck was Private Young, a cannon ball taking off his right arm. I, being close to his right rear, fancied I felt the wind from it as it passed me, I afterwards found I was bespattered with his flesh.... The [Russian] infantry kept up a continuous fusilage as we came opposite them, but the men hung well together, keeping their line and closing in as their comrades fell back wounded or killed. Many riderless horses of the first line were now galloping along with us, forcing their way into the ranks.... As we neared the battery, a square of infantry gave us a volley in flank. The very air hissed as the shower of bullets passed through us; many men were killed or wounded. On looking down I saw that a bullet, which must have passed close in front of my body, had blackened and cut the lace on my cuff.... At a sweeping gallop we passed the guns, our right flank brushing them.... About a hundred yards in rear Colonel Douglas halted us. During the advance we had lost about 50 men, so that we had about 80 left.[32]

To the right rear of the 11th, the 4th Light Dragoons charged into the battery. In their ranks, Private Joseph Grigg, now with 11 years' service, was realizing his boyhood desire to see a battlefield. Through the smoke he saw

a mounted driver. He cut me across the eyes with his whip, which almost blinded me, but as my horse flew past, I made a cut and caught him in the mouth, so that his teeth all rattled together as he fell. I can hear the horrible sound now. Then I made for another driver, cut him across the back of the neck, and gave him a second cut as he fell. Beyond the guns the Russian cavalry ... were coming down upon us howling wildly. We went at them with a rush. I selected a Cossack, who was making for me with his lance pointed at my breast. I knocked it upwards with my sword, pulled up quickly and cut him down across the face. We made for other Cossacks, cutting our way through them as through a small flock of sheep. Then I heard Lord George Paget call out, 'Rally on me!'[33]

At the guns, Sergeant Howes and others of the 4th, with Troop-Sergeant-Major Herbert, surrounded one:

He [Herbert] dismounted with the intention of cutting the traces. We killed all the men belonging to the said gun, and I went to the leading horses and turned their heads round with the view of bringing the gun away, but it was impossible.[34]

Private Samuel Parkes, an old soldier with 23 years' service and Paget's orderly, had lost his horse when he saw the dismounted and sword-less Trumpeter Crawford being attacked by two Russians, whom he drove off. Making their way back on foot, they were attacked by six more Russians whom Parkes, 6 ft 2 in, held off with his sword until disarmed and they were both made prisoners.*

To the 4th's right, Colonel Shewell and the 8th Hussars had taken a slightly different course to outflank the battery's line of fire, but they were enfiladed from their right.

At that moment [an anonymous private felt his] blood thicken and crawl, as if my heart grew still like a lump of stone within me. I was a moment paralysed, but [with] the snorting of the horse, the wild gallop, the sight of the Russians becoming more distinct, and the first horrible

---

* Parkes subsequently received the Victoria Cross. See page 132.

The 17th Lancers, as they appeared to the Russian gunners. After C.E. Stewart.

discharge with its still more horrible effects . . . my heart began to warm, to become hot, to dance again, and I had neither fear nor pity! I longed to be at the guns. I'm sure I set my teeth together as if I could have bitten a piece out of one . . . . I cut clean off the hand of a Russian gunner who was holding up his sponge [staff] against me. He fell, glaring savagely, but I cared little for that. Bodies and limbs scattered in fragments, or smashed and kneaded together, and blood splashed into my face were now no novelty.[35]

Once through the now-silenced guns, Cardigan, considering he had done his duty, rode back alone up the valley, leaving the remains of his regiments trying to rally. The loud Nottinghamshire voice of Corporal Morley* was bellowing for the 17th: 'Coom 'ere, coom 'ere! Fall in, lads, fall in!' [36] All those still mounted could clearly see the need for regaining some formation as squadrons of Russian lancers had now appeared behind them to cut off

their retreat. Three on the south side menaced a group of 17th Lancers but they were charged and routed by the 8th Hussars. On the north side Lord George Paget collected the remnants of the 4th Light Dragoons, then

we went about to cut a way through this regiment which had formed to attack us in flank. I am no swordsman, but was fortunately enabled to disengage myself and get through them, and I had the worst of it, for in the melée I had got on the right flank and my horse was so dead-beat that I could not keep up, and saw the rest gradually leaving me at each step. We had to ride back a mile through the murderous fire we had come through . . . how any of us got back I don't know.[37]

That they did so was largely due to a fine charge by the Chasseurs d'Afrique along the Fedioukine slopes.

---

* A decade later he served as a Union cavalry officer in the American Civil War.

The Light Brigade reaching the guns, with Cardigan engaging a Russian gunner. A painting by T. Jones Barker.

Corporal Grant, 4th, had dismounted to find some means of taking a gun but 'found myself in the rear almost alone, my regiment having retreated'.[38] To his relief he saw the 11th Hussars coming back, pursued by Russians, and joined them. After passing the guns, the 11th had successfully charged some cavalry, chasing them for some distance. In danger of becoming cut off, and with no other help near, Colonel Douglas ordered his regiment to reform on, as he thought, the 17th Lancers in rear. Sergeant Bentley

drew his attention to their being Russian, and not our lancers, when we got his order, 'Fight for your lives!' Thereupon all retired. On passing them I was attacked by an officer and several men, and received a slight wound from a lance. I was pursued by them, and cut the officer across the face. Lieutenant Dunn came to my assistance. I saw him cleave one almost to the saddle and can bear witness to his admirable and gallant fortitude.[39]

Sergeant-Major Smith said Dunn was 'a fine young fellow, standing six feet three, wielding a terrific sword, many inches longer than regulation. His heroic conduct inspired all with courage'.* As the tired 11th went back

we no longer resembled the steady line we had done before. The four [remaining] officers and men being mixed up but still keeping well together, so that we assumed an oval shape. Many men whose horses had been wounded, others whose horses were fagged, were overtaken and killed.[40]

Smith's horse was hit by gunfire and he had to run for it. After some narrow escapes, he found a riderless horse and reached C Troop. Sergeant Lethbridge, waiting with the unused I Troop near the original start line, saw 'the 11th come back alone some little time after the other regiments. We cheered them as they passed'.[41]

Long before this, men who had been wounded,

---

* Dunn subsequently received the Victoria Cross. He owned a large estate in Canada to which he retired after the war with Colonel Douglas's wife (see page 136).

or lost their horses before reaching the guns, had been making their way back under fire. Sergeant Berryman, though himself wounded in the leg, stayed with Captain Webb who was in great pain from a shattered shin. Eventually, aided by Sergeant Farrell and Private Malone, 13th, they carried Webb to safety. Captain Morris, with three head wounds, a cut arm and two broken ribs, was briefly captured by the Russians but escaped and was rescued by the German, Sergeant Wooden, 17th, who helped him back until Surgeon Mouat of the Inniskillings rode forward from the Heavy Brigade to dress Morris's wounds under fire.*

At the start of the charge, Lucan had ordered the Heavies to follow in support but, as they entered the fire zone, their casualties soon exceeded those sustained in their own charge.[†] Seeing the Light Brigade's destruction, Lucan ordered the Heavies to retreat to a position from where they could cover the Light Brigade from any Russian pursuit. The horseless Sergeant Mitchell, coming back alone,

The Light Brigade coming in after the charge. On the left, mounted, is Troop-Sergeant-Major Loy Smith, 11th Hussars. A painting by Lady Butler.

must have thought his earlier prayer had been answered when he first spotted the Greys but then, seeing them 'retiring at a trot, I thought there was no chance now'.[42] However, on reaching the spot, now shelled by the enemy, he found a blinded Grey who had been left behind and together they walked on.

So, some 25 minutes after starting, the Light Brigade came back, in small groups, ones and twos, many on foot, others still mounted or sharing a horse, their once-glittering uniforms, the most decorative in the Army, now soiled, torn and bloodied. Up on the Sapouné Ridge, the headquarters staff, witnesses to it all, were aghast. Nearby Mrs Duberly, the bright little wife of the 8th Hussars' paymaster, thrilled with her spectacular view, stared at the scattered figures and exclaimed, 'What can those skirmishers be doing?' Then

---

* Berryman, Farrell, Malone, Wooden, Mouat all subsequently received the Victoria Cross. Webb died 12 days later. Morris survived.

† During the day's fighting, they lost ten killed, 98 wounded.

realization struck: 'Good God! It is the Light Brigade!'[43]

Of the 51 officers and 610 men who had charged down the North Valley, 9 officers and 93 men had been killed, 11 officers and 116 men wounded,[*] and 2 officers and 56 men had been taken prisoner; the heaviest casualties were sustained by the 17th Lancers – 51 per cent. 362 horses had been lost. Considering the odds and weight of fire against them, the fact that casualties were not higher can only be ascribed to the Russian cavalry's reluctance to engage, which in turn may have been due to its amazement at what the Russian artillery officer, Kozukoff, called 'the desperate courage' of the 'valiant lunatics' of the Light Brigade. Ryjoff asserted that the British cavalrymen had been made drunk, but Kozukoff said he had seen no drunks among the British wounded and that it was 'indeed difficult to imagine that drunken cavalry could have achieved what those English horse actually did'.[44]

Though physically and mentally exhausted, many in pain from wounds or distressed for lost comrades and devoted horses, the Light Brigade's morale still held. When Cardigan rode up with his self-justifying, 'Men! It is a mad-brained trick, but it is no fault of mine', one of them called back, 'Never mind, my lord. We are ready to go again!'[45]

The ensuing recriminations between the higher commanders, and their later apologias, have been as often discussed as the altercation beforehand. Easiest to blame was Nolan, who was past speaking for himself, though undoubtedly his hot-headed contempt for Lucan had been contributory. Cardigan, for once, had obeyed Lucan's order – after rightly pointing out its likely consequence – and led bravely, though his questionable conduct after reaching the guns drew criticism. Lucan had received unclear orders from Raglan. After receiving the last, and most fatal, he lost his temper, misinterpreted its intention and, blaming Raglan for what he knew was madness, launched his cavalry, but without its available horse artillery support.

Had Lucan and Cathcart – who, though out of sight of each other, were only about half a mile apart when the penultimate order was received – made some attempt to locate each other and concert a joint plan to execute it, and had Cathcart shown more sense of urgency and tried to relate his division's task with the operations as a whole, then the fourth order might have been unnecessary. Even after the Cavalry Division advanced, Cathcart, then at No.4 Redoubt, seems to have ignored or failed to find out what was happening in the North Valley. His battery fired a few rounds at No. 3, and the 1st Rifle Brigade skirmished toward it, but otherwise nothing was done that could at least have provided some diversion on the Light Brigade's south flank, as the Chasseurs d'Afrique did on the north. But liaison between divisional commanders seems to have been an unknown concept, and initiative was as lacking as short-sightedness was prevalent in many Crimean generals.

Liprandi had failed to take Balaclava, but by retaining the easterly redoubts he could control the Woronzoff road, thereby confining the British communications between Balaclava and the Chersonese to the Col track; this would have serious repercussions when winter came. Moreover, the already over-stretched infantry divisions on the plateau were further reduced by leaving the entire Highland Brigade under Campbell's command to hold a reduced perimeter round Balaclava. Nevertheless, though British generalship had been faulty, the conduct of the British cavalrymen who charged on 25 October had made a marked impression on their opponents and, with Tennyson's help, has left a memory that has lasted to this day.

---

[*] A survey carried out in 1881 among 74 survivors who had been wounded showed that 21 per cent of wounds had been caused by sabres, 26 per cent by lances, and 53 per cent by artillery and infantry fire (Loy Smith, *A Victorian RSM*, p. 218).

4

The Minié's Murderous Effect

Menshikoff, pessimistic about holding Sebastopol and with scant faith in his subordinates, had felt little inclination for taking the offensive but, pressed by the Tsar to do so, he had sanctioned what appeared at the time to be an attempt against Balaclava. However, a modern historian, with access to Soviet archives, has called the events of 25 October 'a reconnaissance in force, a demonstration rather than a full attack'.[1]

Since the opening of the Allied bombardment, Menshikoff had become increasingly concerned about a powder shortage within Sebastopol and the growing proximity of French batteries to its isolated and tactically important Flagstaff Bastion. By 23 October he had been reinforced by Liprandi's 12th Division of Dannenberg's IV Corps and, although its 10th and 11th Divisions, with Dannenberg himself, were on the way, he had decided that a diversion against the Allies was necessary before they could arrive. Initially he had favoured an attack against the British left, but Liprandi had suggested Balaclava as a less costly objective, though warning he could not guarantee success with the troops available. To this Menshikoff had agreed. Thus, had they taken Balaclava, its capture would have been a bonus, rather than the result of an express design to do so.

The outcome was regarded by many Russian officers as a failure since they believed that, had Menshikoff waited for Dannenberg, Balaclava could have been taken; as it was, the British must now be alerted to the vulnerability of their rear. Liprandi's soldiers, in their first battle against the British, had had a sharp taste of their enemies'

fighting qualities, but those within Sebastopol were told it had been a victory. This, coupled with news of Dannenberg's approach, raised morale within the town.

After Dannenberg's arrival, Menshikoff would dispose of at least 100,000 troops in and around Sebastopol, which would afford him the superiority for a convincing counter-stroke against the Allies' 65,000. On the day after Balaclava, the most promising first objective still seemed to be the British base, using the ground gained by Liprandi as a start-line. He decided that very day to make use of the heightened morale of the Sebastopol garrison by mounting another reconnaissance in force against the right rear of the British siege lines on the Chersonese. This, while distracting attention from Liprandi, would also gauge the British defences in an hitherto-untested area. Colonel Federoff was ordered to establish himself with his Boutirsk Regiment, half the Borodino and four guns on the Inkerman Heights, while his right flank would be guarded by another battalion advancing up the Careenage ravine.

As explained earlier, this region was the responsibility of De Lacy Evans's 2nd Division. Bounded on the east by the escarpment above the Tchernaya valley, and on the west by the Careenage ravine, this ground, from the 2nd Division's camp northwards to where the Heights fell steeply down to the roadstead, was roughly the size and shape of London's Regent's Park. Unlike that park's comparative flatness, however, the northern, western and eastern sides were broken up by re-entrants rising to the high ground: from the roadstead, the

Volovia gorge and, to its west, St George's ravine climbed up due southwards for 1,400 yards (1,280 m) to Shell Hill, a hump rising to 588 feet (179 m) above sea-level; from the Careenage ravine, the Mikriakoff glen and, further south, the Wellway branched off south-eastwards, pointing respectively to the left front and rear of the 2nd Division's camp; and from the Tchernaya valley, the Quarry ravine cut up south-westwards into the escarpment with St Clement's ravine south of and parallel to it, the two separated by a spur. Shell Hill splayed out sideways to two spurs, known as the West and East Juts, above the Careenage ravine and just north of Quarry ravine respectively. From this mile-wide feature, a lower saddle ran southwards, narrowing in width to about a quarter of a mile between the heads of the Mikriakoff glen and Quarry ravine, then broadening out and rising to another east–west feature, 50 feet (15 m) higher than Shell Hill and some 650 yards (590 m) long, known as Home Ridge; this had a north-pointing spur at its eastern end, called Fore Ridge, which gradually descended to St Clement's ravine. From Shell Hill to Home Ridge was 1,420 yards (1,300 m).

Immediately south of Home Ridge was the 2nd Division's camp. The only road traversing the area was the main Post Road from the interior to Sebastopol. This came up the west bank of Quarry ravine from the valley, running roughly parallel to an old track in its bed, went over Home Ridge, through the camp and on south, skirting the head of the Wellway, towards the Guards' camp just under a mile away, and the Light Division camp a mile and a half away. At the head of Quarry ravine, 540 yards (490 m) in front of Home Ridge, a loose stone wall about 4½ feet (1.4 m) high, known as the Barrier, had been constructed across the road. All the ground was covered in boulders and stunted oaks, between 3 and 10 feet (almost 1 and 3 m) high, with some blackthorn, which grew thickest in the ravines.

Behind Home Ridge, Evans had the 3,000 infantry of his two brigades and the 12 guns of B and G Batteries, though some 400 infantry were on trench duty in the siege lines. Following the first bombardment's failure to achieve suitable conditions for an assault, a Guards' captain spoke for all the infantry divisions when he wrote:

The view from Home Ridge looking north towards Shell Hill. A photograph dated 1904.

We are very hard worked, sometimes 3 or 4 nights together out of bed, or rather out of tent (for the ground is our bed), either working in the Trenches, or else on outlying Picquet, or else guarding the Trenches, every day more or less under fire with very little protection.[2]

The campaign looked like dragging on into the winter. The grinding monotony of trench warfare was not helped by the poor food. Some men were still without any change of clothing, having not yet received their knapsacks which had been left on board ship at the landing, and when they got back to the often-leaking tents they had only a thread-bare blanket and a greatcoat between them and the cold, hard ground. Soldiers' greatcoats, with a cape for the shoulders, were made of a cheap, shoddy, grey baize, which compared poorly with the thick Russian coats, but at least afforded another layer of clothing for night duties over the tattered, faded red coatees. Beards were thicker; hair unkempt; faces more cadaverous, now crowned as frequently by dark-blue woollen forage caps of pork-pie shape as by the Albert shakos, many of which had been lost or discarded. The Guards still turned out in their bearskin caps, though at night their sentries were permitted to wear their neat field caps, another innovation of the Prince Consort. Most officers, too, sported their once-smart undress caps in which they had long ago cut a dash with young ladies in distant Dover or Dublin; their elegant, gold-laced coatees, now soiled and tarnished, were often shrouded in voluminous greatcoats of superior cloth to the men's, their expensive, hand-made boots cracked and battered. One officer begged his father to send him out some new boots as he was 'almost barefooted'.[3] It was indeed an altered-looking army from the one which had left England six months previously.

While the 3rd, 4th and half the Light Division manned the trenches and batteries fronting Sebastopol, Codrington's brigade of the Light Division, the 2nd Division and Guards Brigade watched the open north and east flanks, from astride the Careenage ravine, across the Inkerman Heights, and the northern end of the Sapouné Ridge. On the left bank of the Careenage ravine rose the Victoria Ridge, on which a Royal Navy Lancaster gun was sited in a battery pointing north-westwards at Sebastopol; on this, Codrington's right-hand picquet was based. Across the ravine, in the 2nd Division's sector, from West Jut over Shell Hill, were the 'left' picquets of Adams's 2nd Brigade. To their right and southwards, around the heads of Quarry and St Clement's ravines, from the Barrier eastwards to the right bank of St Clement's, known as the Kitspur, then due south along the Sapouné

Undress cap worn in the Crimea by Lieutenant Anthony Morgan, Grenadier Company, 95th Regiment.

Ridge to the right rear of the divisional camp, were Pennefather's 1st Brigade 'right' picquets. From there southwards along the plateau's edge was the Guards' responsibility until the first French picquet of Bosquet's corps was met, 2 miles (3 km) south of Home Ridge. In addition to guarding its sector of the Sapouné Ridge, the Guards Brigade was charged with supporting the 2nd Division, should it be attacked from the north.

Besides the outlying picquets on this front was a novel body of 60 'sharpshooters' from the 1st Division, who had been organized in mid-October primarily 'to pick off the enemy's artillerymen in the embrasures'. They were to operate from behind cover, 'scraping out a hollow for themselves' and remaining 'for many hours (even twenty-four) without relief'. Their movements to firing positions had to be 'rapid, in a scattered order; each man acting for himself and exercising his intelligence'[4] – all in marked contrast to the close-order evolutions of Horse Guards Parade. Under Captain Goodlake of the Coldstream, the Guards' sharpshooters had developed their sniping role into that of a fighting patrol, roving at will beyond their brigade's area of responsibility.

So that what followed may be better visualized, the picquet system must be explained. The task of outlying picquets was to prevent the enemy reconnoitring and to glean intelligence of its movements, but primarily 'to gain sufficient time to enable the

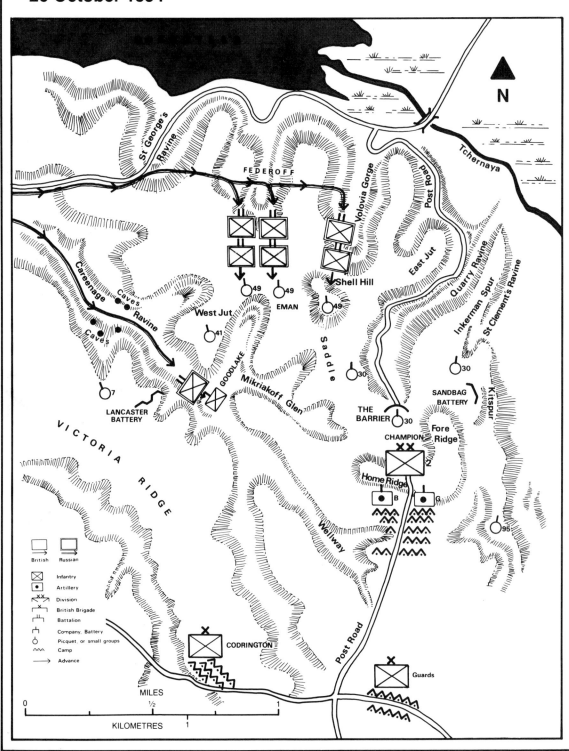

St George's Ravine

FEDEROFF

Volovia Gorge

Post Road

Tchernaya

N

Careenage Ravine

Caves

Caves

49

49 EMAN

West Jut

41

Shell Hill

49

East Jut

Quarry Ravine

Inkerman Spur

St Clement's Ravine

7

LANCASTER BATTERY

GOODLAKE

Mikriakoff Glen

Saddle

30

30

SANDBAG BATTERY

Kitspur

VICTORIA RIDGE

THE BARRIER

30

CHAMPION

XX

2

Fore Ridge

Home Ridge

B

G

95

Wellway

British   Russian

⊠ Infantry

● Artillery

XX Division

X British Brigade

Battalion

Company, Battery

Picquet, or small groups

⌃⌃⌃ Camp

→ Advance

X

CODRINGTON

Post Road

X

Guards

MILES

0   ½   1

KILOMETRES

1

Picquets skirmishing on the heights overlooking the Sebastopol roadstead. After W. Simpson.

main body in rear to get under arms and prepare for action'.[5] Each was of company strength, by then averaging only 60 men. On arriving at its position, it would throw out a chain of double sentries, sufficiently far forward to give timely warning of any enemy approach, but in view or hearing of the picquet commander, who also kept touch with the other picquets to the right and left. By day, each pair was placed so as to have maximum observation towards, but also concealed from, the enemy and in sight of the next pair of the chain; by night they were placed so as to spot the enemy against a skyline, one man periodically patrolling forward to listen, his partner maintaining regular contact with the next pair to the right. The chain would be supplemented by a small, officer-led party which would patrol at intervals along the front and rear of the chain, and always before first light. Sentries would give early warning by rifle signals or by firing, one of the pair running back to report to the picquet commander. Once warned of an attack, the commander would fall in his company in two ranks, extend each file to a given number of paces, usually six, and prepare to engage as skirmishers, the two men of each file working together, one always being loaded and ready to fire while the other reloaded – firing being from a standing, kneeling or lying position depending on the ground. The picquet so formed, and with its sentries called in, would defend its front until its flanks were threatened, when it would retire to the next favourable position, thus delaying the enemy advance while the main body made ready.

Each brigade of the 2nd Division found, by day and night, four picquets (480 men for the whole division). A brigade's picquets, on each 24-hour tour of duty, were either found entirely by one battalion or drawn from two or more. A field officer was appointed to command each brigade's picquets, but as the roster for this duty was kept by divisional headquarters, it sometimes happened that one brigade's picquets were commanded by an officer of the other brigade.

This, however, was not the case on 26 October when the 1st Brigade's picquets on the right were commanded by the 95th's pious Major Champion. He had his headquarters at the Barrier, one company of his own regiment east of Home Ridge above the escarpment, and three of the 30th: one near the head of St Clement's ravine, the second further west, ready to support the third, Captain Atcherley's, which was forward and in touch with the right-hand picquet of 2nd Brigade, Lieutenant Conolly's company of the 49th on Shell Hill. West of Conolly were two more of the 49th and finally one of the 41st on West Jut above the Careenage ravine; all were commanded by Major Eman of the 41st. Across the ravine on Victoria Ridge was the right picquet of the Light Division, found by the 7th Royal Fusiliers, while patrolling along its bed were Goodlake's sharpshooters.

The morning of the 26th, 'a particularly beautiful one',[6] had been quiet except for the distant tolling of church bells and sounds of cheering from Sebastopol. Just after 1 pm Lieutenant Hume of the 55th, who had been relieved on picquet that morning by Atcherley, was standing with his brother and other 55th officers on Home Ridge, taking advantage of the excellent visibility to get a distant view of the positions captured by Liprandi the day before. Suddenly they heard heavy firing from the picquets. 'Soon after we saw some artillery come galloping over the crest of Shell Hill, followed by columns of infantry. "Green guns, by Jove", said Daubeney;[*] and off we ran as hard as we could to camp. We found the division turning out'.[7]

What they had seen were Federoff's six battalions which, having marched from Sebastopol at midday, had crossed the northern slopes of the Inkerman Heights, then wheeled right to advance southwards over Shell Hill. They came on with three battalions as a first line, each preceded by

Major James Eman, when an officer in the 41st's Light Company. He commanded 2nd Division's 'left' picquets on 26 October. He was killed in 1855.

skirmishers, and supported by the other three. The latter were each in the usual Russian column of attack formation: each battalion's four companies one behind the other, each company having its two platoons side by side in the Russians' customary three ranks, thus giving a battalion frontage of about 55 paces.[†] The leading battalions were in a different attack formation, used for advancing through close country: each having three companies in line, each 25 paces apart, one in reserve centrally, 25 paces behind; the companies having two, two-deep platoons one behind the other, both formed of the front and centre ranks of the normal platoons, whose third rank provided a third, two-deep platoon which supplied a number of skirmishers. Each of these battalions had a frontage of some 140 paces, less skirmishers, but of course the thick scrub on Shell Hill disrupted the intervals and dressing of the ranks.

Nevertheless, it was something approximating to

---

* Second-in-command, 55th. Russian guns were painted pea-green, British grey.

† 46 yards (42 m).

On smooth ground.   *In thick brushwood.*

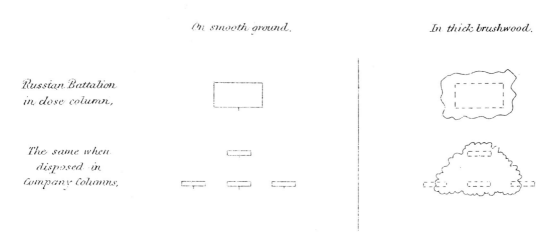

Russian Battalion in close column,

The same when disposed in Company Columns,

Formations used by Russian battalions on 26 October and 5 November. From A.W. Kinglake's *The Invasion of the Crimea.*

these formations which, fronted by skirmishers, were spotted coming up the northern slopes of Shell Hill by the sentries of the foremost picquet, Conolly's. The Russians were 'dressed in long grey coats and cloth caps with a red band. Their coats are so similar in colour to the high brushwood that they are almost invisible at a distance'.[8] Conolly at once extended his company into a skirmishing line, some 195 paces wide,* and opened fire. Since the six enemy battalions totalled 4,300, the 60 men of the 49th picquet were engaging, at first, the 1,620 of the leading nine companies. However, of those, only their 270 skirmishers could fire, whereas every man of the picquet could bring his rifle to bear. Furthermore, the latter all had rifled Miniés, while the Russian muskets found afterwards on the field were 'old, bearing date 1834, converted from flint to percussion'.[9]

Conolly's men disputed every yard of ground 'with an obstinacy that could hardly have been exceeded if, instead of this outpost duty, they had had to defend to the last some only-remaining stronghold'.[10] It came to close quarters and Conolly, throwing off his dark greatcoat so that his men might see his scarlet coatee among the Russian grey, hurled himself into an enemy group, closely followed by Sergeant Owens. When his sword broke, he struck out with his telescope until,

having been seriously wounded, he was rescued by his men. But numbers began to tell and, in danger of being surrounded, his picket fell back to the other 2nd Brigade pickets to its left.[†]

Meanwhile, Champion at the Barrier, seeing Conolly's fierce resistance, advanced with his nearest two 30th picquets to join Atcherley and form a skirmishing line on the southern slope of Shell Hill, ready to engage the Russian first line once Conolly's withdrawal permitted it to resume its advance. At the same time, he detached a small party under Colour-Sergeant Sullivan, 30th, to shoot at Federoff's gunners so as to delay their opening fire. With three companies extended over about a quarter of a mile, Champion was able to present a firing line as wide, if not wider, than the three enemy battalions' frontage. After some furious firing, he saw the enemy force dividing to threaten his flanks and realized it was time to move.

To give time for the picquets to collect, I halted to fire upon the enemy and we gave an efficient fire. At last the artillery playing very sharply upon us, and our left flank being endangered, we retired with all expedition to the

---

* 30 files, each occupying 21 inches (53 cm), extended at six-pace intervals, each of 30 inches (76 cm).

† Conolly and Owens (see page 136) both subsequently received the Victoria Cross.

Lieutenant J.A. Conolly, 49th Regiment, whose picquet was the first to engage the Russians on Shell Hill, holding the telescope with which he fought after his sword broke. Gazetted VC on 5 May 1857.

Barrier, where the three companies collected and continued to keep up a fire.[11]

While this delaying action had been fought, Goodlake had positioned his sharpshooters across the bed of the Careenage ravine some half a mile forward of West Jut, and had advanced with Sergeant Ashton to reconnoitre some caves. While inside, Federoff's hitherto-unseen flanking battalion came round a corner and surged past the caves up the ravine until engaged by the sharpshooters. Realizing he was cut off, Goodlake resigned himself to being captured but Ashton, believing they were marked men for their recent capture of a Russian officer, urged resistance, saying, 'They would kill

us over that picquet "job"'.[12] So, together, they dashed out, shooting or clubbing the nearest Russians, completely surprising them, and ran on up the ravine into the main column, through whose ranks they passed unmolested, their identities seemingly concealed by their greatcoats and the rough, bush-covered ground. Reaching the head of the column, they found it halted by fire from the sharpshooters lining a ditch across the gorge 30 yards (27 m) away. They quickly raced across the gap to safety. Heartened by their leader's near-miraculous escape, the sharpshooters stood their ground on that spot, below and between West Jut and the Lancaster battery, their accurate fire proving a stronger deterrent to the column than its commander's exhortations to charge.

After reaching the Barrier, Champion called in his right-hand, 95th picquet so that he now had all his four companies confronting the three leading enemy battalions. 'We defended ourselves vigorously against the swarms of Russians now appearing everywhere except in our rear. I knew that succour must come shortly and sent to say how hard we were pressed'. Heedless of danger, he jumped up on the stone wall to encourage his men, shouting, 'Slate them, my boys – slate them!' He told them that

supports were coming up to us, and I made them cheer and fix bayonets, which daunted the Russians, who had nearly driven us out by turning our flank. I tried to get up a charge, but it was too much for human nature and the few men I had with me; but they advanced a little, firing a few shots, and the Russians fell back.[13]

These, however, were probably only the enemy skirmishers, for the leading companies continued the fire fight at about 200 yards (180 m) range. 'Here as always the Minié told with murderous effect',[14] but the picquets' ammunition was running out and the three columns of the Russian second line could be seen coming on. More than once Champion must have looked anxiously rearwards for the help he had promised his hard-fighting men.

While the picquets had been gaining him time,

Captain Gerald Goodlake, Coldstream Guards, and the Guards' sharpshooters engaging the Russians. Gazetted VC on 24 February 1857.

Lieutenant-General Sir George De Lacy Evans, commanding 2nd Division.

De Lacy Evans had called the rest of the division to arms and ordered his two batteries to align their guns along Home Ridge, the infantry moving into cover behind it. Word had gone to the Guards Brigade which had sent forward its H Battery and its battalions were marching up. From the Light Division, E Battery was on its way, passing the alerted Naval Brigade where the future field-marshal, Evelyn Wood, then a midshipman, saw them, 'the teams stretched down at top speed, every driver "riding" his horse. I was so impressed by the set, determined look on the faces of the men that I have never forgotten it'.[15] Some guns had opened fire at the Russian artillery on its first coming into view, but it was extreme range. They had then engaged the infantry, but it was difficult to distinguish the extended picquets from the enemy in the thick undergrowth when both were in greatcoats, until Champion's men fell back to the

Barrier; nor were Eman's left picquets easily visible from Home Ridge, so fire had been stopped. ★

Hitherto Evans had refused all requests for help from the pickets, being determined to halt the Russians with his guns from Home Ridge, and then counter-attack with his infantry, whom he was keeping hidden. Now, just as Champion's picquets were down to their last rounds, and the entire enemy force was in full view, he sent forward Captain Paget Bayly's 30th Company to the Barrier and the 41st Light Company to assist Eman. At the same time, B, G and H Batteries opened fire at the Russian second line columns as they came within maximum range. A battery's four 9-pounders' most effective range when firing round shot or shrapnel was 800 yards (730 m), though they could reach out to 1,200–1,400 (1,100–1,280 m), about the distance the second columns were from Home Ridge when fully in view. The two 24-pounder howitzers per battery, firing shell or shrapnel and effective up to 1,025 yards (937 m), may at first have been held in reserve, or used to engage the rear of the foremost battalions confronting the picquets about 700 yards (640 m) from Home Ridge. Watching the blue-uniformed crews' well-practised gun drill – two rounds per minute – was Hume, whose 55th was in reserve:

It was splendid to see our gunners at work. One, a red-haired man, was greatly excited, and used very strong language when he found one of the ammunition boxes could not be opened; he soon knocked the hasp off with a stone.[16]

The relief afforded to Champion's men at the Barrier, first by the 60 rounds per rifle of Bayly's company, then by the crash of 18 guns from Home Ridge and the whistling shot passing overhead, turned to exhilaration when they saw the gunfire's effect on the Russian second line. The easternmost column broke away in some disorder, seeking shelter in Quarry ravine, into which some of Champion's men ran forward to fire. The other two soon retraced their steps behind Shell Hill to get out of range. Despite this setback to their supports, the forward battalions continued firing at the Barrier. Atcherley was disabled by an arm wound

★ The position of Eman's picquets by this time is unclear, but probably they were angled back from West Jut along the lip of the Mikriakoff glen, engaging the Russians' right flank.

and Paget Bayly was shot through the face but stayed with his men.

However, Federoff now ordered a retreat, either feeling he had adequately tested the defences or realizing he could achieve no more. His first line fell back in good order, keeping up a musketry to hold off Champion's jubilant men, now running forward with bayonets fixed. Seeing them go, Evans sent forward the remaining four companies of the 30th and seven of the 95th towards the Barrier and Shell Hill, and the rest of the 41st towards West Jut. The sight of these fresh troops and the sudden loss of Federoff, who fell seriously wounded, caused some of the Russians to lose heart and their retreat became hurried. Others still turned to fire as they went back over Shell Hill. Among the 95th, advancing in column,* was Private Doody who was suddenly hit in the chest and fell, thinking he was shot, only to find the ball had struck the brass plate where his shoulder belts crossed on his chest and glanced off. Surgeon Clarke ran forward to attend a badly wounded man, but was berated by Major Hume[†] for being so slow. 'I am doing my best', replied Clarke, as the balls fell around him. Then the man was hit again and killed. 'I can do no more for him now', the surgeon said stiffly.[17]

An eyewitness sketch by J.A. Crowe, correspondent of *The Illustrated London News*, of the action on 26 October. The nearest infantry must be the companies sent forward by Evans, not the picquets who were in greatcoats.

The main body of the 95th was halted on the south side of Shell Hill, but its Light Company went on in skirmishing order pursuing the Russian rearguard until it came under fire from Sebastopol's guns and ships in the roadstead. The men came back with the Russian soldiers' black bread loaves stuck on their bayonets. On the left, some of the 30th and 41st dropped down into the Careenage ravine where Goodlake's men, later joined by some of 2nd Rifle Brigade under Captain Markham from the Light Division, had held their ground throughout the main fight until the flanking column turned back. Scouting down the ravine, Sergeant Madden, 41st, went into a cave after a Russian officer and 14 men and took them all prisoner.[‡] Sergeant Shaw and Private Andrews, 30th, having captured and sent back some prisoners, went in search of some reward for their efforts and found a wounded, mounted Russian officer whom they escorted back to camp. They managed to get a good price for his sword, saddle and accoutrements, but his horse was killed a few days later by enemy fire before

---

* Each company in line, one behind the other separated by one company's width.
† Of the 95th, not to be confused with the brothers Hume of the 55th.

‡ Madden subsequently received the Victoria Cross.

Royal Navy Lancaster 68-pounder of the type manned by
Midshipman Hewett and his crew. After W. Simpson.

they could find a buyer. These two men had fought
all afternoon, having been with one of the original
30th picquet companies commanded by Lieutenant
Ross Lewin, the son of an old Peninsular officer.
As he led his tired men back to their lines, he met
Brigadier Pennefather who shook his hand and
congratulated them on their success, adding, 'The
30th behaved like gentlemen!'[18]

Some of the last shots at the Russians as they
made their way back to Sebastopol were fired by
the sailors manning the Lancaster 68-pounder on
Victoria Ridge, commanded by Midshipman
Hewett of HMS *Beagle*, and guarded by a 7th
Fusiliers picquet. Earlier in the day the picquet had
been fired on from Shell Hill and by part of the
column in the Careenage ravine. The fire was so
accurate that the picquet had to take cover on the
far side of the battery, the officer ordering Hewett

to spike his gun and leave it. According to one of
the Fusiliers, Private Alfred Oliver, Hewett replied, 'No, sir! Not while we are able to defend it',
and ordered his sailors to demolish the gabions
protecting the right side, so that they could
manhandle the gun, normally pointing forwards,
round to face the threatened flank and open fire.
Later, as Oliver wrote,

the gun did her duty nobly as well as the little Middy
who, when they [the Russians] were going through a
gulley and over a bridge into Sebastopol, in a mass of
columns, swept them away by hundreds. It was really
awful to see the havoc she made among them.[19]★

Two Russian officers and 181 men were found
dead on the battlefield. An observer wrote: 'The
dead men were lying in pools of blood, their faces
and hands like wax; most had been killed by our

★ Hewett received the Victoria Cross for this action and his conduct on 5
November and later became an admiral (see page 136).

Minié rifles. Our heavy conical balls cause frightful wounds; wherever they touch limb, they smash the bone'. [20] How many dead and wounded were carried off is uncertain, though the Russians admitted to a loss of 270. Altogether 80 prisoners were taken, among them a Pole who told an officer that 'to inflame them to fiery conflict with the "red devils", two stimulants, which most powerfully excite the sluggish soul of the Muscovite serf – religious artifice and "quass"* – were freely administered'. [21]

The 2nd Division's casualties were surprisingly light, totalling 84, of whom 12 were killed, the greatest loss falling on the 30th with 7 killed and 25 wounded. The Guards had been standing by in reserve and Captain Wilson of the Coldstream had watched the wounded

as they limped or were carried on stretchers to the rear. Far from drooping in spirit, most were in buoyant spirits. Sometimes a fine youth with badly fractured arm hurra-ed lustily as he passed; sometimes a 'stout Widdrington', whose thigh a round shot had smashed, would, faint as he was, raise himself a little on his litter, and brandish his rifle triumphantly. I observed that nearly every man, whether slightly or sorely hurt, still clutched his musket. A bullet through the heart alone conquers such soldiers. [22]

After the battle, Champion, whose inspiring and combative leadership had so greatly contributed to the day's success, reverted to his gentler nature in a letter to his wife:

I came heated and flushed from a hard-won field, where I had braved death with a prayer to the Almighty, and looked upon death with the hardened eye of a soldier. I felt the tears come into my eyes as I looked to a beautiful sunset in the west, where I knew you were; sweet was the comfort I felt in thanking the Almighty that we were spared to each other again. [23]

Coming as it did the day after the disaster to the Light Cavalry Brigade, which itself had increased the disillusion following the failure of the first bombardment, this combat of 'Little Inkerman', as it came to be known, gave the whole Crimean army a fillip. It had been an almost textbook action. The picquets' dogged resistance; Evans's considered handling and grasp of his battle; the leadership of the company officers; the skill-at-arms of the men, mostly fighting in skirmishing pairs, which called for much greater individual enterprise than the close-order of line and column; the professional work of the gunners; all had not only repulsed a numerically superior force at little cost, but had left the 2nd Division with an immense confidence in its supremacy over the enemy, greatly enhancing its morale for its future guarding of this exposed flank.

However, as the perceptive Lieutenant Morgan of the 95th noted: 'I do not think [the enemy] intended anything more than a reconnaissance in force; they only came to see the nakedness of the land and, as their subsequent moves showed, they attained their object'. [24]

---

* Kvass = rye-beer.

5

The English Shall be Attacked

The battle experience of 26 October, added to that of the Alma and Balaclava, had revealed the strengths and limitations of the Russian soldier, both in attack and defence. British soldiers may have been driven to enlist to escape the hardships of civilian life, but at least they had done so more or less of their own free will. Their Russian counterparts were in the main serfs, living under a harsh and repressive regime, and conscripted for 25 years. British officers were struck by the sameness of their appearance:

Broad-shouldered, sinewy, nearly as tall as Englishmen, there was ever a stereotyped and ugly uniformity of high cheek-bones, snub noses, elongated upper lips and cropped poles with colourless hair of the coarsest texture, thin wiry moustaches . . . fine, stout men but their faces are broad and flat and betoken great ignorance.[1]

To encourage them before the Alma, they were told that, since England was primarily a naval power, the men they saw before them in red would be as useless in a land battle as the two battalions of seamen in Menshikoff's army, whose ineptitude at drill had caused the soldiers much mirth. According to Kinglake, this was believed by some of the more uneducated officers, 'and even, it was said, in one instance by a general of division'.[2]

No strangers to corporal punishment before joining the army, their daily life as soldiers was punctuated by frequent blows with sticks or fists, to punish or encourage, from both officers and NCOs. A Polish deserter, sick of the beatings, claimed that he and his comrades had been warned the Allies would cut off their ears if they deserted[3] –

a risk he had obviously thought worth taking, but a warning which could well strike fear into the simple minds of most conscripts, who were always those who had been unable to buy or talk their way out of the periodic call-ups.

Before the Alma at least, they were eager for action and, according to an NCO of the Taroutine Regiment, 'all of us, officers and men, were confident in our own strength and openly voiced it'.[4] In action, particularly when primed with an alchohol ration, the Russian soldier was brave and stoical, but a British observer felt that 'his courage would seem to be passive not active'.[5] A Russian officer, aware of the fear-based discipline which held his men in thrall, cynically remarked to his British captors: 'No wonder our soldiers are brave! They have so little to lose that they lose nothing when they lose their life. The way to make a good soldier is to make him careless about his existence'.[6]

The regimental officers often appeared as equally careless of theirs. 'They were ever in front of their less adventurous rank and file, urging them on with voice and uplifted sword; they rushed freely on certain death, with the view of inflaming the sluggish spirit of their followers'.[7] In Line regiments (as opposed to Guards) a minority, from the hereditary but landless nobility, came from military cadet schools, but the majority were either sons of military officers and Civil Servants who, before commissioning, had to serve in the ranks as a 'junker' (neither officer nor soldier) and qualify in an examination, or were promoted NCOs with 12 years' service who could pass a simple exam.

HOW THE HOLY MEN OF RUSSIA INSPIRE THEIR SOLDIERS.

John Leach's interpretation for *Punch* of how 'the sluggish soul of the Muscovite serf' was stimulated by 'religious artifice' and alcohol.

Though ready to lead gallantly, most tended to be militarily uneducated, remote from their men, and with any professional enthusiasm atrophied by the boredom of routine in uneventful, distant garrisons, which could only be alleviated by drink, gambling, or complaisant peasant women.

Staff duties were on a par with the British service. Such work was unpopular and most senior commanders had little appreciation or understanding of staff functions, ignoring any trained staff officers they might have had, and relying on their own spontaneous decisions, assisted by a few chosen aides.

The Russian Army was trained and equipped, not so much to fight, as to present an awesome, magnificent and machine-like spectacle. Ever since Nicholas I's accession as Tsar in 1825 had been threatened by a military coup, led by officers who had acquired liberal ideas in Western Europe after the fall of Napoleon I, every aspect of Russian life

had become increasingly regimented. From his army, Nicholas expected the unquestioning obedience which could only be obtained by the enforcement of the most rigid, brutal discipline, and the endless practice of close-order drill, in which an exaggerated parade-march, or goose step, predominated. Nicholas had the soul of a drill-sergeant which delighted in the slow, stately manoeuvres of huge blocks of splendidly dressed automata, the theory being that 'in unblemished formal parades lay the guarantee of success in war'.[8]

As they had trained in peace, so they performed in war, and hence the ponderous columns of companies, battalions and regiments already seen

Russian infantry attacking with the bayonet through scrub-oak.
A watercolour sketch by Captain H.H. Clifford.

at the Alma and Little Inkerman, 'the obstinate but soulless action of their massy formation', as one British officer described it.[9] Little time and money was devoted to musketry. The great Suvoroff's late-eighteenth century maxim that 'the bullet is a fool, but the bayonet a fine fellow'[10] still held good, and in any case their smooth-bore muskets, whose effective range was little more than 150 yards (137 m), were often unserviceable from excessive polishing with brick-dust and loosening of fittings to rattle impressively at drill. There were a number of Rifle battalions which could be attached to infantry divisions to provide a more skilled company of skirmishers for each regiment, but many of these were armed with a Belgian-made version of the Brunswick, used by British Rifle regiments until the introduction of the Minié, of which it was said that 'the force required to ram down the ball was so great as to render a man's hand much too unsteady for accurate shooting'.[11] However, the Russian infantry's weakness in firepower and reliance on massed bayonets was balanced by a well-armed and trained divisional artillery, whose pieces outgunned and outranged the British field batteries; unfortunately its handling by higher commanders was not always as good as its technical expertise.

The inadequacies already noted in some British generals could be matched by those of the Russian Army. If the British military system had suffered too long from the ageing influence of the Duke of Wellington, so had the Russian from the rigid despotism of Nicholas I which discouraged ideas and initiative. Menshikoff in his time had been a general, an admiral, an administrator and a diplomat, but was master of none of these professions. Rich, ambitious and arrogant, he had enjoyed the Tsar's confidence but was distrustful and contemptuous of his subordinates and his troops, secretive about his intentions, and had few powers of leadership. Liprandi, one of the more capable generals, he considered 'a Greek intriguer'.[12] Towards Todleben, only a colonel and of German origin but perhaps the most competent senior officer in the Crimea, who had reorganized Sebastopol's defences, Menshikoff was dismissive and irritable. Among his subordinates at the Alma,

Gortchakoff was elderly and cautious, Kiriakoff was incompetent, a drunken braggart, and possibly a coward as well. Between Menshikoff and Dannenberg, his new deputy appointed by St Petersburg, whose IV Corps arrived on 2/3 November, there existed a hearty and mutual dislike. The latter, like some of his British counterparts, was an ageing, once-able veteran of the Napoleonic War, but on the Danube against the Turks his command of IV Corps had been undistinguished.

It was this unpromising partnership which was to launch the great counter-offensive. The objective was not, as hitherto favoured by Menshikoff, Balaclava, but, on the Tsar's personal instructions, and as expressed in Menshikoff's orders of 4 November: 'Tomorrow the English shall be attacked in their position, in order that we may seize and occupy the heights on which they are established'.[13]

Menshikoff's plan envisaged a two-pronged attack on the sector reconnoitred by Federoff on 26 October, supported by a sortie from Sebastopol against the French siege lines by Timovieff, and by a strong demonstration across the Balaclava plain to distract the defenders of the Sapouné Ridge from reinforcing the British defenders of Home Ridge to their north, and ultimately to link up with the main attack.

Soimonoff's 10th Division (the 12 battalions of the Katherinburg, Tomsk and Kolivansk Regiments) was marched into Sebastopol on 3 November, where it was increased to corps strength by the addition of the Vladimir, Sousdal and Ouglitch Regiments (16th Division) which had fought at the Alma, the Boutirsk (17th Division), present at Little Inkerman, half the 6th Rifle Battalion, 289 sappers, 100 Cossacks, and 38 guns; a force of just under 19,000 men (28½ battalions). This corps was to be the right, or western prong, advancing from Sebastopol, parallel to the Careenage ravine, towards the Inkerman Heights. The left, or eastern prong, was Pauloff's corps, consisting of his own 11th Division (Selenghinsk, Iakoutsk, Okhotsk) plus the Borodino and Taroutine Regiments (17th Division), also veterans of the Alma, half the 4th Rifle Battalion, and 96 guns; nearly 16,000 in all (20½ battalions). This corps, encamped on the heights east of the Tchernaya, was to cross the river, march west parallel to the roadstead and ascend the heights via St George's ravine, there to

Left: General P.A. Dannenberg, commanding IV Corps. Right: Lieutenant-General F.I. Soimonoff, commanding 10th Division.

join up with Soimonoff, prior to attacking southwards together under Dannenberg's joint command. *

The force to operate against the Sapouné Ridge was under Gortchakoff's command and consisted of troops who had fought at Balaclava: Liprandi's 12th Division, 7,000 cavalry, and 88 guns; some 22,000 men strong. Gortchakoff was ordered to draw the Sapouné Ridge defenders (the Guards Brigade and Bosquet's corps) upon himself, to try and seize one of the routes up to the ridge, and to hold his cavalry in readiness to ascend the heights as soon as practicable.

Soimonoff, who had proved competent against the Turks, received these orders, not from Dannenberg, hitherto his superior, but direct from Menshikoff's headquarters at about 5 pm on 4 November; he was thus given no time to reconnoitre ground he had never seen, and which he would have to traverse in the dark. However, one of Menshikoff's staff explained that he was to advance up the eastern side of the Careenage ravine towards Shell Hill, so as to protect Pauloff's right, prior to linking up with that corps near the head of St George's ravine. Soimonoff later received written instructions from Dannenberg to attack at 5 am, instead of 6 am, and up the Victoria Ridge (that is, on the western bank of the Careenage ravine). This put Soimonoff in a quandary, which

---

* Kinglake, quoting Todleben, gives Soimonoff 18,929 and Pauloff 15,806, both excluding gunners. Another Russian account gives Soimonoff 16,200 and Pauloff 13,500 infantry.

only Menshikoff could resolve. Unable to obtain a ruling, and since he would not come under Dannenberg's command until after joining up with Pauloff, he decided he should adhere to the first order.

All being well, therefore, the two corps – less Pauloff's Borodino and Taroutine Regiments which were to advance up the Volovia gorge towards East Jut as left flank protection – would unite near the top of St George's ravine, establish themselves on the Shell Hill feature, prior to the whole 35,000 with its 134 guns attacking southwards against the 2nd Division, 3,000 strong with 12 guns.

If a humble subaltern like Morgan of the 95th could assess the purpose of Federoff's sortie the week before, it should not have been beyond the generals and staffs to see the need for clothing the nakedness of the Inkerman Heights with extra men, guns and defences. A Russian breakthrough here would not only threaten the rear of the British

siege lines and camps and cut them off from Balaclava, but could, in conjunction with Gortchakoff's corps, menace the French right flank and rear. Raglan, for all his faults, was not a fool and was aware of the vulnerability of this flank, and how stretched his forces were to guard both it and Balaclava, at the same time as prosecuting the siege. He had 6,000 Turks under his command but, after their abandonment of the Balaclava redoubts on the 25th, he refused to use them, even for digging defences. He had asked for French help but Canrobert, who had already detached one of Bosquet's brigades to assist the Highland Brigade's defence of Balaclava and the foot of the Col, said he could spare none. Yet Bosquet's other three brigades, behind man-made defences, and with the Guards to their north, were employed watching the approaches to the Sapouné Ridge from a naturally much stronger position than Home Ridge, guarded only by the 2nd Division's two brigades. They, it was true, could look to the Guards for support and had Codrington's Light Division brigade to their left, but Codrington's task was specifically to guard the approach up Victoria Ridge. Other than the Guards, therefore, the 2nd Division could only be reinforced by drawing men from the siege operations (that is, the 3rd and 4th Divisions and

The Russian view from Shell Hill towards Home Ridge. The Post Road is visible (centre) emerging from Quarry ravine, behind the nearmost trees, and disappearing over Home Ridge on the right centre of the horizon. A photograph dated 1904.

Buller's Light Division brigade), respectively three, two and a half, and one and a half miles away.

However, Raglan was keenly aware that his army's main aim was the capture of Sebastopol and soon, if he and his men were to be spared a Russian winter on the Chersonese for which they were not equipped. Indeed, a meeting had been arranged with Canrobert to discuss plans for an assault, provisionally fixed for 7 November. So, in the week after Federoff's attack, the minds at Raglan's headquarters were focused primarily on the siege works and preparations for the assault, leaving 2nd Division to take care of itself.

Without additional troops, De Lacy Evans had no choice but to adhere to the defensive arrangements existing before the 26th which, in effect, as Federoff had proved in broad daylight, allowed the Russians access to Shell Hill unhampered by any resistance other than that which could be offered by the picquets. Only by occupying its northern spurs, which would have required far greater strength than was available, could this have been avoided. So the defence of the sector remained based on Home Ridge with the picquet line as before. To give some cover for their guns when positioned on Home Ridge, the gunners of the two batteries began constructing a wall of stones and earth, some 100 yards (90 m) long. The ground was rocky so no trench could be dug and soil had to be fetched from further away. As few infantry could be spared to assist the gunners, by 4 November it was little more than 2 feet high.

The loose stone wall of the Barrier, at the head of Quarry ravine, was shorter but 1 to 2 feet higher and extended across the Post Road into the scrub on either side. Some 500 yards (450 m) in front of the Barrier, the surface of the road, where it emerged round a bend in the ravine, had been broken up to impede the passage of guns. Ideally, fields of fire should have been cleared through the brushwood, but there was not the manpower and, as proved on the 26th, it afforded cover for defenders as well as hindering the solid formations of the Russians; in any case, as on that day, a mobile, rather than a static defence was envisaged, with Home Ridge and the Barrier providing rallying points rather than redoubts.

The only other construction in 2nd Division's sector was an earthwork, sited 600 yards (550 m) east of the Barrier on the Kitspur, which jutted out

south of St Clement's ravine. Known as the Sandbag Battery, it had been erected some weeks before to house two 18-pounders, positioned to silence a gun across the Tchernaya valley. Their task completed, the guns had been withdrawn, but the battery remained. Being 9 feet (2.7 m) high, with only two embrasures and no fire-step, it was useless for infantry, other than as a windbreak for the picquet stationed there. Standing up prominently on the Kitspur, just to the right front of Fore Ridge, it was soon to assume a terrible significance.

The arrival of Dannenberg's corps, with Soimonoff marching into Sebastopol and Pauloff camping across the Tchernaya, had not passed unreported by the 2nd Division picquets, whose long hours of watching had become, as Champion wrote, increasingly 'severe, when you have to keep awake half the night', with a sudden change in the weather bringing 'a cold north wind and rain'.[14] Their reports, as well as deserters' tales, spies' messages, warnings from sources as far away as Berlin – all indicating a coming enemy offensive – found their way to Raglan's farmhouse on the Chersonese, 3 miles (5 km) south-west of the 2nd Division, yet none distracted its occupants from their planning for the assault. Colonel Calthorpe, one of Raglan's ADCs, expressed the general disbelief that the Russians 'will have determination and courage enough to overcome British firmness and French gallantry'.[15] The staff were more interested in the effects of the Allied bombardment, which opened on 1 November, and arranging the joint Council of War convened for the 4th, at which the 7th was settled as the day for the general assault on Sebastopol.

At that meeting, Canrobert assured Raglan he would reinforce the 2nd Division position but without making any specific commitment. Had De Lacy Evans been present he would surely have emphasized the urgency of the matter, but unfortunately he was aboard ship in the harbour, recovering from a fall. His division was temporarily under the 1st Brigade's commander, John Lysaght Pennefather. Aged 54, the third son of a Tipperary parson, he was known in his brigade as 'Old Blood and 'Ounds', from one of his favourite expletives, of which he had a wide and colourful repertoire.[16] In the 1840s he had been a notable commanding officer of the 22nd, which he had led into action at the Battle of Miani in 1843, receiving a serious

An Allied Council of War at the British headquarters. Raglan is seated at the far end of the table. After W. Simpson.

wound.* He had both command and staff experience and, as commander of the 1st Brigade, Hume of the 55th recorded that 'officers and men liked him, he was always so cheery and ready for any amount of fighting'.[17]

He had not been summoned to the Council of War, so he spent that Saturday afternoon riding through the heavy rain which had been falling most of the day, visiting his picquets to glean any new information about the enemy dispositions while daylight lasted, as was his daily custom. The right picquets that day were all provided by the 95th, but commanded by Major Grant of the 49th, who was at the usual field officer's post at the Barrier, with Lieutenant Carmichael and his men. When Pennefather reached them, they drew his attention to the heights across the Tchernaya whereon, according to Carmichael, 'the enemy was showing in great force. There had been a review in the course of the day and it was remarked to him that the enemy,

when in skirmishing order, advanced with fixed bayonets, which was entirely opposite to the practice in the British Army';[18] a point of minor tactics which may have suggested that even Russian skirmishers had more faith in their bayonets than in their firearms.

Through his telescope, Pennefather observed a yellow carriage in the enemy camp. He could not know, of course, that this had brought the Grand Dukes Nicholas and Michael, the Tsar's sons, to inspire by their presence the Russian soldiery's forthcoming effort. Nevertheless, the combination of the review and the sudden appearance of such an unusual vehicle for a military camp suggested to him that something important might be brewing. Before leaving the Barrier, he ordered Carmichael to keep watch from the furthest point of the spur between the Quarry and St Clement's ravines, during the last half hour before dark, and report personally to him any alterations in the enemy dispositions. In due course Carmichael reported a new body of cavalry on the river's far bank, south-east of his post, and a large flock of sheep which had been herded around the ruins of the old Inkerman village below the enemy camp.

The left picquets were commanded by Major

---

* During Napier's conquest of Scinde.

Brigadier-General J.L. Pennefather, commanding 1st Brigade, 2nd Division, but temporarily in command of the Division from 4 November.

A British infantryman dressed for picquet. Under the greatcoat's cape is slung, over the left shoulder, his ammunition pouch and water-bottle, with mess-tin attached to its strap, over the right his haversack; a bayonet (not visible) is suspended from his waistbelt. A photograph by Roger Fenton.

Goodwyn, 41st, and found by the 2nd Brigade regiments, though on this occasion for some reason their right-hand picquet on Shell Hill was commanded by Captain Vialls of the 95th. Having been more or less soaked by rain all day, with no shelter other than what could be found under the scrub-oak, the prospect of continuing the watch on through the night cannot have been enticing. After dark, the rain diminished to a steady drizzle, but with a thick mist adding to the difficulty and strain of observing, listening and maintaining contact to right and left. In such conditions officers found 'they could not keep their men awake; they *would* sleep, in spite of all they could do to prevent them'.[19]

In the 95th picquet east of the Barrier, Captain Sargent, conscious of the effect of damp on his men's rifles, made them reload. In so doing, one of his sentries, tense and fumbling in the darkness, accidentally discharged his rifle, bringing the whole picquet line to arms. Carmichael, visiting his sentries, suddenly ran into Major Goodwyn and

Anthony Morgan, 95th, photographed in 1902 in the kit he had worn as a subaltern at Inkerman.

Others, too, heard the church bells, 'slow and solemn as if for some great and mournful event',[21] but thought nothing of it as it was Sunday morning. Sargent from his post and Morgan in the Sandbag Battery also heard the rumbling, creaking wheels and reported the sound to Grant, but all thought it was merely one of the Russians' nightly supply trains which they, like Carmichael, had often heard before. Sergeant-Major Williams, whose 55th was providing the right picquets on the 5th, had visited the line after midnight, presumably to check routes and positions in the poor visibility since the new picquets customarily joined the old an hour before daylight. He had crept forward to listen on his own account and had been 'quite certain he heard in the direction of Sebastopol the rumblings of heavy wagons or artillery, either by supplies entering the city, or by guns coming out towards the Inkerman valley'.[22] He reported this to Grant and to his own officers who were due for picket. On Victoria Ridge a Light Division sentry also heard the sound of wheels down in Sebastopol but, so familiar was this, that he did not report it at the time.

So, huddled in their sodden greatcoats, trying to keep warm in the clammy mist, the tired picquets kept their watch through those enervating hours before dawn when a man's spirits are at their lowest, thankful their 24 hours' turn of duty was nearly over. Wherever they were posted, and however alert, the mist, thickening to fog, prevented any observation in the dark, and the sounds they heard, though reported, were not so unusual as to warrant any alarm. These were indeed the early hours of a Sunday morning when Sebastopol's church bells would customarily ring. The picquets were not to know they heralded special services to pray for success and to hearten the devout peasant soldiers in their great enterprise; their clangour echoing, as it were, other bells in distant St Petersburg, where the Tsar prayed throughout three hours for the Almighty's aid in ejecting the invaders from his lands. Nor could the weary sentries know that the grumbling wheels announced no harmless train of forage carts, but the heavy guns of Soimonoff and Pauloff, trundling along behind the dense marching columns in the foggy darkness, before the climb began up the northern slopes of Inkerman.

Vialls with his picquet. Vialls told him privately that Goodwyn, against his advice, had decided to withdraw his sentries from the crest of Shell Hill to its base on account of the mist but that, having gone astray in the scrub, they had made for the road to get their bearings. Sometime later Grant told him to rest while he kept watch, but Carmichael recalled,

tho' I laid down on the ground, I slept very little. I remember hearing the clang of church bells in the town and the rumble of wheels in the valley, but the latter noise raised no suspicion in my mind as it was a nightly occurrence and it was well known the enemy used the road during the night.[20]

PART

III

THE SOLDIERS' BATTLE

Remember, remember
The fifth of November,
Sebastopol, powder and shot;
When General Liprandi
Charged John, Pat and Sandy
And a jolly good licking he got!

PUNCH, VOL. XXVII, 216

6

Facing Fearful Odds

As the bells tolled to inspire Soimonoff's infantry tramping out of Sebastopol, the 2nd Division was roused from its leaky tents to parade for the customary hour's stand-to before daylight, quite unaware of the masses marching against it. The new picquets, all 55th under Lieutenant-Colonel Carpenter, 41st, for the right, two each of the 41st and 47th under Lieutenant-Colonel Haly, 47th, for the left, marched off into 'the thick, damp fog, which made it impossible to see anything beyond a few yards', and in which 'they had great difficulty in making out the position of the old picquets'.[1]

By the time he had been relieved at the Barrier and marched his tired men back to camp, shortly before 6 am, Carmichael found the division had been dismissed from stand-to and the usual wood and water fatigue parties sent out.

I went into my tent which I shared with Macdonald, then acting as Adjutant, and do not think I was in it three minutes when we heard some smart musketry in the direction, as I thought, of the Lancaster Battery.* My servant, No. 2500 John Smith, came in with a tin of very hot ship's cocoa, but it was so hot I could not take it.[2]

He asked Macdonald what he thought the firing meant. ' "Only the new picquets mistaking a bush for a party of Russians"', replied the Adjutant, but almost at once they both heard how 'the firing became regular and continuous, then in volleys. In a second everyone knew what it meant and "Stand to your arms!" was called out from one regiment to

another'.[3] Without his cocoa, without breakfast, without any rest after 24 hours' picket Carmichael, like others in the same situation, ran to fall in. Even men who had had what passed for a night's sleep on the unwelcoming ground had not yet had breakfast, before the distant picquets raised the alarm.

The most advanced of the new picquets was the 41st's Grenadier Company, 53 strong, under Captain Hugh Rowlands. With him was Lieutenant Allan, who had been on a working party from four the previous afternoon till one that morning. As they had passed through the night picquet, Rowlands thought he had seldom seen

a more cheerless aspect. On arriving I halted the company and went out to plant sentries about 150 yards over the hill. I returned to the company, which had just piled arms, when the sentries commenced firing in a most determined way. One shouted out there were columns of Russians close to them. I stood to arms and advanced in extended order, thinking it was a sortie like 26 October. On getting to the top of the hill I found myself close upon, very truly, thousands of Russians. I immediately gave the order to retire for about 200 yards . . . . I halted on the next high bit of ground and lay down quietly waiting for them. Fitzroy came up with the Light Company [which] I extended to reinforce my own. The Russians came on with the most fiendish yells you can imagine. We commenced firing. To my dismay half the firelocks missed fire, which dispirited the men.

Grossly outnumbered, and with the enemy closing in, Rowlands had to fall back again, the 47th pickets to his left conforming. Then, seeing

---

* On Victoria Ridge, see Chapter 4.

some 200 of the 30th doubling up from the rear,* 'I begged Colonel Haly to allow me to charge, and after a little hand-to-hand work, we drove them back about 500 yards'.[4] Haly cut down three Russians in this charge, but was unhorsed and bayoneted. Rowlands, with Privates Kelly and McDermond, both 47th, dashed forward to rescue him. Kelly was killed but Rowlands, though wounded in the arm, and McDermond managed to fight off Haly's attackers and drag him clear.[†] This sudden counter-attack earned them a respite until the Russian infantry came on again, edging round their flanks and forcing them to retire.

Captain Hugh Rowlands, second from the right (profile), and Lieutenant William Allan, second on the left (seated), with other officers of the 41st, some in the new 1855 uniform. Rowlands was gazetted VC on 24 February 1857. A photograph by Roger Fenton.

To Rowlands' right, Captain Robert Hume's 55th picquet was also beset by defective rifles. Having been loaded for some time, the damp had affected the powder in the nipples which failed to ignite when the hammers fell on the percussion caps. Hume was soon wounded and had to hand over to Lieutenant Elton, but continued to make himself useful by having the wet rifles brought to him, unscrewing the nipples and putting in fresh powder; an example of coolness under fire and indifference to his wound which his brother

---

* Major Patullo's wing (i.e. a half-battalion, four companies).

† Both later received the Victoria Cross for saving Haly's life; Rowlands' award also being for his 'great pluck' in command of his picket.

Private McDermond, 47th, saving the life of Lieutenant-Colonel Haly, for which he later received the VC, gazetted on 24 February 1857. A painting by Chevalier Desanges.

thought 'encouraged his men to face the fearful odds against them so bravely'.[5]

Despite the picquets' resistance, the Russian columns lumbered forward through the fog and presently their guns came into action. Elton's men

retired gradually and soon had most desperate work, almost hand to hand in the thick brushwood with the guns playing on us in a most fearful way, and ours answering them over our heads, while we were firing into each other at between 15 to 30 paces distance, now and then charging and driving them back, and then being driven back by superior numbers again.[6]

The troops which had loomed up against Hume's and the left picquets were Soimonoff's eight battalions of the Tomsk and Kolivansk Regiments, preceded by the 6th Rifles, and supported by the Katherinburg Regiment and 22 12-pounders. Each of the two leading regiments had two battalions forward, both in the close-country company columns used on 26 October, with their other two,

and all the Katherinburgers, in battalion close columns. Thus, what the picquets saw coming through the mist-shrouded scrub was, first, the Rifles' skirmishers, then 12 companies in line with a second line of four companies, followed by four rectangular blocks of battalion columns in line, and lastly the four Katherinburg columns, two by two. Some way in rear and out of sight of the picquets were Soimonoff's other 16 battalions and 16 lighter guns.

So, at this stage, as Soimonoff's 12-pounders, covered by their infantry, went into action on Shell Hill, from which ranges had been carefully calculated on 26 October, some 300 picquets, firing and falling back in their skirmishing pairs, were doing their utmost to hold up the advance of nearly 10,000 men on the western sides of Shell Hill and the saddle leading to Home Ridge.

As soon as the Russian guns opened fire on the 2nd Division camp, 'life was not worth ten minutes' purchase as [they], having got the accurate range, were throwing in a storm of shot and shell, and their fire was incessant'.[7] The tents had been struck on the alarm being given and the six battalions, less those on picquet, had been doubled forward to lie down behind Home Ridge. Thus,

5 Battle of Inkerman: Dawn to 7.30 am

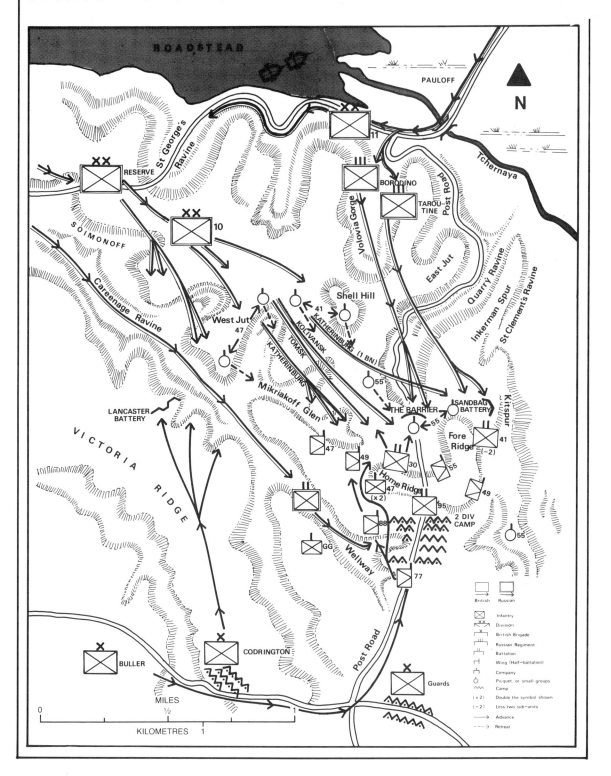

ROADSTEAD

PAULOFF

N

St George's Ravine

Tchernaya

RESERVE

BORODINO

TAROU-TINE

Volovia Gorge

Post Road

SOIMONOFF

10

East Jut

Quarry Ravine

Inkerman Spur

St Clement's Ravine

Careenage Ravine

Shell Hill

West Jut
47

41
KATHERINBURG

KOLIVANSK

(1 BN)

Kitspur

KATHERINBURG

TOMSK

55

SANDBAG BATTERY

LANCASTER BATTERY

Mikriakoff Glen

THE BARRIER

55

Fore Ridge

41
(-2)

VICTORIA RIDGE

47

49

30

55

Home Ridge
47
(x 2)

95

49

2 DIV CAMP

55

88

GG

Wellway

77

Post Road

BULLER

CODRINGTON

Guards

	British	Russian
		Infantry
		Division
		British Brigade
		Russian Regiment
		Battalion
		Wing (Half-battalion)
		Company
		Picquet, or small groups
		Camp
(x 2)		Double the symbol shown
(-2)		Less two sub-units
		Advance
		Retreat

MILES
0   ½   1

KILOMETRES   1

although the fire caused much damage in the abandoned camp, casualties at first were few.

Two 9-pounders of the divisional artillery were kept permanently hooked in, ready for immediate action. These galloped up through the 95th, lying down in line either side of the road, and they were the first to return fire. According to Carmichael,

They fired at the flashes of the enemy guns on Shell Hill, but soon drew a heavy fire on themselves. Some of their men fell, and I remember one round shot tore into my company, completely severing the left arm and both legs off a man in the front rank and killed his rear rank man without any perceptible wound. I called some bandsmen to carry the poor mutilated fellow away but they said they were too busy with other wounded.[8]

The 95th was being held in reserve by Penne-father, who had quickly decided how to fight his battle. Realizing he was facing a major attack, far stronger than Federoff's, he knew reinforcements must come, but that he must hold with his greatly inferior numbers until they arrived. Evans's plan, successfully implemented on the 26th, had been to let the picquets come in, then fight from Home Ridge. Pennefather, however, conscious of the distances reinforcements must march, and aware there was no suitable defensive position rearwards of Home Ridge, decided to use the fog and brushwood to conceal his numerical weakness, and to strike the enemy as hard and as far forward as possible by feeding the picquets' resistance, first, from his own division, then with whatever troops and guns came to hand. He retained on the ridge as a reserve his 12 guns, the 95th, two 47th companies and the balance of the 55th not on picquet. Tactical reasoning apart, this was typical of his combative spirit.

Hence the dispatch of Patullo's wing of the 30th to the left picquets, while the other wing under

A sub-division of a Royal Artillery battery, showing the 9-pounder and limber, with its ammunition wagon and limber beyond. After G. Campion.

section; each lurking in the scrub, waiting for the 'blank, dazed faces'[9] in the Russian columns heaving forward out of the swirling mist, before checking them with Minié fire or a short, savage bayonet charge. Brigadiers and generals would be present, but it would mostly be regimental officers who would confront each crisis, all spurred on by the indefatigable Pennefather's cheerful oaths.

Arriving near Home Ridge at about 7 am, Raglan, who had learned of the attack from the Light Division, saw no reason to interfere with Pennefather's arrangements. He realized that all planning for the assault on the 7th must now take second place but, having ensured that all possible reinforcements were on the way from the Light and 4th Divisions, and the Guards, and that the 3rd Division would watch all exits from Sebastopol, there was little he could do but observe. However, aware of the weight of Russian gunfire from Shell Hill, he ordered up two 18-pounders from the siege train a mile and a half (2.4 km) away. They should reach Home Ridge within the hour.

The Light Division had been alerted by Codrington, who had been riding round his picquets when the first shots were fired. Buller had most of his brigade in the trenches, but he immediately sent off four companies of the 88th (290 strong) under Colonel Jeffries towards Home Ridge, following shortly after with his ADC, Henry Clifford, and four companies of the 77th under Colonel Egerton. Moving up at the same time was Townshend's P Battery, Royal Artillery, from the 4th Division. Codrington had deployed his old and new picquets, plus such troops as were not on trench duty, on the eastern side of Victoria Ridge, to give whatever fire support he could to the 2nd Division's left flank across the Careenage ravine, and to prevent any enemy advancing up Victoria Ridge, as Dannenberg had wished Soimonoff to do.

Had Soimonoff complied, he might have been able to push through these 1,100 men of Codrington's so as to cut off 2nd Division from the other British formations and place his corps across its rear, while Pauloff attacked frontally. On the other hand, he had received Dannenberg's orders so late

Lieutenant-Colonel Mauleverer went to the Barrier. A wing from each of the 47th and 49th, respectively under Majors Fordyce and Grant, who had been up all night with the right picquets, advanced to the head of the Mikriakoff glen as a fall-back for the left picquets. The right picquets, all 55th, had not yet been attacked, except for Hume's. However, mindful of the great host he had seen across the Tchernaya the previous afternoon, Pennefather sent towards Fore Ridge Brigadier Adams with the rest of the 41st, to be supported by Bellairs' wing of the 49th from the east end of Home Ridge. All, sooner or later, would be heavily engaged.

This was the way the Battle of Inkerman began for the British, and so it would continue: not fought like the Alma in the formations of the Manual – brigades and divisions with all battalions in two-deep line – but by bodies seldom larger than a wing and often as small as a half-company or

The junction of the Mikriakoff glen and Careenage ravine, seen from Victoria Ridge looking towards the saddle between Shell Hill (left) and Home Ridge.

that the necessary change to his own orders would more likely have resulted in confusion. As it was, he had gone straight into action to establish his guns on Shell Hill, but at the expense of getting his leading infantry heavily engaged by Pennefather's skirmishing tactics before there was any sign of Pauloff. Not knowing that the latter had been delayed, due to misunderstandings over responsibility for repairing the Tchernaya bridge across which Pauloff had to march, Soimonoff decided to wait for him. However, seeing the ground south of Shell Hill for the first time, he realized how little space there was to deploy two corps on the Saddle leading to Home Ridge. He decided, therefore, to use the delay to send a reconnoitring column south-eastwards across the spurs and gulleys falling from the western side of the Saddle into the Careenage ravine and Mikriakoff glen; this would be protected on its right by another small force which had been advancing as flank protection up the Careenage ravine.

The reconnoitring column pushed on unopposed through the oaks. Suddenly, there in the mist was a line of rifles. This was the 49th wing under Grant, who shouted: 'Give them a volley and charge!'[10] Some 245 Minié balls smashed at close range into the surprised and closely-packed Russians, leaving them in no state to resist the yelling 49th as they sprang forward with bayonets levelled. The column

broke right back to the slopes of Shell Hill, Grant cheering his men on in pursuit. The Careenage column, seemingly unaware of this reverse, continued on up the ravine's bed, heading towards the Wellway.

There was now less fog on Shell Hill than on the lower ground, and the unexpected sight of Grant's four companies in line below him changed Soimonoff's mind about waiting for Pauloff. Out of Grant's view, just over the crest, waited the Tomsk, Kolivansk and Katherinburg Regiments, realigned from their previous formation after their earlier brush with the picquets. The 49th, getting their breath back after their exhilarating advance, then heard 'a multitudinous stirring as of a host, followed by myriad hurrahs which gave voice to the rage of a close-gathered soldiery'.[11] A line of flat caps appeared, then the 12 leading companies heading the blocks of battalion columns, all plodding down the slope, bayonets advanced. Faced by such odds, Grant's men had no choice but to melt away into the brushwood, firing as they fell back.

All this while Soimonoff's guns had continued to thunder out against Home Ridge from where Pennefather's two batteries had done their utmost to reply, though both sides' gunners were hampered by the fluctuating visibility. Soimonoff's leading infantry could see the British gun flashes and to avoid them they followed the route taken by the reconnoitring column. In doing so, their right became more advanced from the remainder and, since the brushwood was thicker in the Mikriakoff glen, the ranks of the company and battalion columns lost their alignment, the formations degenerating into masses of men all jumbled up together. This, to a soldiery drilled and drilled like the Russians, weakened the cohesion such drilling was designed to attain.

It was one of these masses which suddenly spilled out of the fog down the side of the Mikriakoff glen, straight at the centre of the four 88th companies, separating one half from the other. Having reported their arrival to Pennefather near Home Ridge, they had been ordered to advance towards the left front. They had met a 2nd Division officer, probably Grant, who pointed out the enemy's general direction, and had been advancing in extended order through the glen when the Russians fell on them. The Grenadier and No. 5 Companies on the right were forced back, but the

Light and No. 7 opened fire, then charged, driving their opponents back, right up to the southern side of West Jut. There they were halted by a 5-foot (1.5 m) high wall, behind which eight battalions and artillery of Soimonoff's reserve were massed.

Undaunted, the Irishmen threw themselves at this obstacle, but 16 of them died on the Russian bayonets. Captain Crosse was

surrounded by a knot of Russians; having just taken out his revolver, he was ready for this onslaught and shot four; a fifth bayoneted Captain C. in the leg, and fell over him, bending the bayonet in the wound, and pulling Captain C. on top of him; a sixth charged him but, with his sword, he was enabled to cut along the Russian's firelock on to his hands. Captain C. got up and made off, but was again attacked by [this] Russian and again drove him back; he then fell in with Privates Samuel Price, John Gascoigne and Pat Daly who had come to look for [him].[12]

These three defended Crosse against the pursuing Russians until they encountered some 49th bandsmen with a stretcher, on which they placed him; then they rejoined their companies, which had been falling back. Owing to the hurried retreat from the wall through the dense scrub, the two companies were in no sort of order, nevertheless individuals periodically turned to fire to keep the enemy at a distance. They could hear their regimental call and 'Assembly' being repeatedly

Officers and men of the 88th (Connaught Rangers), photographed by Roger Fenton in 1855.

sounded by a bugler with their other two companies, which had retreated to the head of the glen, where eventually all four were reunited.

The Light and No. 7 Companies owed their escape in part to Lieutenant Miller and the crews of three guns of P Battery on the southern spur above the glen. Some of the 88th ran back through them, but when two Katherinburg battalions came up over the lip through the mist, they only had time to fire one round of case-shot* before the enemy was on them. Miller immediately spurred his horse into them, slashing with his sword, followed by his gunners laying about them with rammers and short swords, 'finding vent for their rage in curses and shouts of defiance'.[13] The leading Katherinburgers halted as though frozen into disbelief at the gunners' foolhardiness, but then the momentum of the mass inexorably pushed them on, over the 20-odd battling artillerymen, until the guns were in their hands.†

Their way forward now seemed clear, but somehow the capture of such prestigious trophies struck these battalions as an end in itself, and there

---

* A tin container filled with musket balls; also called canister.
† Miller survived and subsequently received the Victoria Cross.

they halted, simply watching the 88th disappear into the scrub. It was as well they did, otherwise they would have walked straight into the fire of Grant's 49th wing, now lying in wait under the bushes some 300 yards (270 m) behind the guns.

Another Katherinburg battalion, to the right of these two, had been less lucky. As it tramped down into the Mikriakoff glen, it was watched by Fordyce of the 47th who had extended his wing among the oaks. With 140 files, he overlapped the 50-yard (46-m) frontage of the enemy column by about 75 yards (69 m) on either side. At 80 yards (73 m) range, he ordered file-firing. At the moment Fordyce's command rang out, the Russians must have been forcing their way through the waist-high scrub, tripping and stumbling over roots and boulders, their long greatcoats catching in the thorns and twisted branches, stronger men pushing the weaker aside to find an easier passage, officers and NCOs shouting and striking out to maintain some formation. Into this throng tore a consecutive fusillade from Fordyce's 280 rifles, each front-rank man firing, followed by his rear-rank comrade, the Minié bullets lancing frontally and obliquely through the 800-strong mass, cutting down its front and flanks, where most of its officers marched. Within a very short time the stricken battalion was floundering back up the slope, as Fordyce herded them away with rifle-fire, until he halted on the lip where the unfortunate Katherinburgers had first appeared.

Meanwhile the concealed Careenage column, unhindered by the gunfire and series of miniature battles above and behind it, was approaching the head of the Wellway. Some 100 yards (90 m) beyond lay the rearmost tents of the 2nd Division camp, from where a determined surprise attack on the rear of the gun line could effectively assist Soimonoff's frontal assault. But now its fortunes changed.

Just nearing the camp was Buller with Egerton's 77th. When the short-sighted Buller saw grey figures emerging from the Wellway, he was unsure who they were. Clifford, riding at his side, had no doubts. 'In God's name,' he said, 'Fix bayonets and charge!' Turning to the nearest 77th men he yelled, 'Come on, my lads!' He later wrote:

The brave fellows dashed in among the astonished Russians, bayoneting them in every direction. One of the

bullets in my revolver prevented it revolving and I could not get it off. The Russians fired their pieces within a few yards of my head but none touched me. I drew my sword and cut off one man's arm who was in the act of bayoneting me . . . a second was running out of my way when I hit him over the back of the neck and laid him dead at my feet. About 15 of them gave themselves up and the remainder fell into the hands of the 77th. Out of the small party with me [12], 6 were killed and 3 wounded, so my escape was wonderful.[14]★

This onslaught finished the head of the Careenage column. Its main body was dispatched by a Guards' outlying picquet which was always stationed on the spur south of the Wellway, and this day was manned by Prince Edward of Saxe-Weimar's company of the 3rd Grenadiers. Hearing Clifford's action, he doubled his guardsmen to the edge of the Wellway and opened fire on the packed column below, with an impact as immediate and decisive as Fordyce's. Thus a potentially dangerous threat to Pennefather's rear was averted and nothing more was seen of the column.

The right of Soimonoff's attack, mainly Katherinburgers, had now been repulsed or held. Meanwhile the Tomsk and Kolivansk had been advancing south-eastwards through the fire of Pennefather's batteries and the musketry of the 2nd Brigade picquets and Patullo's 30th wing, though both the latter were running short of ammunition. Some had been in action for over an hour, and the 60 rounds carried in each man's pouch, if fired off one after the other, could be discharged in about half an hour. Moreover Soimonoff's left had now been extended by the first of Pauloff's corps, the Borodino and Taroutine Regiments, which had advanced separately via the Volovia gorge. These two had unaccountably linked up with the fourth Katherinburg battalion which had gone astray. Thus Home Ridge was now menaced by 17 battalions.

To the left, or east, of the three Katherinburg battalions held by Grant and Fordyce, was the right of this mass of infantry: two Tomsk battalions, the first in company columns, the second behind in close column, some 1,500 men, nearing the west end of Home Ridge with little to bar their way but the bayonets and near-empty pouches of some picquets. Suddenly, over the rise in front of them,

---

★ Clifford subsequently received the Victoria Cross.

Thomas Egerton, 77th (left), when a major, with Private
Alexander Wright of the Grenadier Company, who won the VC
in 1855. A painting by D. Cunliffe.

there appeared through the murk, at almost
point-blank range, a few scattered mounted figures
rising above a grey line, some 75 yards (68 m) long,
from which an English voice shouted: 'Give them
one volley on the knee and load!'

The voice was Thomas Egerton's, the tall and
highly capable officer whose 77th was one of the
best trained battalions in the army. After dealing
with the Careenage column, his four companies
had skirted the 'scene of ruin and desolation' of the
2nd Division camp, wheeled into line, and were
advancing towards the right of Grant's 49th confronting the Katherinburgers, when Egerton saw
the Tomsk immediately ahead. With his front rank
kneeling, the volley from 260 rifles crashed out as

the Minié bullets tore through their heavy column from
front to rear, and shook them to their centre. Our men
rose up and loaded their rifles with as much steadiness as
if on parade. Colonel Egerton then gave 'Prepare to
charge – Charge!'[15]

The lethal volley, the double line of bayonets
springing forward, halted the first Tomsk battalion
in its tracks. Its leading ranks fired and thrust
forward their bayonets ready to stand, but the
disciplined, cheering fury of the 77th would not be
denied. The Russian flank men, on the fringes of

the charge, reloaded and fired again, but back and
back went the centre, piling into their sister
battalion's close column, causing more confusion.
A 77th officer recorded:

A terrible scene of slaughter took place for our men plied
them fiercely with fire and steel; driving them through
the oak copses in our front, we sent the remains of the
shattered columns headlong down a small ravine, about
450 yards from where the fight commenced.[16]

Egerton's line inevitably became broken up by the
undergrowth and the stiffer resistance on the
flanks, but all pressed on in small groups under
subalterns and sergeants, taking their direction
from their field officers who, being mounted, had a
better view over the bushes. At the foot of Shell
Hill Egerton called a halt, reformed line and
ordered his men to lie down out of sight of the
Russian gunners who were beginning to inflict
casualties.

As Sergeant Connor, who had charged with the
left flank company, told his brother: 'This brilliant
service saved the whole of our left flank being
turned'; however, he confessed 'these were awful
moments. I knew not the moment I should fall,
probably never to rise; but God protected me, and
the guardianship of His Holy Mother shielded me
in these trying dangers'. At the same time he
mourned the loss of his best comrade and of his
captain, John Nicholson, 'one of the nicest gentlemen in the Army'.[17] Nicholson, aged 27, had only
obtained his captaincy shortly before and had
looked forward to 'leading a company of my own to
glory', but had been conscious that 'it may be my
turn next to be called hence and stand before the
judgement seat'.[18]

The two Katherinburg battalions checked by
Grant, seeing the Tomsk men's rout and now
vulnerable to Egerton on their left, Grant in front
and Fordyce on their right, turned and went back,
leaving the three captured guns behind. Grant
advanced, supported by the reformed 88th companies, halting just out of canister range of the
enemy's guns on West Jut between Fordyce and
Egerton, on the northern side of the Mikriakoff
glen. In this advance a lucky long shot felled a
conspicuous mounted Russian officer; the firer
could not know, but he had mortally wounded
Soimonoff, whose fall further discouraged these
beaten battalions of his right.

Meanwhile, the other two Tomsk and four Kolivansk battalions, either unaware of, due to fog, or ignoring Egerton's counter-attack, had got almost up to Home Ridge, owing to the 2nd Brigade picquets' failing ammunition and their masking of their own gunners' fire. The situation was critical. Then Sergeant Conway of Turner's G Battery ran forward, bellowing at the picquets to lie down. Though the Russians were almost on them, the picquets obeyed, and over their heads Turner opened with case. At such close range the leading Tomsk battalion was shattered and broke back into its companion, which was forced to halt. To their left, three of the Kolivansk also ground to a halt under the fire. Seeing their hesitation, the picquets sprang up and charged.

The fourth Kolivansk, having swung to its left towards the east end of Home Ridge where the guns had been silenced, was out of Turner's line of fire and was pursuing some scattered picquets who, out of ammunition and without officers, were running for safety. Once again one quick-witted man saw the danger. At the bend of Home Ridge with Fore Ridge lay Bellairs' 183 men of the 49th. With bayonets fixed and without firing a shot, they leaped over the breastwork and charged down the slope, hurling themselves into the Kolivansk column. Just as the Minié fire and sudden, shouting charges on the extreme left had first disrupted, then unnerved the ponderous, rigidly drilled Russian formations, so now the bayonets in front of Home Ridge did the same. Back went the Tomsk and Kolivansk, right back to where they had started and beyond. Soimonoff's first line was finished.

A quarter of a mile behind this last attack, and while it and the actions to the west had been going on, fighting had raged between the Barrier and the Sandbag Battery. Pauloff's left wing of the eight battalions of the Borodino and Taroutine, out of touch with their main body and unaware that it had been delayed, had crossed East Jut and descended into Quarry ravine. Seeing the solitary Katherinburg battalion, which had wandered over from the west, crossing its front eastwards, the Taroutine followed, making for what looked like a tactically important position – the Sandbag Battery on the Kitspur. They swarmed up to it in fine style, to discover only a sergeant and six men of the 55th, detached from Lieutenant Barnston's picquet high-

Mark Walker (seated), Adjutant of the 30th, with, from the left, a private, sergeant of the Light Company and the sergeant-major. Walker was gazetted VC on 4 June 1858.

er up the spur. These man hurriedly decamped, covered by Barnston who opened fire before retiring towards the Barrier. The Taroutine remained about the Battery, waiting for the Borodino to come up Quarry ravine on its right. Both regiments were in the same formation as Soimonoff's, with the Katherinburgers between them.

At the Barrier the 55th picquet had been reinforced by Mauleverer's wing of the 30th; 400 yards (366 m) to the right, Brigadier Adams with the 41st under Major Eman* watched the Taroutine. On this side of the heights visibility was clearer and, seeing the leading six companies of the Borodino trudging up Quarry ravine either side of the road, Mauleverer ordered his 200 men to open fire. Like elsewhere that morning, many of the caps misfired. With over 2,000 massed Borodinos looming larger every second over their useless rifle muzzles, the frustrated 30th became uneasy. Immediately Mauleverer, whose peacetime party trick was vaulting the Officers' Mess billiard table, leaped over the Barrier and ran alone at the enemy. His Adjutant, Mark Walker, at once followed suit. With a yell, the 30th charged down the road behind them. Mauleverer fell wounded, two officers were

* The whole battalion, less those with 2nd Brigade's picquets. Its commanding officer, Carpenter, was commanding 1st Brigade's picquets.

killed and Ross Lewin, praised by Pennefather after Little Inkerman, mortally wounded. But, like Bellairs' 49th, the 30th's onrush threw the Borodino into confusion and retreat.*

Seeing the Borodino repulse, Adams ordered the 41st to advance in line against the Taroutine and the Katherinburg battalions. With some 250 files, the 41st was the strongest individual body yet encountered by the Russians that morning; in its ranks were some veterans of the First Afghan War, 12 years before. In the centre floated their Colours, borne by Lieutenants Armar Lowry and John Stirling who, though sick, had insisted on parading.

The Taroutine, unlike Soimonoff's regiments, had felt such lines' fire at the Alma. As the first volleys struck them, their buglers started sounding 'Left about'. They, like the Borodinos, having received no orders, had more or less drifted into action undirected, after a fatiguing and uncertain advance in the dark. They had heard or seen the Borodinos' fate, and the immediate priority of their leading companies, which quickly communicated itself to the mass, was to escape those dreaded Minié volleys. As the 41st's bayonets came down to the charge, the shortest way to safety for most was down the steep sides of the Kitspur, where any control was soon impossible.

Seeing his own companies already losing formation in the scrub, Adams sounded the halt, confining any pursuit to rifle-fire only. Once his front was completely clear, he ordered the 41st to reform and return to the Sandbag Battery, where he was joined by Bellairs' three 49th companies.

It was 7.30 am, an hour and a half since fighting began. The 2nd Division, just under 3,000 strong, with 550 of the Light Division, had so convincingly repulsed nearly 10,000 of Soimonoff's corps and not quite 6,000 of Pauloff's, that these battalions were, for the moment, a spent force, due to their casualties, particularly in officers: three regimental commanders, one being the Katherinburg's which also lost all its battalion commanders and two-thirds of its officers, while two Kolivansk battalions returned with only one captain.

The fog, which had swirled about most of the battlefield, isolating many of the confrontations,

The right flank of the battlefield. At the extreme right is the Sandbag Battery with, above it across the valley, the Inkerman ruins. Left centre, below the horizon is Shell Hill. Fore Ridge is in the foreground. After W. Simpson.

had affected both sides. It had assisted the British by not only concealing from the enemy the thinness of their lines and numerical inferiority, but also concealing from them the enormous numbers coming against them which, if visible, might have daunted the bravest. On the other hand it had prevented them exploiting the superior range of their Miniés.

The fog's opaqueness, combined with the close country, must have confused the Russian infantry, who were not trained for this sort of bush fighting. Soimonoff's regiments, in particular, had never seen this ground before, nor had they previously experienced the British mode of fighting. To them, a line of rifles emerging from the fog would have suggested, not a thin array only two ranks deep, but the leading rank of a column similar to and, since it frequently overlapped their own frontage, stronger than theirs, leading them to believe they were outnumbered.

The Minié fire, so much more destructive than their own musketry, killed their leaders and penetrated the depths of their solid formations, causing these brave but simple-minded men to huddle even closer together for mutual protection,

---

* Walker was subsequently awarded the Victoria Cross on Mauleverer's unselfish recommendation.

The camp of the 3rd Grenadier Guards, a mile south of Home Ridge. A watercolour by Orlando Norie.

thereby presenting a still more vulnerable target to the men who sprang up behind bushes to shoot them, dressed not in the red coats they had doubtless been told to expect, but in grey greatcoats not dissimilar to their own.

Notwithstanding the success won by steadiness, determination and superior training, this, as Adams had realized when restraining the 41st, had only been the first round. Soimonoff's 16 reserve battalions remained unbloodied on West Jut and Shell Hill with his guns still largely intact, and

Gortchakoff's host was spreading across the Balaclava plain towards the heights. Dannenburg had at last assumed command, nearly 90 guns were emplaced between West and East Juts, and Pauloff's 12 new battalions were already advancing.

With the fog lifting to reveal these fresh forces, the 2nd and Light Division men, reduced by casualties, hungry, and tired by their exertions, must have looked anxiously round for reinforcements. Someone said the Guards were coming. 'All right,' said the sardonic Private Williams of the 41st, as contemptuous of the Household troops as he had been of the Cavalry in September, 'let them do some fighting for a change!'[19]

7

Load, Fire and Charge!

7.30 to 8.30 am

The Guards were indeed approaching, preceded by their batteries, Paynter's and Woodhouse's, but their advance had been delayed by uncertainties about Gortchakoff's intentions on the plain below. Cathcart too was approaching with elements of his 4th Division. On the way he met Sir George Brown and together they encountered Bosquet. The experienced French general, a veteran of North African campaigns, had by now assessed that Gortchakoff's manoeuvrings were no more than a feint; already he had ordered two battalions to march northwards. Meeting the two British generals he offered assistance but they, both veterans of the Napoleonic War, loftily denied any need, suggesting he would be best employed guarding the British rear. Assuming this rebuff was founded on better knowledge of the situation than he possessed – which was not so – Bosquet reversed his battalions' march. Later, beckoned by the crescendo of battle to his north, and with his tactical judgement reinforced by a pleading message from Raglan, he again sent off the two battalions, followed by five more with 24 guns. Nevertheless, the arrogance of two British generals had ensured that Pennefather's hard-pressed men would have to hold the line alone, at least until the Guards could arrive.

Just under half of Pennefather's 2,900 men consisted of the 47th and 49th wings which were guarding the left and rear approaches to Home Ridge, reinforced by the 600-strong 77th and 88th companies, and the original 2nd Brigade picquets plus elements of the 30th and 55th, which had supported them, all somewhat disorganized and weakened by casualties, many without ammunition, and now rallying between the camp and the Ridge. The remainder were Mauleverer's 30th wing at the Barrier; three batteries on the ridge and behind it the 95th, three 47th companies, and some hundred 55th; to their right front, the 41st and Bellairs' portion of the 49th; some 1,600 in all. As Williams of the 41st looked angrily round for sight of the despised bearskins, and then to his front, it was clear to him – indeed to them all – that Pauloff's 10,000 would reach them first.

Covered by 90 guns emplaced between Shell Hill and East Jut, four Okhotsk battalions, with one of Sappers, followed by eight of the Selenghinsk and Iakoutsk, were advancing south-eastwards, in the same formations used previously, with the clear intention of turning the British right around the Sandbag Battery. Despite the uselessness of that structure, much blood of both sides was about to be spilled in a ferocious struggle for its possession.

Though hoping for a respite after their recent dispatch of the Taroutine, the 700 men of the 41st and 49th again formed line under their brigadier, Henry Adams, a huge man on a huge horse and a veteran of the China War, to face the 4,000 Okhotsk and Sappers clambering up the Kitspur. Out went Nos. 3 and 4 Companies of the 41st as skirmishers. Opening fire, they drove in the Russian skirmishers, then charged down at the leading companies. But the Okhotsk, unlike the Taroutine, were unaccustomed to British soldiers and, seeing how few they were, met them with fire and bayonets.

Skirmishing line and company columns dis-

6 Battle of Inkerman: 7.30 to 8.30 am

200 Yds

440 Yds

RUSSIAN
RESERVE

(4 x ⊠)

Shell
Hill

IAKOUTSK   OKHOTSK   SELINGHINSK

Post Road

Quarry Ravine

St Clements Ravine

N

Kitspur

SANDBAG
BATTERY

Mikriakoff Glen

THE BARRIER

Fore
Ridge

GG

SFG

88   77

21

21

63

95

47(−)   55(−)

RB

30

Home   Ridge

Zouaves

41

49

RB

95

CG

20

68
46

57

20

20

6

7

G O R T C H A K O F F

Wellway

47

49

4

Guards

British	French	Russian

Infantry

Division

British Brigade

Russian Regiment

Battalion

Wing (Half-battalion)

Company

Picquet or small groups

Camp

Advance

Retreat

incomplete

GG   Grenadier Guards
SFG   Scots Fusilier Guards
CG   Coldstream Guards
RB   Rifle Brigade

YARDS

0   220   440

200   400 METRES

solved into a furious mêlée among the bushes. Captain Richards was bayoneted to death after killing six Russians who had demanded his surrender. Amazingly, some Okhotsk and 41st soldiers suspended their killing to form a ring within which Lieutenant Taylor and a Russian officer fought with swords; having simultaneously dispatched each other, their soldiers set to again. In danger of being overwhelmed, the remains of the two companies broke back towards their line. Looking round, some 41st saw Lieutenant Swaby still fighting and called to him to come. 'No!' he shouted, 'I will fight to the last!'[1] His body was later found with nine wounds.

As the skirmishers cleared his front, Adams ordered volleys into the oncoming infantry. Though temporarily shaken by this fire, these Russians were more determined than the earlier attackers; conscious of their five to one superiority and ignoring their casualties, they simply plodded on up the Kitspur, some pushing into Adam's centre, others feeling round his flanks.

Private Hyde of the 49th said

they came on like ants; no sooner was one knocked backwards than another clambered over the dead bodies to take his place, all of them yelling and shouting. We were not quiet and what with cheering and shouting, the thud of blows, the clash of bayonets and swords, the ping of bullets, the whistling of shells, the foggy atmosphere, and the smell of the powder and blood, the scene where we were was beyond the power of man to imagine. We had to fight to save our lives.[2]

The need to face right and left as well as forwards, the irruption into their centre, their own casualties and the undergrowth, all broke up Adam's two-deep line into small, desperately fighting groups, mostly with butt and bayonet at close quarters. John Stirling with the 41st's Regimental Colour was shot dead. Sergeant Daniel Ford saw the Colour fall:

I picked it up. A Russian seized the pole end, and we had a regular tug of war until I drove him through with my bayonet. Another came up and I drove the butt of my rifle into his face. I then followed Lieutenant Lowry [Queen's Colour] up the hill. We met an officer who told us the Colours were to go to the rear.[3]

The 41st's Colour Party on the Kitspur. Centre top, Lieutenant Stirling as he was shot. Detail from the Welch Regiment's silver centrepiece, made in 1897.

Rallying to their regimental call being sounded, the 41st again managed to halt the Okhotsk but in the ensuing pause they were struck by renewed enemy gunfire. Adams was everywhere, striving to hold the line, until he was shot. As the Okhotsk surged forward again, the survivors of the 41st and 49th went back on to Fore Ridge, their retreat covered by the timely arrival of three guns of Paynter's battery under Captain Hamley. The Okhotsk, with the Selenghinsk coming up on their left, now had the Sandbag Battery – but not for long.

Meanwhile, the four Iakoutsk battalions were ascending Quarry ravine astride the road towards Mauleverer's 30th at the Barrier. Like Adams's men, they would have to hold until help could reach them. What happened will be discussed later, but between the fighting there to contain the Iakoutsk and the increasingly bloody struggle for the Sandbag Battery, there developed an undefended quarter-mile gap at the north end of Fore Ridge, which was to have dangerous implications for both fights and Home Ridge itself.

Hardly had the Okhotsk got their breath, when a new force descended on them: 500 tall men made taller by their black bearskins, advancing with measured tread down the east side of Fore Ridge – the 3rd Grenadier Guards, seven companies in line, their Colours in the centre. When they had formed for their attack on Home Ridge, George Higginson had felt 'a momentary shock of despair on seeing beneath us the grey coats of the huge column of the enemy'.[4] Artillery fire struck them, then musketry. They halted; a volley – more wet caps, even in the Guards – reload; front rank at the charge, rear rank at the slope and – forward! The thudding boots of big, heavy men at the double, the levelled bayonets, the great bearskins, the bearded, cheering faces were suddenly too much for the brave Okhotsk. They abandoned the Sandbag Battery, seeking the safety of the dead ground below the ledge in front of it. The Grenadiers halted, facing eastwards.

The Scots Fusilier Guards, 392 strong, had advanced to their left rear. The 1st Coldstream were some way behind, having mostly just come off picquet when the brigade marched. Unfortunately they were all under dual command, being accompanied not only by their brigadier, Bentinck, but also by their divisional commander, the Duke of Cambridge, who, though brave enough, was not at his best in a crisis – and one immediately occurred. Spotting two enemy battalions coming up out of St Clement's ravine towards the now-halted Grenadiers' left rear, the Fusilier Guards marched to check them, only to be ordered angrily by Cambridge to swing right towards the Grenadiers, thus offering their left flank to the Russians. No sooner had the Fusiliers wheeled, than Bentinck ordered them back to drive the two battalions away. This they did with a volley and a short charge – but only the Guards' discipline could have achieved this without muddle. They then formed line on the Grenadiers' left, so that both battalions presented an inverted L hinged on the Sandbag Battery.

The Fusiliers had arrived in the nick of time for the Okhotsk and Sappers, having safely reformed in the dead ground, came on again over the northern end of the Kitspur. The Selenghinsk surged up over the eastern side against the Grenadiers, some moving south along the steep slope to get round their right, only to be frustrated by the arrival of six Coldstream companies. So these three battalions, each averaging 440 men, stood their ground against repeated attacks by nine Russian battalions, each averaging 750 men.

They presented not the ordered double ranks which the London crowds had seen nine months before, but rather a thin, uneven line bent round the scrub and rocks of the Kitspur; men in pairs or small groups, some loading, others firing. Sergeant McMillan said 'we kept firing away as fast as we could, kneeling on the ground to keep out of the line of fire'.[5] Around them, their dead and wounded piled up. Colonel Walker of the Fusiliers, already twice wounded, was shot through the jaw. Lieutenant Sturt fell severely wounded with the Grenadiers' Queen's Colour but clutched it until Lieutenant Turner could prise it from him. Captain Hon. Henry Neville, whose brother, Grey, was dying in hospital from his Balaclava wounds, was shot through the spine and bayoneted. Captain Wilson of the Coldstream saw his colour-sergeant killed: 'Never can I forget the look that dying man cast upward at me. It was horrible in its intensity'.[6] A war correspondent was struck by the 'grim, painful frown' on Guardsmen's faces killed while charging; an officer also finding their 'look of determination' unforgettable, while their opponents' corpses 'had a more placid expression'.[7]

When the Russian infantry fell back to reform,

their artillery opened up. Soon the Guardsmen would again see 'the columns swarming through the bushes, the officers in front waving their swords and shouting to the men. Directly they saw us, they fired quickly and nervously, generally over our heads'.[8] The Guardsmen would open fire,

The Grenadier Guards attacking the Okhotsk in the Sandbag Battery. A painting by W. Simpson.

the Miniés blasting them like flashes of lightning. After a minute or two the columns would waver a little; then to the right about and retire. Nevertheless, no sooner had one corps made off, than its supporting battalion started up before our view, with the same stereotyped yells.[9]

They pressed us hard but not a yard would we yield. The groans of the wounded, officers yelling, soldiers shouting, and the firing almost deafened one. One of the most remarkable things about Russian troops is the noise they make in action, and I think it is catching, as I never heard our men make such yelling as they did all this day.[10]

When their pouches were empty, they refilled them from their dead comrades' or hurled rocks. If the Miniés at close range could not hold a column, it was time for the bayonet, remembering to thrust at the throat, as the thick Russian coats would turn or bend the point. The air was so thick with powder smoke and the residual fog that 'no man could tell what was going on fifty paces on either side of him. The mortal strife was now backward, now forward, now sideways'.[11]

Amid the appalling noise and such intensity of slaughter, with only brief respites between each onset – since the ground in which the Russians reformed was so close – Wilson found it impossible to gauge time, yet the time in which the Guards fought alone for the Sandbag Battery was probably no more than 30 to 40 minutes. Within that period, however, that worthless rampart changed hands four times.

Notwithstanding their mounting losses and periodic setbacks, the Guardsmen were holding firm, though Cambridge was increasingly concerned about the undefended gap, through which at any time Russians might attack his left rear, and had ridden back to seek reinforcements from Pennefather. The latter, more intent on the Russian right's threat to Home Ridge than the Sandbag Battery, nevertheless offered Champion's wing of the 95th, which he had been keeping for the ridge.

Cathcart had arrived with the first of his 4th Division and had presented to Pennefather a wing of each of the 1st Rifle Brigade, which he had known in South Africa in 1853 and claimed 'could do anything', and of the 20th, once described by the Duke of Wellington as the most distinguished regiment in the service;[12] these Pennefather also offered to Cambridge for the Kitspur. Cambridge asked Cathcart to fill the gap with his other troops, but Cathcart had other ideas, as we will see. Cambridge then saw, behind Home Ridge, two blocks of blue uniforms – Bosquet's first two battalions, from the 6ème Ligne and 7ème Léger, 1,660 strong.* But neither his requests, nor Pennefather's more fiery urgings, would induce their commanders to move forward without their superiors' sanction. Thus, although Cambridge returned with some 500 reinforcements for his embattled Guardsmen, the gap remained open.

Cambridge had intended these troops to protect the Guards' left, but somehow the awful lure of the death struggle around the Battery beckoned too strongly. Crofton sent two of his 20th companies to the Coldstream, his other two into the Battery. Champion ranged the four 95th companies to support the Fusiliers. Only Horsford with his 140 Riflemen took a more independent line, 'running to the front in a very scattered order' past the 95th to the head of St Clement's ravine.[13]

With the Rifles was the Waterloo cavalryman's son, Corporal John Fisher:

Fizz! Fizz! fly the bullets about us, but we could not see where they were coming from. Whack! comes a round shot close to us, then a shell which bursts and huge lumps of iron go whizzing through the air like horrid demons to enter their victims. We come to some bushes; we discern figures groping about, hardly knowing which way to turn, so it appeared to us. We are in skirmishing order. Pop, pop, bang, we are engaging them. We soon make them retire on their main supports. We lay down under the bushes. The enemy come blundering towards us again. Our men seemed to have lost all patience. I had a feeling allied to madness creeping over me and jumping up, said, 'Come on, let's get at them!' But I was not aware that Major [Horsford] was so near, who told me to lie down until I got the order. At last we made another move towards them, making them retire into a hollow.[14]

Horsford continued to hold the head of St Clement's by keeping his men skirmishing at a distance. To his right, despite the arrival of the eight 20th and 95th companies, the close-quarter savagery around the Battery was unabated. Though the structure itself had been lost more than once, the line around the Kitspur still held; but since Cambridge and his officers had forbidden any follow-up to each successful repulse for fear of losing control of their depleted files, the Russians, also depleted but still numerically superior, could reform unmolested by rifle or artillery fire. Unless this pattern was somehow changed, their numbers, supported by their heavier guns on Shell Hill, must ultimately prevail.

The soldiers in the fighting line had learned by now how useless the Battery was as a defensive position, yet their natural stubbornness, and perhaps a desire not to betray their comrades who had died for it, still drove them on to eject any equally stubborn Russians who got into it. But the frustration of having to do the work again and again, with no decisive result, was beginning to strain the bonds of discipline which held them to their officers' restraints. Then came the spark which ignited this pent-up fury from right to left.

After handing over the wings of Rifles and 20th, Cathcart, having conferred with Pennefather, had dispatched the rest of Goldie's brigade to reinforce the left and centre, then under attack from Quarry ravine, keeping Torrens's brigade under his own hand. However, Windham, his AQMG, judging the left to be more critical, had also ordered the 63rd in that direction, leaving Torrens with only four companies of the 68th Light Infantry and two of the 46th, the regiment which had incurred so much obloquy over the Perry case – 400 in all.†

When Cathcart had refused Cambridge's request to fill the gap with Torrens's men, he had spotted what he conceived as a more pressing task: the extreme left Selenghinsk battalion ascending the slopes to turn the Coldstream's right, which then was the extreme right of the Guards Brigade. He had already ordered Torrens to open fire, when Airey galloped up, bearing an order from Raglan for Cathcart to turn about and fill the gap. 'Those are Lord Raglan's orders,' he added.[15] Irritated by

---

* Each French infantry regiment had two battalions.

† The rest of the 68th were in the trenches and most of the 46th had not yet disembarked at Balaclava.

Two sketches by Captain Henry Torrens of Cathcart's counter-attack down the eastern side of the Kitspur: 1 and 2 = 68th and 46th, led by Brigadier-General Torrens; 3 = Russians attacking; 4 and 5 = Guards at Sandbag Battery, attacked by Russians (6); 7 = Russians on East Jut.

Airey's 'quick, inconsiderate manner',[16] and unwilling to concede that Raglan's tactical judgement was superior to his own, he turned away and ordered Torrens to advance against the Selenghinsk.

Down the slope obliquely went the six companies in line, 68th on the right. Having earlier discarded their greatcoats, they were the only regiment fighting in red, which showed clearly amid the scrub to the Russian gunners on East Jut, who opened fire. Captain Torrens, acting as ADC to his father, wrote:

It was only as the smoke occasionally cleared away that we could discern the dark mass of long greatcoats, flat caps and cold blue steel approaching us. We charged and drove them back before they reached the top of the hill, taking them partially in flank.[17]

The Selenghinsk would not stand but then, proving the wisdom of the restraint hitherto imposed on the Guards, the 46th and 68th pressed on in pursuit, their excited ranks becoming increasingly disordered by the undergrowth, until they reached the bottom of the Kitspur.

Seeing his divisional commander's action, Crofton urged his 20th wing forward from the Coldstream. He had intended only a volley and a controlled charge, but he fell wounded and his men too went on down the hill. Killed in this rush was Lieutenant Dowling. He should have been safely on camp guard that morning, but when his men asked to fight, rather than mount guard, he told his captain: 'The men request to be led to the front and I would rather go too'.[18]

Wilson's Coldstream company next to them followed, pursued by him yelling for them to return, but to no avail. Alerted by Wilson's plight, the other captains were able, for the moment, to hold back their men.

The Grenadiers were still hard pressed by the Okhotsk around the Battery. Loath to abandon it, yet hampered by its height, the men's frustration found expression in one Guardsmen who shouted, 'If any officer will lead us, we will charge'. Sir Charles Russell felt he

could not refuse such an appeal. I jumped into the embrasure and said, 'Come on, my lads; who will follow me?' I rushed on, fired my revolver at a fellow close to me but it missed fire. I pulled again and think I killed him.

Sir Charles Russell Bt and Private Palmer, Grenadier Guards, outside the Sandbag Battery. Both were gazetted VC on 24 February 1857. A painting by Chevalier Desanges.

Just then a man touched me on the shoulder and said, 'You was near done for'.[19]

Unknown to Russell a Russian had got behind him with bayonet raised when Private Anthony Palmer, the only man at first to follow, had killed him.* Russell and Palmer, now joined by other Grenadiers and some Fusiliers, fought their way to the right, where Captain Edwyn Burnaby had also charged out with Private James Bancroft, followed by five more. All were immediately engaged in desperate hand-to-hand conflicts, of which Bancroft's may stand as an example:

I bayoneted the first Russian in the chest; he fell dead. I was then stabbed in the mouth with great force, which caused me to stagger back, where I shot this second Russian and ran a third through. A fourth and fifth came at me and ran me through the right side. I fell but managed to run one through and brought him down. I stunned him by kicking him, whilst I was engaging my bayonet with another. Sergeant-Major Alger called out to me not to kick the man that was down, but not being dead he was very troublesome to my legs; I was fighting the other over his body. I returned to the Battery and spat out my teeth; I found two only.[20]

Fired by the example of the few, men of all three battalions surged forward into the stolid enemies who had tried them so hard, driving them down all sides of the Kitspur. Cambridge, standing with the Grenadiers' Colours, bellowed at them to keep to the high ground, but only the nearest Grenadiers, about a hundred, could be restrained.

Part of the 95th wing had been kept back by Champion on the western side of the Kitspur, but then, seeing a column coming up St Clement's ravine untouched by the headlong pursuit to its left, Sargent attacked it with the Grenadier company. The column would not stand and went about as the 95th charged on, deaf to Champion's and Sargent's commands. Champion rode down to check them. Dismounting to negotiate some boulders, he was mortally wounded by a chance shot. In

* Both subsequently received the Victoria Cross.

one of his last letters to his wife, this devout and devoted husband had written: 'I am truly glad I have never yet with my own hands taken the life of any fellow being; may I be spared doing so, except in self-defence'.[21] Never seeing his assailant, his wish was granted.

The rest of the 95th wing under Carmichael and Vialls had charged from the Battery with the Guards. Carmichael saw how

the enemy turned at once, several threw away their arms, and knelt down asking for mercy – 'Christos!' The pursuit continued into the ravine. I thought the battle was won and the men were exultant, Lance-Corporal Purcell saying, 'We are driving them again, Sir!' The men got very scattered and were beginning to run short of ammunition. I noticed that those following us were turning back and soon after cries were raised, 'Come back! You are cut off!'[22]

Some time before, when the reinforcements first reached the Guards, the two right-hand Okhotsk battalions had been so strongly repulsed that they had fallen right back, well down St Clement's ravine, and had remained out of the battle for some time. Now, however, they had been reorganized and, having advanced round the head of the ravine, were bearing due east towards the Battery, overlooking on their left the lower slopes of the Kitspur where their late opponents were scattered. To their right one battalion of the Iakoutsk, which had hitherto been attacking the Barrier, had swung east across the gap and advanced unopposed until it overlooked the scene of Cathcart's charge. Thus all the troops who had charged down, as well as Cambridge and his 100 Grenadiers, were now separated from Home Ridge by three Russian battalions.

Cut off and fired on from the heights to their rear, enfiladed by Gortchakoff's artillery across the river, disorganized, intermingled and with empty pouches, the pursuers had become the trapped. Cathcart, the architect of their fate, was killed, almost his last words expressing what all must have felt: 'We are in a scrape'.[23] Such a reversal of fortune after very severe fighting could have induced thoughts of surrender. Some skulked, others ran. Windham discovered 'the difficulty of stopping men running under heavy fire'.[24] Sergeant McMillan believed 'it was all up'[25] and Sergeant

The view from the Tchernaya valley looking south-west up to the Kitspur, above dark trees, with the Sandbag Battery near the top facing left. The dark V-shaped area in the centre is St Clement's ravine.

Campbell of the 20th that they needed 'the greatest miracle in the world'.[26]

But notwithstanding their predicament, most, given a lead, were not yet prepared to give up. In small groups, all mixed together, Guards and Line began the steep and difficult climb. 'With greatcoats on, and pretty well blown, and impeded by the stiff oak brushwood, we made but slow progress'.[27] Lord Henry Percy of the Grenadiers, though wounded in an earlier, heroic lone charge at the Battery,* found a sheep track to lead men round below the Iakoutsk. Fifty of the 20th, reaching the Okhotsk, simply pushed through them with butts and bayonets; though many were killed, some got through. Major Wynne of the 68th, 'as good a man to hounds as ever crossed a horse' was killed as 'he tried to boil up a charge'.[28] Sargent with his 95th and Wilson with his Coldstreamers – one too distant, the other too close to Gortchakoff to risk a move – decided to lie concealed to await events.

---

* Subsequently awarded the Victoria Cross.

In the abandoned Battery, Drummer Thomas Keep of the Grenadiers, a boy of 10, had made a fire to brew tea for the wounded. Assistant-Surgeon Wolseley of the 20th had done what he could for them when some of his regiment, with some Coldstreamers, came in without officers. Seeing the Okhotsk approaching, Wolseley went back with them.

We had not gone fifty yards when we found a line of Russians drawn up. In consequence of the mist they were not visible until we were within 20 or 30 yards of them. They appeared to me as a very close line of skirmishers and were firing rapidly at us. I was the only officer in sight and gave the order, 'fix bayonets, charge and keep up the hill'. We charged through losing, I should think, half our number.[29]

This unexpected charge out of the mist surprised the Russians, probably the left-hand company column of the Iakoutsk. This battalion, hitherto firing down the Kitspur's east flank, had suddenly spotted, behind the Sandbag Battery, the 100 Grenadiers with their Colours under Cambridge. Wheeling left, the Iakoutsk had been advancing against them, firing, when Wolseley struck them.

Facing forwards, the Grenadiers had been unaware of this force at their back. George Higginson felt a bullet pass through his bearskin from behind and thought they were being fired on by their own troops. He quickly perceived their peril. Capture of the Duke of Cambridge, and indeed the Grenadiers' Colours, was unthinkable, so the order was given to march through the Iakoutsk, but keeping along the Kitspur's eastern side to avoid being outflanked on their left. Thus they were headed at the Russians' right as Wolseley's band went at their left. Cambridge and his ADC, being mounted, managed to ride round the enemy's flank in a flurry of shots and got clear, though Cambridge's horse was hit. Higginson, in a long life, never forgot their retreat:

Clustered round the Colours, the men pressed slowly rearwards, keeping their front full to the enemy, their bayonets ready at the 'charge'. As a comrade fell, his fellow took his place and maintained the compactness of the diminishing group that held on in unflinching stubbornness. More than once from the lips of this devoted band came the shout, 'Hold up the Colours!', fearing no doubt they might lose sight of those honoured emblems. The two young officers, Verschoyle and Turner, raised them well above their heads and in this order we slowly moved back, exposed to a fire, fortunately ill-aimed, from front, flank and rear.[30]

The Iakoutsk maintained its fire but, as the distance between its right and the Grenadiers narrowed, for some reason – perhaps intimidated by the unyielding Guardsmen's Minié fire – it began to veer leftwards. So, while the nearest Grenadiers had to cut and shoot their way through, those on the outer flank had only to march on. The Iakoutsk left was also assailed at this time by Wolseley's handful; nevertheless this almost passive acceptance by a battalion, 700 to 800 strong, of the 100-odd Grenadiers' grim determination to get through, can only be ascribed to the bovine inflexibility of Russian units.

Though the Iakoutsk seemed bemused by what had happened, the two Okhotsk battalions also had the Grenadiers' Colours in their sights and had been advancing on their right rear – hence the fire from that quarter mentioned by Higginson. Hurrying to catch up his battalion was Burnaby, who had regained the heights with a mixed group, only to see his Colours retreating up the hill. Spotting the Okhotsk coming on to aid the Iakoutsk, Burnaby halted his men to face the Okhotsk skirmishers. They were no more than 20: Bancroft was still there, Isaac Archer, Joseph Troy, John Pullen, Edward Hill, William Turner, all Grenadiers; a Line sergeant whose name is lost; and another dozen, Guards and Line. At Burnaby's command, they ran at the skirmishers and 'knocked them out of the way'.[31] The Okhotsk came on. Burnaby shouted: 'Get close together and charge them once more, my men!' Bancroft thought 'it perfectly useless, but for all that I did so'.[32] They all sprang forward. Against 700 men, with a similar number behind, what hope had 20? They fought and fell, until only seven remained, all wounded, lying amid the Russian bayonets.

Then, with an urgent flourish of bugles, blue coats came down the slope at the Okhotsk's flank. The French had moved at last. Ordered forward by General Bourbaki, the 6ème Ligne drove the Okhotsk away, down into St Clement's ravine. Further to their left Horsford's Riflemen ran forward firing at the Iakoutsk, retreating towards Quarry ravine. Sergeant McMillan, who had struggled up from below, where he had often felt he

Captain Edwyn Burnaby, Grenadier Guards, dressed for picquet. An 1855 photograph by Roger Fenton.

The British right had been saved, but at a cost of nearly half the 2,800 men who had fought for it. The survivors, tired and hungry when they started, were now exhausted and completely intermingled. To their left, however, the fight was by no means over.

When the first attack against the Sandbag Battery had begun an hour before, Mauleverer's 30th at the Barrier had been confronted by all four Iakoutsk battalions. Having only recently repulsed the Borodino, they numbered less than their original 100 files and could only operate as a picquet line, firing as they slowly fell back over the 540 yards (494 m) to Home Ridge, where they ran in behind its low stone wall to join the remains of their other wing under Patullo. Despite the thunder of both sides' guns, many fell fast asleep.

Their resistance had given time for reinforcements to reach the ridge: Hume's left wing of the 95th and the other wing of the Rifles. Both immediately advanced in line, firing. Their musketry halted the Iakoutsk and turned it back to Quarry ravine, except for its right-hand column. This got round between the 95th's left and Egerton guarding the Mikriakoff glen a quarter of a mile away, and ascended the ridge's west end. At almost point-blank range, three guns of Turner's battery opened with case-shot, throwing the column into confusion. Some of it, however, managed to swing left away from the guns, heading further along the ridge. A few yards from them, deaf to the battle's din, slept the exhausted 30th. Suddenly a voice – probably Pennefather's – roared out, 'Up, 30th, up!' Seizing their rifles the 30th leaped over the wall and drove their disturbers away.

So the Iakoutsk's first attack was held, though not defeated. After reforming in Quarry ravine, they soon came on again, this time towards the right of Home Ridge where only some guns, under fire from Shell Hill, barred the way with no formed body of infantry. The combined strengths of the detachments, then defending Home Ridge, only yielded 300-odd files which, if combined in one line at normal distance, would cover about 210 yards (190 m), thereby leaving a quarter of a mile of the ridge unguarded. Such a gap could be covered by Minié fire under good conditions, but visibility was still poor and the fields of fire had not been cleared. Also open to attack was the undefended gap over Fore Ridge towards the embattled Guards, across

would 'be shot down or taken prisoner and cruelly murdered after', saw the French charge: 'I cannot express the joy I felt, many a man burst into tears as soon as the danger was over'.[33]

The French battalion did not pursue the Okhotsk but, after some hesitation and further exhortations from Bourbaki, occupied the spur between St Clement's and Quarry ravines.

Burnaby and his seven, rescued in the nick of time, rejoined the now safe Grenadiers' Colours for which they had offered their lives. The terrible fighting round the Sandbag Battery – 'quel abattoir', as Bosquet described it – the plunge into, and subsequent retreat from, the ravine, were over.

Captain William Inglis, seated, who assumed command of the 57th after Captain Stanley's death, with other officers of the regiment. An 1855 photograph by Roger Fenton.

they too had one of those talismans so treasured by the British infantry to sustain them at crucial moments. Second in command to Stanley was Captain Inglis, whose father had exhorted the 57th to 'die hard' in the bloodbath of Albuera, 43 years earlier; nearby was Sergeant Grace, another son of an Albuera man. To such men, Stanley's shout of 'Remember Albuera!' was all they needed to give a lead to which the young 57th responded in full measure. Stanley and many others fell in the fierce struggle that ensued, but their opponents joined the rest of their regiment in Quarry ravine.

With this counter-attack, and the subsequent withdrawal to Home Ridge by the 20th and 57th – accomplished not without loss due to the Russian gunners re-opening fire – this sector had been stabilized at about the same time as had the right. It was half-past eight.

8.30 to 9.15 am

Dannenberg's first offensive with Pauloff's corps had cost the Iakoutsk, Okhotsk and Selenghinsk some 1,000 casualties, perhaps more, but they were by no means demoralized, like those of Soimonoff's first attack had been. The 9,000-strong reserve of 16 battalions still remained untouched on Shell Hill with 100 guns. If Dannenberg could break through to the plateau behind Home Ridge, then Gortcha-koff's unused 22,000 might be induced to ascend the escarpment.

Using the Barrier as his start-line, Dannenberg now planned to smash through Home Ridge along the line of the road, using the four Iakoutsk Battalions, one behind the other in a solid column, but screened by strong advance and flank guards. Who provided these is unclear. The Selenghinsk were not available as they were still recovering from the Kitspur battle below St Clement's ravine. Some may have been from the Okhotsk, but one officer mentions 'the Chasseurs of the 10th Division' (Soimonoff's)[35] – that is, the Tomsk and Kolivansk who were so designated.[†] If so, they must have been reorganized after Soimonoff's repulse and brought up from the rear. Their eight battalions, added to the Iakoutsk's four, would account for the

which one Iakoutsk Battalion was marching, as noted above.

Fortunately, as so often in this battle, a crisis found its saviours. Into the breach marched part of Goldie's brigade: 90 files of the 20th's left wing under Colonel Horn followed, to their left rear, by a similar number of the 57th, all sent forward by Raglan. They were immediately hit by Russian gunfire but, quickly extending, they advanced and opened fire at the Iakoutsk. Like all the 4th Division, except the Rifles, the 20th and 57th had no Miniés, only smooth-bore muskets[*] which, although they permitted a slightly higher rate of fire because they were easier to reload, lacked the Minié's penetration. Thus only the Russian fore-most ranks suffered casualties and more urgent measures became necessary.

Nearly a hundred years before, the 20th, with five other regiments, had broken the massed French cavalry at Minden. Over the years they had evolved a 'strange and unearthly' battle-cry, known as the 'Minden yell'.[34] This the Iakoutsk's left now heard as the 20th's bayonets came at them, pushing them back in disorder towards Quarry ravine.

As the 57th went at the Iakoutsk's right, their commander, Captain Stanley, sensed a hesitation when his men first saw the odds against them. But

---

† Russian infantry regiments were designated either 'Musketeers' or 'Chasseurs/Jagers', the only difference being in uniform. The Okhotsk, Borodino and Taroutine were also Chasseurs.

---

* The 1842 percussion pattern.

12 which British officers who observed the attack assessed as its strength.

To meet this onslaught, Pennefather had the same troops who had repulsed the last one on Home Ridge. He was also being reinforced by the 21st's right wing under Ainslie and Swyny's 63rd which, when the Russian advance guard appeared, were approaching the west end of Home Ridge. The 21st's left wing, under Lord West, had been dispatched to the Mikriakoff glen to relieve Egerton's 77th, which was to march back to Home Ridge. Though the Russians had not used the covered approaches of the Mikriakoff and the Wellway since Soimonoff's attack, Pennefather could not risk leaving them unguarded, hence the continued positioning of Egerton (now West) at the former, and Fordyce's and Grant's 47th and 49th wings at the latter.

Rather than awaiting the attack on Home Ridge, where his slender resources would be hammered by the Russian guns, Pennefather sent forward skirmishing parties from the remains of the 30th and left wings of the 20th, 95th and Rifles to delay the advance from in front and on the flanks. Also among these was Bellairs, with the remnant of his three 49th companies; having reorganized after the first Sandbag Battery attack, he had now come over to the west. On Home Ridge itself Pennefather retained, on the left flank, 100 and 50 files respectively of the 47th and 55th, and on his right 80 files of the 57th, plus the last two companies of the Coldstream, which had been on picquet but had now come up. His centre was empty, but to fill it was advancing the 900-strong 7ème Léger.

Outnumbered by the Russian screening troops, the skirmishers could only fall back, harassing the flanks from the brushwood. The scrub, however, also served the enemy flankers, for one party, quite unobserved, suddenly rushed the extreme west end of Home Ridge where there were three unprotected guns of Turner's battery. Some gunners ran, others were killed, but Sergeant-Major Henry and Gunner Taylor drew their swords to defend their guns until Taylor was bayoneted and Henry fell unconscious, stabbed 12 times.* Elated with their trophies, these Russians, like those who had earlier captured Townshend's guns, made no attempt to advance further. This was not only a missed opportunity

Sergeant-Major A. Henry of G Battery, Royal Artillery, defending his gun and receiving 12 wounds. Gazetted VC on 24 February 1857. A painting by Chevalier Desanges.

but their undoing. A company of Zouaves surprised them from the scrub and drove them from the guns.[†]

Behind these Zouaves came the 300 files of the 21st and 63rd. Having carefully observed the rest of the Russian right-flank guard, Ainslie and Swyny waited until it wheeled left towards the ridge, then advanced firing in one line, the 21st on the left, against its right rear. Private George Evans of the 63rd wrote later: 'As fast as we could run and load our pieces, so fast they fell, for we could not miss them, they were so thick'.[36] This attack cleared the west end of Home Ridge but, having advanced some 200 yards (180 m) beyond the recaptured guns, the line came under artillery fire. The two colonels jointly halted, facing north-east, and made their men take cover in the scrub.

Further east along the ridge it had been touch and go. Under cover of the gun smoke part of the enemy vanguard broke through the 55th, taking prisoners, but were then hit by their own artillery. Turner's other three guns fired case until the last

---

* Henry survived, subsequently to be awarded the Victoria Cross.

† Two battalions of Zouaves were marching up from the rear towards the right flank, but this company seems to have been acting independently.

possible moment before limbering up just as the Russian infantry reached the gun line. In the centre the 7ème Léger, arrayed in line to which they were not accustomed, came face to face with the enemy vanguard, faltered – and turned back. The Russians crowned the ridge, some even advancing down the other side. Then they too fell victims to their own gunners, whose observers, 1,400 yards (1,280 m) away, had imperfect vision through the battle smoke. Into this infantry's surprised ranks tore a counter-attack by the now-rallied 55th. Behind the ridge, as the French officers cursed at their men, reforming them in their familiar columns, Egerton's stalwart 77th arrived from the Mikriakoff, calmly forming line from column on the left of the 7ème Léger. When French and English were ready, both went forward together. The briefly victorious Russian vanguard, first shaken by their own guns, then by the 55th, and now by the sight of these 1,100 Allied troops, lost heart and fell away from the crest.

Now the main Iakoutsk column came on, still with its flank guards. By one of the quirks so prevalent in this battle of small groups against solid masses, it was preceded by a few skirmishers led by Bellairs and Vaughan of the 20th, who somehow had been bypassed by the vanguard. They fell back firing, the files covering each other. Their proximity to the leading Russians spared them from the enemy gunfire, but they also masked the front of the British batteries, except for the howitzers which could reach the rearmost Iakoutsk battalion. The officers of the 7ème Léger yelled at them to clear the front and they ran in, forming behind the Frenchmen.

Keeping the 77th in reserve, Pennefather had induced the French battalion to line the forward slope in double company columns, and brought forward the 57th from the right to lengthen the French line on the left, so that both battalions stood in the Iakoutsk's path.

By the time the French opened fire, the leading Iakoutsk were close and reeled from the first volley. But the mass pushed on and, seeing the bayonets so close as they reloaded, the young French soldiers began to waver and fall away. Pennefather and his staff rode among them, exhorting them to stand; French officers and the Zouave company tried to give a lead, while Bellairs and Vaughan closed their men up to stiffen the French ranks. However,

Sergeant Walker leading the 55th in Daubeney's counter-attack against the Iakoutsk. An illustration by Stanley Wood for *British Battles by Land and Sea*.

panic is infectious and the 7ème Léger was crumbling. The foremost Russian companies surged forward with their endless 'hurrahs'. Suddenly, in the moment of victory, uncertainty, then confusion struck them. The second battalion in the column was in disarray.

As the first battalion had come up to the French, Daubeney of the 55th, out on the left, had run forwards and to the right, yelling at his men to follow. Some 30 did so. Accompanied by this handful, Daubeney plunged into the right flank of the second Iakoutsk. With Sergeant Walker, 'a fine, powerful man',[37] wielding his rifle like a club in the van, these few 55th men managed to claw their way right through the close-packed, dull-witted ranks, causing bewilderment and commotion. The effects of this savage little surprise attack spread outwards like a rock flung in a pond. The two rear battalions, which had been about to deploy sideways, hesitated. The foremost, sensing

The advance of the 21st Royal North British Fusiliers under Lieutenant-Colonel Ainslie (mounted), with Sergeant-Major Vousden to his right rear. A watercolour by Orlando Norie.

an attack from the rear, began to turn. The French drummers and buglers ran to the front, sounding the *pas de charge*. Their men rallied and went forward, Zouaves, 20th and 49th mingling in their ranks, cheering them on, herding the unfortunate Iakoutsk back to Quarry ravine.

Out to the left front, the Russian flank guard had again threatened the 21st and 63rd, so Ainslie and Swyny ordered their two regiments together to drive it in towards the Barrier. Among the 21st, an 18-year-old Etonian, Lieutenant Vaughan Lee, carrying the Regimental Colour, heard Ainslie's "'Fusiliers, prepare to charge!'" Up we all got, gave a cheer and rushed through the brushwood with fixed bayonets, I with my sword drawn in one hand, and pistol loosened in my holster'.[38] Nearing the head of the ravine, and now outstripping the French pursuit, they met stronger opposition from the Iakoutsk rearguard. Swyny and several 63rd officers were killed or wounded. Close to Private Evans 'fell poor Mr Clutterbuck, who was carrying the Queen's Colour, and cheering the men on. I never saw a braver man than him in the field that day; it is with sorrow that I have to record his death'.[39]

The enemy rearguard gradually retreated into the ravine. Haines, senior captain of the 21st's right wing, wrote admiringly of his men in this attack: 'I have never seen troops behave better, my great anxiety was to steady and keep them together, the thick brush tending to break our formation'. With some 40 21st and a few 63rd, he advanced past the Barrier, down the road for about 500 yards (450 m) until he saw an enemy column drawn up, with another lower down to its left. 'We opened a brisk fire, paying special attention to the officers prominent on the flanks. The nature of the ground and our thin formation favoured us, whilst their dense masses were fully exposed to our fire.'[40]

Haines's men were sheltered from the enemy guns by a steep bank on their left, but the opposing musketry killed two officers and mortally wounded Sergeant-Major Vousden. Ainslie was shot while bringing up supports, leaving Haines in command. He decided to fall back to the Barrier, where he found a mixed group of Coldstreamers, Rifles and Line, with whom he was able to halt the enemy which had followed up.

This last push against Haines showed that, notwithstanding their recent repulse, the Iakoutsk remained a resilient, formed body which still showed fight. Nevertheless, another major attack, which had nearly succeeded, had been held off from Home Ridge by the leadership and quick thinking of regimental officers, the determination and self-confidence of their men, and – as always – the untiring efforts of Pennefather. He knew what was going on, but most knew nothing 'beyond the personal contest in which he himself was engaged. The only orders given – and unflinchingly obeyed – were "load", "fire", and "charge!"'[41]

8

A Hell of a Towelling

9.15 to 11.00 am

From around 9.15 am Haines began an epic defence at the Barrier, but as this was to last nearly six hours it will be returned to later. On the right, where British and Russians had been reorganizing since 8.30, fighting flared up again with a Russian assault on the 6ème Ligne holding the spur between Quarry and St Clement's ravines. In due course this would involve the main French effort in the battle, including the removal of the 7ème Léger from Home Ridge. First, however, a new element entered the fight which was greatly to influence the future course of the struggle.

When Raglan had first arrived on the scene at about 7 am, he had ordered up two 18-pounders from the siege train to supplement the outgunned and outranged field batteries in their uneven duel with the superior numbers of 12-pounders and 32-pounder howitzers on Shell Hill. These should have materialized by 8 am but, owing to a misunderstanding, the staff officer who carried the message applied first to the wrong officer. By the time this mistake was rectified and the message reached Colonel Gambier, commanding the siege train, valuable time had been lost. Gambier had been keeping two guns, with loaded ammunition wagons, ready for such an eventuality since the 26 October sortie. Now, however, he had no draught horses to pull them. Accordingly, some 150 men of the 6th and 7th Companies, 11th Battalion Royal Artillery, set to with drag ropes to haul them 'over one and a half miles over rough ground and up a steep hill to the scene of the action.'[1]

As they neared the battle, they came under artillery fire and Gambier was wounded. Lieute-nant-Colonel Collingwood Dickson, the son of Wellington's artillery commander in the Peninsula and a veteran of the Carlist War, assumed command. Finding some field-battery horses, he had the 18-pounders pulled into position on the bend between Home and Fore Ridges, facing north-west, where there was an emplacement which afforded some slight protection. To give these valuable guns some infantry defenders, the Guards Brigade, reformed after its dreadful fight on the Kitspur but reduced to about 600 effectives, was stationed nearby.

The 18-pounder, weighing 42 cwt (2,134 kg) and mounted on a four-wheeled carriage, had a long, 9-foot (2.7 m) iron barrel which, with a 6-lb (2.7 kg) powder charge, could throw its shot with great accuracy and power up to 2,000 yards (1,830 m). Thus all the Russian batteries between West and East Juts were within its range. The first ranging shot was fired at 9.30 and the next found its mark. This heavier metal, striking the enemy guns for the first time, provoked a storm of counter-battery fire, round shot ploughing into the ground around the 18-pounders, the howitzer shells 'tearing into fragments, crying for blood with their harsh, grating, truculent "scrisht" – the most hated of all battle sounds'.[2] Despite badly mangled casualties, the British gunners never flinched. With both guns laid each time by an officer, and the Russian batteries clear on the skyline, they began to cause such destruction that, after a while, the enemy battery commanders started moving their guns about which, with damage and casualties, slowly diminished their volume of fire. By 10 o'clock

An 18-pounder gun of the Royal Artillery. After G.B. Campion.

Dickson's men had achieved complete fire superiority over the enemy gun line.

The 18-pounders' fire was soon joined by Boussinière's 12 French 12-pounders from the north end of Fore Ridge. The first six of these had gone into action following the Russian attack from Quarry ravine on the 6ème Ligne, and the appearance of another column once more ascending to the Sandbag Battery. Despite bringing across the 7ème Léger and the guns' effective fire, Bourbaki sent back word to Bosquet that more reinforcements were vital if further retreat was to be avoided.

Bosquet was approaching with 4,600 infantry and, on receiving Bourbaki's plea, sent on 450 Chasseurs à Pied at the double, following with five battalions: one of Tirailleurs Algériens, and both of the 3ème Zouaves and 50ème Ligne. In the rear rode the Chasseurs d'Afrique and the 200-strong remains of Cardigan's Light Brigade, under Paget since its gallant commander had not yet surfaced from his yacht. *

Before receiving Bourbaki's message, Bosquet's intention had been to relieve the British on Home Ridge. On reaching the battlefield he saw, not the frenzied contest he had expected on the ridge, but a few British infantry resting after their recent exertions. The guns were firing and sounds of fighting could be heard to the left front where Haines was holding the Barrier. What struck Bosquet was the dearth of any formed troops to the right front, a void made more ominous by the alarmist tones of Bourbaki's excitable messenger.

In fact, the Russians who had attacked the 6ème Ligne had failed to pursue their advantage, once again displaying that hesitant complacency that seemed to affect them after the smallest success. Nevertheless, Bosquet ordered the Algerians and a

* The British cavalry had moved camp up to the plateau on 28 October.

110

N

95

SELINGHINSK

Kitspur

St Clement's Ravine

Quarry Ravine

Post Road

East Jut

SANDBAG BATTERY

Fore Ridge

Guards

18 pdr

4

Home Ridge

77

6

OKHOTSK

IAKOUTSK

THE BARRIER

49

21

RB

63. RB

20. RB

2

77

RUSSIAN GUN LINE

Shell Hill

VLADIMIR

SOUSDAL

21

88

Mikriakoff Glen

OUGLITCH

West Jut

BOUTIRSK

RUSSIAN RETREAT

Careenage Ravine

CODRINGTON

LANCASTER BATTERY

50

Wing. Half-battalion

Company

Support or small groups

Rallied remnants of 2 and 4 Divisions

Camp

Advance

Retreat

18-pounder

Russian

Infantry

Division

British French Brigade

Russian Regiment

Battalion

British   French

YARDS
0   220   440

METRES
0   200   400

111

General Bosquet (centre) commanding the French corps on Sapouné Ridge, with members of his staff. An 1855 photograph by Roger Fenton.

Zouave infantry. Despite the North African dress, many were Europeans at this date. An 1855 photograph by Roger Fenton.

Zouave battalion, with the Chasseurs à Pied, to deploy on to the spur previously held by the 6ème Ligne. It was a fatal move, particularly as they did not know the ground. Against their left rear, from Quarry ravine, came a Iakoutsk battalion, and against their right rear, from the Kitspur, came the Selenghinsk. Back went the Algerians, the Zouaves followed, and the 6ème Ligne and 7ème Léger went right back – to behind Home Ridge. The Chasseurs d'Afrique and Light Brigade galloped up and were shelled. Only Boussinière's guns prevented a complete catastrophe, receiving a terrible hammering from East Jut for their pains. Once again, disaster did not strike because of the Russians' reluctance to exploit success, deterred perhaps by the continued thunder of Dickson's guns and the few, but unbroken, British remnants on Home Ridge.

However, French troops were always mercurial. What deterred Russians could as quickly restore French confidence. When the enemy failed to come on, Bosquet again launched the Zouaves and Algerians, this time at the Selenghinsk, once more occupying the Sandbag Battery, keeping the other Zouave battalion and the 50ème Ligne in reserve. Now there was no mistake. Eager to avenge their reverse, both battalions went at the battery in the *pas de charge*, bugles blowing, drums beating. As they tore into the Selenghinsk, the Zouaves received a small reinforcement. From the slopes below emerged Wilson with his Coldstream company to join the attack alongside the Zouaves, with whom they had an affinity forged long ago at Varna. Out went the Selenghinsk and down the slopes charged the Zouaves and Algerians, driving them not only to the bottom of St Clement's ravine, but out of the battle. Seeing their line of retreat at last opened by the French, Sargent's trapped 95th company arose from hiding to greet their rescuers.

This flank was now clear and, unlike Wilson and Sargent, the two victorious French battalions could reascend the ravine unhindered to rejoin Bosquet. He reported to Canrobert who, with the arrival of three more battalions at 11 am, then disposed of 8,000 infantry, which he deployed along Fore Ridge and down to the Kitspur.

Another factor influencing these events had been the continued defence, from 9.15, of the Barrier by Haines's men, supported on either flank from time to time, when ammunition permitted, by small skirmishing parties from the 20th, Rifles, and mixed groups from regiments earlier engaged and collected together under whatever officers could be found. Their action served to fix the attention of the Iakoutsk and Okhotsk columns in Quarry ravine, who continued to make periodic attempts to force the Barrier or outflank it.

The 21st Fusiliers' wing commanders in later life. Left: Lord West, in 1860. Right: Frederick Haines, in 1876, when Commander-in-Chief, India.

Though only a company captain in the 21st, Frederick Haines, aged 35, also held a brevet lieutenant-colonelcy and had seen much service in the Sikh Wars, when he and Lord West, commanding the 21st's left wing, had been on Sir Hugh Gough's staff. Only a few days before, they had had the foresight to study carefully the ground on which they were now engaged. With Ainslie severely wounded, command of the 21st as a whole had devolved on the senior major, Ramsey Stuart, but he, with 'his big red face, fearful red beard and whiskers',[3] was regarded as something of a joke by subalterns like Vaughan Lee, while Ainslie had always been reluctant to delegate anything to 'that lubber Stuart'.[4] As the 21st Fusiliers were now the foremost British regiment in the field, it was as well it was operating by wings, both commanded by thoroughly competent officers.

On first falling back to the Barrier, after his foray down Quarry ravine at about 9 am, Haines had drawn up his 70-odd 21st behind its stone wall, posting a small party of the 63rd, some of whom had Miniés, behind a bit of wall to the left with orders to 'fire deliberately' at the Russian gunners on Shell Hill. Until the 18-pounders came into action behind them, Haines's men 'were subjected to a very heavy cannonade and attacked frequently by [columns on] the road and the ravine'.[5]

When the 6ème Ligne had first been attacked, some of them had descended into the ravine. Haines ordered a sortie to assist them. Vaughan Lee recalled:

We rushed out with a cheer and charged the Russe who fled double quick. We had again to retire and poor Hurt was struck, and I was so done up I could not retire and fell, struck down by a stone splinter. A sergeant took my arm and I only escaped being made a prisoner by a few yards.[6]

Private McGuire was confronted by three Russians. He shot one, bayoneted another and brought in the third as a prisoner. Lieutenant Hurt was thought to be dead but, seeing his body move, Sergeants Higdon and Rutherford volunteered to run out under a very heavy fire and brought him in, though he died soon after.* Lee 'laid down under the breastwork and when the Russians came up to within 20 yards, I gave them five barrels of my revolver with great gusto'. He picked up a Russian musket and 'lent it to one of our men who had fired his own musket until it was too hot to hold. I had no time to fire myself, as I had to run about serving ammunition to all the men'.[7]

Repelling these attacks left the 21st dangerously short of rounds. Major Rooper came up with some Riflemen so, temporarily handing over command to him, Haines hurried back to ask Pennefather for ammunition and reinforcements. The former was

---

* Haines later recommended both sergeants for the Victoria Cross, but his report was not approved.

supplied, though at first only Minié balls which were no use for the 21st's smooth bores, but of the latter all Pennefather would spare was Lieutenant William Acton's company of the 77th. However Haines felt this had 'the best effect as it showed we were in communication with our own people and not cut off, as the men were beginning to imagine'.[8]

On returning to the Barrier, Haines found that Rooper had been severely wounded, and that Brigadier Goldie, having earlier sent back Ramsey Stuart to bring forward whatever men he could find, had arrived at the Barrier to take command. Haines asked his permission to visit the 63rd party on the left and found they had attracted so much grape-shot that they had ceased fire. To save lives, Haines agreed and returned to the Barrier, only to learn that Goldie had been killed and he was again in command.

When Dickson's guns began to get the upper hand, the Barrier's defenders suffered less from artillery fire, though the enemy infantry still kept up the musketry duel, occasionally trying to push

through. Each time, however, the 21st and other detachments lined the wall and shot them down. Lee saw the Russian dead and wounded 'lying 4 or 5 deep as every shot told on their columns'. Nevertheless, with at most only 150 men against two Russian regiments, seriously weakened though those were, men were falling all the time. Soon Lee found that he and Haines

were the only two [21st] officers, the rest being killed or wounded. We only escaped by the providence of God, for indeed it was a fearful sight to see so many brave men falling around one. I was covered in blood from a man whose brains were dashed out by a round shot.[9]

Bit by bit, reinforcements turned up. Acton's 77th company came in and Horsford's diminished wing of Rifles added their Miniés to provide longer range fire against the Russian guns. Astley's company of the 49th also arrived. He had been looking for a battle all morning. At day-break he had been manning a detached post, known as the 'Hay Picquet', to the south-east of the 2nd Division camp. Hearing the never-ending roar of battle to his north, he decided to abandon his post and marched along the escarpment towards the Sand-

The defence of the Barrier by Haines and the 21st's right wing. A painting by Marjory Wetherstone.

114

bag Battery. He met some Guardsmen retiring, whose gloomy reports inclined his men to follow. Astley would have none of it and marched on, eventually reaching the Barrier to join Haines's force which, according to Lee, now included men of several regiments.

With such intermingling it may have been here, or possibly earlier at the Battery, that one young officer, anxious to observe the social niceties despite the turmoil around him, pleaded with one of another regiment: 'My men can hardly stand their ground. Would you object to bringing yours into line with ours? I had the pleasure of being introduced to you at Lady Palmerston's last summer'.[10]

As Dickson's 18-pounders had gained ascendancy over the Russian artillery, so too did Haines's unyielding infantry come to dominate the head of Quarry ravine by their superior musketry. By 11 o'clock 'the efforts of the enemy to dislodge us [had] become weak' and, seeing Canrobert's large force deploying on the right, Haines believed 'an aggressive movement seemed feasible'.[11] The question was, where and with what?

11.00 am to 1.00 pm

Near to Haines in the ravine were the Iakoutsk and Okhotsk, still unbroken but greatly reduced and, having been in action with little respite for nearly four hours and with nothing to show for it, might yield to a strong push. However, aligned between West Jut and Shell Hill still stood the unused 16 battalions of the Vladimir, Sousdal, Ouglitch and Boutirsk, as well as the Russian artillery. The latter, though much battered by the 18-pounders, were about to have a new lease of life as Dickson's gunners had fired off all their ammunition. Such a force could hardly be attacked by the few companies and odd detachments of different regiments at Haines's disposal.

Since daybreak some 7,000 British infantry, from 18 battalions or parts thereof, had come into action between the Careenage ravine and the Sandbag Battery. By 11.00 a third of them were casualties, but the survivors by no means formed a cohesive whole. Because of the makeshift method of resisting successive attacks, because seven divisional and brigade commanders and 18 battalion or wing commanders had been killed or wounded, the divisional, brigade, and battalion organization had ceased to exist, except in the reformed Guards Brigade, now mustering only one weak battalion's worth of men.

In addition to the casualties were the non-effectives. Though some men's reserves of courage are greater than others, no man's is infinite. When his belly is empty, when he is short of sleep, when he has endured moments of fearful danger and scenes of terrible slaughter – in which comrades of many years have perished – then, however bravely he may have fought initially, his reserves are likely to be exhausted sooner rather than later. Thus it is not surprising that there were men who found in the wounded an excuse to help them rearwards or to carry their rifles or pouches. There were some who took advantage of the fragmented nature of the battle, the smoke and undergrowth, the absence of officers and NCOs, to conceal themselves until danger passed. In 1854 there were not the regimental aid posts, casualty and straggler collecting posts, and battle police of later wars. There were others who, without ammunition and officers to tell them where to get some and what to do, did not go back but just waited.

As men found themselves without officers, so officers found themselves without men. Carmichael of the 95th, on returning from below the Kitspur, had rounded up some men 'all pretty well exhausted and without ammunition'. By the time he found an ammunition mule, his party had reduced itself to a dozen. He attached himself with these to the Algerians, but soon after realized, 'I had not a man belonging to our army with me'. He ran into Patullo of the 30th who 'like myself had no following whatever' and together they made their way to the back of Home Ridge, where they found 'a good number of officers and men of all regiments'.[12] The 95th, or what was left of it, did not reform as a regiment till the battle was over.

But for every man who skulked or waited to be told what to do, there were the others, equally tired and hungry, who 'behaved admirably, many smoking a little black clay pipe during the engagement',[13] and attaching themselves of their own accord to the nearest unit, however small, of any regiment. John Campbell of the 30th said:

You might find yourself with a party belonging to several regiments pursuing the Russians. Presently you ran against a stronger party and it was now your turn to fall back, but your party diminished, some found their own regiments, some dispersed to collect ammunition from the pouches of the killed and wounded, some wandered and a few might go the rear, not many, for the men were full of resolution. Presently you might come across groups of men sometimes under non-commissioned officers, sometimes not, then you would all join and advance to have another go at the Russians.[14]

Wilson of the Coldstream recalled an Irishman of the 20th who, thinking Wilson was ordering him to rejoin his own regiment, replied, 'O yer honor, don't be after sinding me off. I'd like to go on fightin' wid the Guards'.[15]

So it was that the 2nd and 4th Divisions were, by 11 o'clock, merely a collection of under-strength companies and smaller detachments, most of them willing enough, but lacking the cohesion and chain of command that a properly organized counter-offensive would need to succeed – even under such an indomitable and energetic commander as Penne-father.

He was as aware as Haines that now was the time for attack, and had sent a message to Raglan that he could hold his own and that, if reinforced with fresh troops, he would follow the enemy up and 'lick them to the devil'.[16] The most obvious fresh troops were the 8,000 infantry, 700 cavalry and 24 guns of the French, poised on the right front of Home Ridge. When Raglan ventured a literal translation of Pennefather's spirited message to Canrobert, the Frenchman exclaimed delightedly: 'Ah! Quel brave garçon! Quel brave homme! Quel bon général!'[17] But when he discovered the condition and numbers of Pennefather's troops, from whom he would expect support for any attack he launched, his mood changed. The French batteries would continue to give fire from where they were; the French infantry and cavalry would merely hold their ground. Raglan could only concur and Penne-father, who had himself brought the report which had influenced Canrobert, could hardly defy his commander-in-chief and risk the remains of two divisions on their own.

Canrobert's decision left Raglan no choice but to remain on the defensive. With French aid his troops had foiled every Russian attempt to break through and beckon Gortchakoff up to the heights. Now that Canrobert had at last made good his undertaking of 4 November to reinforce the 2nd

Division position, he could doubtless do so again. But this vital flank of the siege operation – the Allies' chief priority – was far from secure, what with Gortchakoff's large force looming on the right rear, and Dannenberg, still disposing some 14,000 infantry and considerable artillery, continuing to dominate from Shell Hill the vital Home Ridge.

Dannenberg was also in something of a quan-dary. Since he had been unable to bludgeon his way through the under-strength 2nd Division with two fresh corps, it was unlikely that his reduced and tired force could yet succeed now the French had arrived in strength. It also seemed unlikely that Gortchakoff would come up to his aid until he was in a position to offer him a helping hand, unless the commander-in-chief, Menshikoff, exercised his authority – which up to now he had not done – to force Gortchakoff into action. For the time being, therefore, Dannenberg's best course of action was to hold fast on the dominating ground of Shell Hill, strengthening his position with entrenchments, and at the same time endeavouring to dislodge that obstinate little force which still controlled the exit from his most covered line of approach up Quarry ravine.

Haines had continued to resist the Iakoutsk's periodic forays upon the Barrier. Mostly they just fired, sometimes they came on at the wall, as Corporal Fisher described:

I dropped on my knee, ready for a shot. In a few moments a large body showed themselves. We commenced firing and so did they. Our party being weak, some having no rifles, others slightly wounded, the enemy came close up to the wall, so that we had not time to load but threw old bayonets, stones and other things at each other, for we did not give the Russians time to load or they did not give themselves the trouble for fear of getting a bayonet thrust. A young officer in a red coat jumped on the wall and called to us to follow, which we did and in a few moments the enemy lay in heaps.[18]

When ammunition ran short, Sergeant Ellis of the 21st 'ordered the men who had knives to cut the pouches from the dead Russians, and exchanging rifles, we went after them, firing at them with their own weapons'.[19] However, if the two opposing commanders were prepared, at least for the pre-sent, to accept a stalemate, one regimental officer of the 21st Fusiliers was not.

Sensing how increasingly half-hearted these

attacks had become, Haines had appreciated that the enemy gunline, weakened by the 18-pounders, was a worthwhile objective within his capability. He went back to suggest this to Pennefather, but the latter was unwilling to spare men from Home Ridge to replace the force at the Barrier. However, a little later, Haines decided to act on his own responsibility.

Keeping the men with muskets to man the Barrier, he ordered Astley to take all those with Miniés and 'advance in skirmishing order through the brushwood towards Shell Hill and harass the gunners as much as possible'.[20] He next went across to Acton's 77th company on his left and gave him similar orders so as to bring fire on the westernmost battery, some 800 yards (730 m) away.

Acton took this as meaning he was actually to attack the battery, which at the time was firing round shot. Though the balls were passing overhead, his men proved reluctant when he gave the order to advance. 'Then I'll go by myself', he said and walked forward some 30 yards (27 m). His men

The Russian view up Quarry ravine looking towards the Barrier, near the skyline, centre. Post Road is on the right, the old track in the ravine's bed. Inkerman Spur is on the left. A photograph taken in 1904.

watched uneasily, until Private James Tyrell ran out, calling, 'Sir, I'll stand by you'.[21] Another man ran forward as well and the three marched on alone, up the slope, through the scrub, towards the muzzles of the Russian guns. The suspense must have been agonizing, but then their example worked and the company ran up. With huge relief Acton spread out, sending two sections under sergeants towards the battery's flanks, while he led the rest on at a steady run at its centre. The gunners changed to canister and some fell, but they went on, dodging through the bushes. Astley's men, after some hesitation, were now moving up on the right, followed by Horsford's Riflemen whom Haines had dispatched in support. And then came the most heartening reinforcement of all: far in rear the 18-pounders, now resupplied with ammunition, opened fire once more, their heavy

117

William Acton, 77th, photographed after the war as a captain, *c*.1857.

rounds shrieking over the advancing infantry's heads to crash among the battery. *

Fearful of having his guns destroyed or, worse still, captured by the infantry, the battery commander called up his teams. Though men and horses were blown to pieces, his gunners worked like demons to limber up and get away. Their determination was rewarded. When Acton's breathless men finally reached the abandoned position, the only recompense for their gallant attack was one shattered gun carriage and two limbers. Astley and Horsford, coming in on the right, captured eight wagons.

As the 18-pounders switched to other parts of the Russian gunline, Acton, Horsford and Astley were joined by the 21st's No. 1 Company. Thus some 300 British infantrymen stood again on Shell Hill, nearly seven hours after it had been abandoned. Their position, however, was precarious. To their left, on West Jut, and to their right front were the four regiments of the Russian reserve, the nearest little more than 200 yards (180 m) away. Apart from the 18-pounder fire, the closest support of any

substance was over three-quarters of a mile (1.2 km) away, from Home Ridge, or the immobile French. Had Haines judged wrongly?

1.00 to 4.00 pm

Three-quarters of a mile (1.2 km) off in another direction, on Victoria Ridge, Brigadier-General Codrington of the Light Division saw the Russian guns pulled away. Looking at his watch, he noticed it was 12.45 and sent a galloper off to Raglan.

Since day-break he had kept 1,200 of his brigade[†] guarding the east side of Victoria Ridge from any attack up the Careenage ravine, and giving whatever fire support they could across the ravine against West Jut which, when the fog cleared, was within Minié range. One small infantry attack against Hewett's Lancaster gun had been quickly driven away by a company of 2nd Rifle Brigade, but the gun position endured heavy enfilade gunfire from West Jut. Because the parapet had been rebuilt since 26 October, the Lancaster could only fire forward so that the enemy guns had to be engaged with rifle fire alone.

Private Oliver's company of the 7th was in skirmishing order. He took cover from the fire, 'like hailstones', but found 'I could not make my rifle tell upon them'. He and his corporal decided to make for the Lancaster battery,

but it was impossible to proceed any further, the shells and balls came around us so; we fell flat on the ground in a small hole ... after a short time I said, 'Well Jack, you can stop but I'll chance it and run for the Battery'. 'Agreed on', he says, and we ran for our lives. We gained the left of the Battery and commenced firing against the Russians on the opposite hill. I shifted my position again to the right of the Battery and had scarcely left the last place when a shell burst where I had been and killed 4 men.[22]

In the battery was Major Sir Thomas Troubridge Bt of the 7th:

6ft 1 inch and stout in proportion, the best soldier and calmest man in danger I ever saw. A shot came and took the Major's two feet off and one leg of an ensign of the 23rd. The blood and flesh came all over me. It was a

---

* Kinglake (Vol. V, p. 423) attributes responsibility for Acton's advance to Lord West but, according to Haines's biography, he was misinformed by an officer who confused West and Haines. In any case, Acton had been placed under Haines's command by Pennefather, and West was 600 yards (550 m) away in the Mikriakoff glen (see Rait, pp. 145–6).

† Elements of 7th Royal Fusiliers, 23rd Royal Welch Fusiliers, 33rd, 2nd Rifle Brigade; later joined by part of the 19th and five guns.

dreadful sight. Our poor Major stood his post bravely – he only gave a groan. They wanted to take him home. 'No, men', he said, 'I command you still'. As long as I live I shall never forget that man.[23]

When Troubridge later lay with his amputated stumps thrust into gunpowder barrels to staunch the bleeding, he remarked ruefully to a brother officer, 'this is what's called glory!'[24]

While maintaining their position on Victoria Ridge, Codrington's men lost 180 killed and wounded from the enemy guns. But when he saw the Russian gunners attacked by Acton limbering up at 12.45, he was witnessing the beginning of the end. Though as yet only one battery was on the move, its departure from the gunline, and the renewed 18-pounder bombardment, so dismayed Dannenberg that he changed his mind. At 1 o'clock, without consulting Menshikoff, who was only five minutes' ride away with the Grand Dukes, he decided to retreat. He ordered the Vladimir Regiment forward, behind which the batteries were to pull out one by one, the heavier and hardest-hit guns going first, the lighter batteries to follow, supported by the other 12 battalions of the reserve.

Sir Thomas Troubridge Bt, 7th Royal Fusiliers, 'the best soldier and calmest man in danger'. An engraving from a photograph.

Once the Vladimirs had advanced to their covering position, the hard-tried Iakoutsk and Okhotsk were to retreat down Quarry ravine.

Menshikoff, who had not even left his quarters that morning until 6.30, had exercised no command function whatever during the battle, but when he realized what was happening, he rode at once to Dannenberg and ordered him to stop the retreat. Dannenberg replied that his men had done their best, had suffered terribly, and that to countermand the retreat, now it had begun, would invite disaster; if Menshikoff wished otherwise, he should assume command himself. According to Grand Duke Nicholas, who was present, this 'completely unnerved' Menshikoff,[25] who turned his horse without a word and rode off.

The courage and devotion to duty of the Russian gunners, as they stood their ground under Allied artillery and rifle fire until it was their turn to move, was beyond praise – particularly in view of what befell their covering infantry. The commander of the Vladimir was either a fire-eater or misunderstood his orders; instead of merely presenting a threatening front, he formed his battalions into a massive column and advanced to attack. As this hitherto unbloodied regiment stumped down the forward slopes of Shell Hill, the 18-pounders smashed into it; soon it was very bloody indeed and stumbling back.

Apart from pursuing the enemy with gunfire, the weary British were in no better order to advance than they had been at 11 o'clock – at least not without support. Surely now the French would be willing to exploit the Russian retreat? But not until 3 pm, when the last Russian battery limbered up and rode off, did Canrobert send forward a battery with two Zouave battalions to East Jut. What may have seemed Canrobert's missed opportunity when the Vladimir retreated may, after all, have reflected his sound judgement. When the last Russians had cleared Shell Hill, a barrage of fire fell on its eastern slopes. Anchored in the head of the Sebastopol roadstead, two warships had opened fire with broadsides.

As the Russian batteries wound their way down the heights back to Sebastopol, their tired gunners doubtless giving thanks for their deliverance, they suddenly heard what one Russian called the 'characteristic ricocheting "ping"'[26] of Minié bullets. Rifle fire came from the scrub on their left, felling

The 18-pounders in action from Home Ridge. French troops are on the right. After A. Maclure.

drivers and horses. After so much, it seemed they were still not safe.

A company of the 50th under Colonel Waddy now appeared at this late hour to harass the retreat. Part of the 50th had been dispatched earlier from the 3rd Division to reinforce Codrington on Victoria Ridge, from where Waddy had been observing the retreat. Sensing an opportunity, he led forward No. 7 Company, crossed the Careenage ravine, climbed the slope in extended order, and opened fire just as the leading battery was brought to a halt by a blockage on the road. His men, in action for the first time that day, could not miss such a dense target. Unable to see their assailants except for the muzzle flashes, and unable to move on because the draught-horses were falling fast, the artillerymen began to panic. Then amid the noise and confusion appeared the calming figure of Todleben. Ordering up a company of the Ouglitch, he sent them forward as skirmishers, followed by the whole Boutirsk Regiment. With only 28 files to hand, Waddy realized it was time to go. They slipped away as quietly as they had come, firing as they left the last shots of the British infantry at the Battle of Inkerman.

The scattered remains of the regiments that had fought so hard rallied to the bugles sounding the regimental calls in the bleak, fading afternoon, and their sergeants began the doleful task of calling the rolls. In his company of the 20th, Colour-Sergeant Geraghty

did not find more than 20 men to answer their names. When absentees were called, the reply was killed, missing, wounded in hospital or in tents. There were so many wounded that the whole camp was nearly transformed into a Hospital.[27]

It had been what one survivor called 'a pell-mell curiosity of war';[28] the battlefield, said another, resembled 'an abattoir and an earthquake blended – bruised, gashed, disembowelled man-flesh and horse-flesh commingled with broken instruments of war'. It had been won by 'the indomitable persistence of the regimental officers'[29] and, as one of those truly said, by 'the courageous British soldier who fought all day without direction or hint from superior authority, only the example of his officer who was left equally without guidance'.[30]

Inkerman has rightly been called 'the Soldiers' Battle' for of generalship there was little or none; only the endlessly cheerful optimism and tireless drive of the ubiquitous Pennefather. By whatever means it was won, as he justifiably claimed afterwards, 'I tell you, we gave 'em a hell of a towelling'.[31]

PART IV

AFTERMATH

I saw the Valley of Death, where thousands lay low;
Not half of whom ever fell by the hands of the foe;
The causes are many, as well known to the State,
But I might give offence if the truth I relate.

I saw the Valley of Death, and going to the trenches,
I looked on the graves and thought of the wenches
In silence lamenting some dear friend or brother,
I thought of the orphan and the heart-broken mother.

SERGEANT TIMOTHY GOWING
7TH ROYAL FUSILIERS

9

The Reckoning

To break through the British position on the heights of Inkerman, Menshikoff had launched nearly 35,000 infantry, supported by some 4,500 gunners. By the end of the day they had failed and suffered 10,729 casualties, just over a quarter of the force deployed. In contrast, Gortchakoff's corps, which seeing no breakthrough had remained on the plain below, lost 15.

The combined British and French casualties sustained in repelling this attack, including Codrington's contribution from Victoria Ridge, were about a third of the Russian losses. From first to last, the British had deployed nearly 10,200 men, a curiously similar figure to the enemy casualties, and which included over 1,200 gunners and the Light Cavalry Brigade's 200; the French contribution was just under 10,000. Yet expressed as a percentage of their numbers deployed, the 2,573 British casualties * – 25 per cent – was only slightly less than the Russians' 27 per cent. The heaviest British losses had been borne by the Guards Brigade, whose three battalions had each lost over 40 per cent of their fighting strength, though the hardest hit, individual regiment was the 20th with more than half of its men deployed being killed or wounded. Most of the 2nd Division battalions, which had borne the brunt in the early stages, had lost between a quarter and a third of their men, while Horsford's Rifles had suffered nearly as severely as the Guards in proportion to their numbers engaged. The casualties on both sides among senior officers – battalion commanders

upwards – testified to their willingness to give a lead and share their men's dangers.

The horrific scenes strewn across the battlefield affected the most seasoned soldiers. Old Colonel George Bell had been through the Peninsular War but some of the sights he saw after the battle

shocked my nerves. What ghastly wounds! What varied positions! That man was in the act of loading his firelock. His left hand grasps the barrel, his right raised to ram down the charge; he holds his firelock fast. That one lies on his back, white and livid, all his blood beside him in a pool. This body is riddled with shot. This man's jaw-bone is carried away; his comrade's knee-cap is shot off. There is a multitude of dead here, many of whom passed away in agony; others look as if peacefully asleep. Hear those piercing cries! Men don't often cry but now they rend the air with life's last shriek of agony.[1]

Gunner Love had not been in the battle but, searching for fallen comrades that evening, thought 'seeing the field after the battle was worse than being in it'. He and his fellow searchers looked with horrified fascination upon a man of the 77th, with

nothing on but his shirt and trousers, laying down in a circle of eight Russians, and one of the Russians had his bayonet through him and he had his bayonet through the Russian, and he was lying with one hand grasping the Russian's coat collar and the other clenched in a boxing attitude. There were three Frenchmen outside of the circle with their bayonets through three of the Russians. I think they must have come to his assistance.[2]

But why, one wonders, was he only in shirt and trousers?

---

* For a breakdown, see Appendix B.

The war correspondent of the *Morning Herald*, N.A. Woods, was particularly appalled by the effects of gunfire:

One poor fellow of the 95th had been struck by two round shots in the head and body. A shell afterwards burst on him and tore him to pieces, and it was only by the fragments of cloth, with the regimental buttons attached, that you could tell the rough bloody mess had ever been a human being. Some had their heads taken off at the neck, as if with an axe; others their legs gone from their hips; others their arms, and others again hit in the chest or stomach, literally as smashed as if they had been crushed in a machine.[3]

It was upon Home Ridge and the ruined 2nd Division camp that the Russian guns had caused most damage,

the earth ripped up, furrowed, corduroyed by the iron tornado. In one place half a dozen men would seem to have been felled by the same round shot. In another, splinters of a single shell had rent an entire group limb from limb; multitudes of killed artillery horses, ammunition ponies, ambulance mules, gave variety to the grim picture.[4]

One of the most piteous sights Woods encountered was 'English women whose husbands were missing hurrying about with loud lamentations, turning the

Graves of 4th Division officers killed at Inkerman with headstones erected in 1855, including Major Wynne's, 68th (nearest the sentry), and Sir George Cathcart's (large cross to the right rear). From Dickinson's 'Officers' Portfolio'.

faces of our dead to the moonlight, and eagerly seeking for what they feared to find'.[5]

Many survivors commented on how peaceful some men struck by musket balls looked, compared with those who had been bayoneted, 'their features convulsed, leaden orbs bulge from their sockets; their mouths wide open, their blackened tongues protrude; mud and grass are held in their clenched fists'. The worst, and the majority, of such corpses lay around the Sandbag Battery – 'layer upon layer, sometimes three or four deep'; not only bayonet wounds but 'the shocking aspect of faces, every feature beaten down into purple jelly, bears witness to bludgeoning with butt ends'. That writer, Wilson of the Coldstream, must have reflected the thoughts of countless soldiers – then and since – when he remarked that 'politicians would talk less lightly of war, could they sometimes step from their libraries into a field like this'.[6]

Many of the dead had not been killed outright but, after falling wounded, had been finished off by Russian bayonets. Lieutenant Macdonald of the 95th, for example, having been shot through the

British and French soldiers collecting Russian dead for burial after the battle. A watercolour by Captain H.H. Clifford.

Lieutenant and Adjutant Macdonald, 95th, receiving the first of his multiple wounds, in the knee. Detail of a silver centrepiece owned by the 2nd Battalion Sherwood Foresters.

knee, was propped against a bush when Russians approached him. He tried to make them understand he was incapacitated but they prodded him several times with their bayonets and finally knocked him senseless with their butts. Miraculously he survived, but many did not. Even after the battle bearer and burial parties, retrieving not only Allied but Russian casualties as well, were fired on by Russian guns from Sebastopol. So numerous were the reports of such brutalities, that Raglan and Canrobert were constrained to send a remonstrance to Menshikoff under a flag of truce. That reprisals were not taken, and that indeed every kindness was shown to the Russian wounded, 'was mainly owing to the generous nature of the English soldier'.[7]

The plight of the wounded was such that, unless their injuries were slight, many may have envied the dead. The luckier ones, if not helped to the rear by comrades, were collected by the regimental bandsmen – 20 per regiment – or, in Guards' battalions whose regimental bands remained at home, by the drummers and pioneers; each battalion only had ten stretchers. Their task was as dangerous as any. A Scots Fusilier Guards corporal-drummer wrote how, after being told to find the best shelter they could, he and the drum-major 'were lying down behind a small bush, the bullets passing within a few inches of our heads, breaking off the branches as we lay there. We both expected every moment to be shot'. The first of five men he carried back had his thigh broken in two places.

We would get five yards, when a round shot would come. We would drop down as well as we could, then we would get up and run. Then a shell would come and down we would go again. Poor fellow, he knew how we were situated and did not complain.[8]

Each regiment was supposed to have its own two doctors and a hospital-sergeant – of varying degrees of skill and sometimes sobriety – to whom, if they could be found, the wounded walked or were carried. One doctor wrote how, having

made, as I thought, convenient arrangements for the wounded, I was compelled to abandon from the solid shot and live shell falling thickly around me. I fell back on my own camp where, having a tent, I established as comfortable a hospital as could be wished, and where I was soon in requisition by a host of applicants of all ranks. I was soon however again compelled to beat a retreat, the Russians having advanced into such a position that they regularly enfiladed the whole camp.[9]

The regimental doctors, or surgeons as they were styled, could only apply dressings, staunch bleeding and carry out minor surgery and treatment. Casualties beyond their competence had to be conveyed to the divisional staff surgeons. The trouble was, so inadequate was the logistic planning of the Crimean Army, that there was no properly organized system of casualty evacuation. A hurriedly formed ambulance corps had reached Bulgaria in July, but since it was manned entirely by elderly and often drunken pensioners, it was a total failure. Some country carts, a few pack animals, the odd artillery limber or wagon, or four men each holding the corner of a blanket, these were the only means of evacuating desperately wounded and crippled men to the staff surgeons' hospital tents. Fortunately for some, the French

Surgical instruments used by Surgeon Huthwaite, Grenadier Guards.

had a well-organized medical service which helped with transport when it could.

If a badly wounded man had escaped the Russian bayonets and been rescued by his bandsmen or – if he had had to survive a night of pain in the open and was still alive next morning – by the search parties combing the battlefield under artillery fire; if he had outlived the regimental surgeon's ministrations; if he had been transported by whatever painful means – then he would face, as like as not, the horrors of amputation without anaesthetics in the 'shambles of the hospital tents. On all sides surgeons, their naked arms smeared with blood, hacking, sawing, gashing, probing, plastering. On all sides shrieks of agony mingled with dying moans and incoherent prayers'.[10] Sergeant Connor believed that 'when the amputation of a leg or an arm takes place, which is frequently done, in seven cases out of ten the patient dies from exhaustion'[11] – in other words, from shock. If the unfortunate victim survived that, he still had to face the pain of, and probably death from, a septic wound since the theory of antisepsis was then unknown.

Sergeant Ellis of the 21st had received a musket ball through the muscle of his right arm and still had one embedded between the calf and bone of his left leg. The second bullet was extracted and he was sent to his own tent 'where I lay for seven days

The Barrack Hospital, Scutari. The cemetery lay in front of the timber building in the foreground.

getting worse'. He was taken back to hospital where 'it was considered necessary to amputate my leg and arm, but I strongly protested. One of the doctors said he had treated a similar case without amputation, so I was allowed to retain those useful appendages and gradually became convalescent'.[12]

Dressings and medication were in short supply. There were no properly trained orderlies or nurses, and only a few ordinary soldiers to hold the patients down and bury the severed limbs – 'a dreadful task', thought Private Hyde of the 49th, while admitting that 'many of our men had become so callous' after seeing so many amputations.[13] The Fusilier Guards drummer, 'after some supper and a drop of rum, went and helped the doctor dress the wounds – an awful sight to see, but I can stand anything now, I am as hard as flint'.[14] The only other helpers were some of the wives, like the 95th's Mrs Nell Butler, met earlier, who, according to one grateful soldier, 'worked like a Trojan, attending to those who needed it'.[15] Another 95th

wife was Mrs Polley, whom George Cavendish Taylor, an ex-officer of the regiment in the Crimea as an observer, found in the 95th's hospital, kneeling on the ground – there were no beds – with her wounded husband's head on her lap. He had known both in England and asked her what had brought her to the Crimea. 'She told me she had been at the camp at Chobham, and thought this would be much the same!'[16]

The wounded who required further treatment and longer convalescence were transported by whatever rough and ready means were available down the awful, jolting Col track to the Balaclava hospital, where conditions were chaotic. Then, as happened to Sergeant Gowing,

we found ourselves on an old steamer – packed on board anyhow – to live or die; many died before we left the harbour. The sea was boisterous. Many of our poor fellows had had not the slightest thing done for them since they were wounded ... their poor mangled bodies were infested with vermin. Between decks men were shrieking with pain, some were lying in a state of putrefaction, others in a morbid state and some were consigned to a watery grave.[17]

An improved ward in the Barrack Hospital, after the arrival of Florence Nightingale, standing in the centre. After W. Simpson.

Gowing was lucky as, on reaching Constantinople, he was shipped on to Malta where there were good hospitals. For most, their final destination – in both senses – was either the General or Barrack Hospital at Scutari: 4 miles (6.4 km) of rickety beds with unwashed mattresses on rotting floors, vermin everywhere, sewage overflowing, overworked and insufficient doctors, acute shortages of everything, gross overcrowding, filth, stench, gangrene, death and hopelessness. Such were the base hospital facilities provided by one of the richest and most powerful countries in the world for the wounded soldiers whom it had sent out to fight. It was said that once a man entered here, all that was left for him was to pull his still muddied and bloodied blanket – if he had one – over his head and await his end. To this feared hell-hole had come the sick from Bulgaria, the wounded and dying of the Alma and Balaclava. Here too came the heroic men of Inkerman. But unlike those who had preceded them, they could soon expect some comfort for the dying and, for some, a chance of survival. The day before they had fought their battle, a party of 38 nurses had landed at Scutari, led by a redoubtable Englishwoman, Miss Florence Nightingale.

II

The day after the battle, the combatants began to take stock. Despite having amassed, for the first time in the Crimea, a decisive superiority in men and guns, the Russians had failed to achieve the aim set out by Menshikoff of seizing and occupying the heights on which the English troops were. established. To placate the Tsar, rather than implementing any strongly held views of his own on the need to attack – which he lacked – Menshikoff had devised a plan, complex but basically sound and feasible. However, he had promulgated it without clarity, and executed it without the essential overall command and coordination. Despite his numerical superiority, only about a third of his total force was committed to the main thrust. His subordinate commanders, who had only just arrived, were given no time for reconnaissance of difficult ground unfamiliar to them, which would have to be traversed in the dark and of which there were no maps. By confining Dannenberg's command over Soimonoff and Pauloff until the moment when the two corps had linked up on the heights, he virtually allowed Soimonoff a free hand in the early stages which, compounded by Pauloff's delay in coming into action, resulted in Soimonoff's premature attack – with the results seen. Pessimistic by nature, without confidence in his troops, subordinates and even himself as a field commander, Menshikoff had simply let events take their course, his only intervention being his attempt to halt Dannenberg's retreat. According to Grand Duke Nicholas, he provided himself with no headquarters staff during the battle, and neither sought nor received any reports from his commanders. After it, he blamed everyone but himself for the failure and accused the troops of cowardice.

The elderly Dannenberg had attempted to put some flesh on Menshikoff's skeletal orders, including his belated and, as it turned out, ignored order for Soimonoff to attack up Victoria Ridge. But, inhibited by his superior's dislike, lack of confidence and restrictions on his command responsibilities, and with deployment of his large force limited by the formation and size of the battlefield, he had been unable to launch a coordinated offensive and the attacks had been made piecemeal. First Soimonoff, then part of Pauloff's corps, had been held and convincingly repulsed by Pennefather's 2nd Division alone before 7.30, leaving only Pauloff's other three regiments to continue the battle, including the wasteful struggle for the Sandbag Battery, for nearly another six hours, while the four regiments of the reserve remained uncommitted.

Dannenberg's dismay at Gortchakoff's inactivity, emphasized by his negligible casualties, was understandable, but the latter's orders had only enjoined him to draw upon himself the enemy forces holding the escarpment, to try and secure one of the ascents up it, and send up his dragoons 'at the first possibility'.[18] As to the last, Gortchakoff could claim that no possibility had arisen, but his execution of the rest had been so ineffective – for which he blamed his subordinate, Liprandi, with whom he was at odds – that he had completely failed to prevent Bosquet's timely reinforcement of the embattled British.

Considering the animosities between the senior Russian commanders, their poor planning, imperfect control and waste of resources, it is surprising and indeed creditable that most Russian units fought as bravely and as stoically as they did. The Iakoutsk and Okhotsk Regiments, in particular, were used and used again, yet still retreated rather than ran at the end. In the circumstances – and remembering the vulnerability and rigidity of the way they were trained to operate, and their reliance on the bayonet necessitated by their obsolete muskets – it ill became Menshikoff to blame his defeat on their cowardice.

For the future, he saw no alternative but to remain on the defensive, trusting in the winter to defeat the Allies. Apart from a failed attack against a strong Turkish force holding Eupatoria, the Allies' original landing place, in February, the Russians would not take the offensive again until August. By then, however, Menshikoff had been dismissed, and Tsar Nicholas, broken by failure, was dead.

That would be many months ahead. The only advantage accruing to the Russians immediately after Inkerman was that the casualties they had inflicted, particularly on the British, put paid to the plan discussed by Raglan and Canrobert on 4 November for an assault against Sebastopol on the 7th. Indeed De Lacy Evans was so struck by the disparity of strength between the Russian forces and the remaining British, that he felt compelled to urge Raglan to abandon the siege. Raglan could not agree, but it was clear the Allies too would have to remain on the defensive until major reinforcements could arrive. And that, as Menshikoff had hoped, would condemn them to winter on the Chersonese Plateau, for which the British certainly were in no way equipped.

Nevertheless, apart from the heavy loss inflicted on the Russians, the Allies had averted what could have been a major tactical disaster with far-reaching strategic implications. Had the Russian plan succeeded, Raglan's army would have been cut off from its Balaclava base, which itself would have become more vulnerable than it had been on 25 October. The entire British position before Sebastopol could have been attacked both from the rear and the town, forcing Raglan to withdraw what remained of his army into the French sector and transferring his base to Kamiesch – if facilities there permitted. Whether the Allies could have continued to prosecute the siege successfully on the

Some of the men who stood firm at Inkerman. Survivors and wounded of the Coldstream Guards and 20th returning to camp. Detail from a print after Lady Butler's 'Return from Inkerman'.

relatively narrow front afforded by the French lines is questionable. They would have had to contend not only with the town's defenders, but with a powerful force permanently poised on their open flank with free access both to the town and the interior. If it had come to failure, the only course would have been evacuation – assuming its feasibility – leaving Russia the victor, at least in the Crimea. One could speculate endlessly about what might then have ensued: encouragement of further Russian expansionism; the effect on Turkey, Austria and upon Napoleon III's position in France; the implications for Britain's communications with the East and for her prestige and power, particularly in India. Notwithstanding what might have happened had the men of Inkerman not stood firm, the fact remains they did, thereby saving their country's honour and ensuring their army's survival before Sebastopol.

If their endeavours had received some help from faulty Russian generalship, their success could hardly be ascribed to its British counterpart. Raglan had been present throughout but had exercised little influence on the outcome, apart from the important and effective decision to order up the two 18-pounders. Sir George Brown, the martinet commander of the Light Division and Raglan's chief confidant, had also been present but had done little except rebuff Bosquet's early offer of help and sustain a wound in the arm. Sir George Cathcart, Brown's partner in the Bosquet incident, had disobeyed orders and got himself and a good many of his men killed in an ill-conceived counter-

Left: HRH The Duke of Cambridge, 'who led nobly to the charge'. Right: Sir George Cathcart, who did the same, but contrary to orders.

attack, from which the survivors had considerable difficulty extricating themselves. Sir George De Lacy Evans had conscientiously ridden up from his sick-bed, but sensibly had refrained from interfering with his subordinate, Pennefather's handling of the battle. Codrington and Sir Richard England, commanding 3rd Division, though not, in the event, attacked, had not been able to discount the possibility of a foray from Sebastopol – as made against the French lines by Timovieff – so they had rightly maintained watch on that flank but doing what they could to assist the main battle. The Duke of Cambridge had followed, rather than influenced, events; he had been unable to prevent the heavy losses sustained by his Guardsmen, by which, one said, 'he seemed sadly hurt',[19] yet had won their esteem for the way 'he had led us nobly to the charge', thereby proving himself 'a fine specimen of what family he belongs to'.[20]

Such generalship as had been evident was Pennefather's. His methods – akin to damming a growing number of holes in a flood-threatened dyke with whatever materials lay to hand – may

have been more unconventional and disruptive of regimental cohesion than Evans's handling of Little Inkerman, but he had been faced with a far stronger force, and from the start he could not know what reinforcements would reach him and when. All he could do was to win as much time and space as he could with his own understrength division by confronting the enemy well forward and utilizing the difficulties of the terrain. Once he had got all the reinforcements he was likely to receive – a large part of which, through no fault of his, became sucked into the fight around the Sandbag Battery – his only option then was to inspire his men to hold on, either until the Russian will to continue was broken by their casualties, or until the French arrived – not unlike Wellington waiting for Blücher at Waterloo.

Up to a point, his dawn picquets had been caught unawares by the enemy advance but, given the fog, the extent and ruggedness of the ground combined with his lack of numbers, it is difficult to see how it could have been otherwise. Nevertheless, they put up a sufficiently stout resistance to give Pennefather time to reinforce them with whatever wing or battalion came first to hand.

Pennefather's methods proved effective enough to prevent a Russian breakthrough. In the end, the efforts of some enterprising infantry and the

18-pounders provided the catalyst which persuaded Dannenberg to break off the contest. That the Russian retreat was not exploited into a rout cannot be blamed on Pennefather, for by then he was bound to defer to Raglan, who in turn was hamstrung by Canrobert's unwillingness to continue.

III

While not detracting from Pennefather's achievement, the fighting conditions – poor visibility caused by fog and subsequent battle smoke, plus the brush-covered terrain with its gullies and ravines – made it impossible for even such an energetic commander as he to exercise control over events other than those occurring wherever he happened to be at any one time. Thus it was that so much of the outcome depended on the regimental officers and their ability to judge what needed to be done to stem the flood, and to carry their men with them in furtherance of their resolve. Though always outnumbered, they were quick to appreciate how the solid, ponderous Russian masses could first be confused, then halted, and finally turned back by their own supple, and agile, but thin, formations. These could make best use of their superior musketry, on the principle that the way to stop a steamroller was not by opposing mass with mass, but by the irruption of small missiles into its working parts from many directions.

Battle obviously induces fear into all men, and British officers and men were no braver than their Russian counterparts. But the latter's reliance on mass bred a sheep-like mentality; the more open British methods encouraged enterprise and initiative, not merely among the officers, but in the men as well. One officer observed admiringly 'how quick of invention and rich in resource were the non-commissioned-officers and privates, despite a military education shallow and imperfect'.[21] In peacetime the British infantryman had been drilled and drilled, as had the Russian. This had inculcated the necessary discipline but, having learned how to survive on the battlefield at the Alma, Little Inkerman and during the constant picquetting duties, the British soldier's more independent character had asserted itself, without losing the engrained obedience which is a prerequisite for military success.

That men, most of whom were tired and hungry when they started, could so overcome their natural fears as to endure the concentrated horrors and dangers of a battle like Inkerman and still function effectively as soldiers under orders, against superior numbers and artillery, cannot be wholly attributed to the drill-based discipline acquired on the barrack square, nor even to better skill-at-arms than the enemy's. In his book, *The Face of Battle*, John Keegan has skilfully suggested what motivated men to keep going at Waterloo, a very different battle tactically, fought nearly 40 years earlier, but nevertheless with some characteristics similar to Inkerman. Most of the British infantry at Waterloo began the battle tired, hungry and wet through, probably even more so than at Inkerman, which suggests their morale may have been at a low ebb. Yet Keegan speculates whether their physical fatigue may not have partially anaesthetized them mentally against life-threatening fear.[22] No evidence of this is readily apparent from the Inkerman accounts, yet perhaps men felt that the quicker the fighting was concluded, the sooner could their physical deprivations be made good, assuming of course one survived; running away was likely to increase, rather than alleviate the problem, apart from the consequences of being caught. In any case, in the Crimea there was nowhere to run to, except the enemy, and his treatment of the wounded may have suggested to ordinary soldiers that a similar fate awaited prisoners or deserters – Sergeant McMillan for one had certainly believed

Some of the types of men to whom the victory was due. Coldstreamers, all wounded at Inkerman, after the war.

Loyalty to comrades: Private Parkes, 4th Light Dragoons, saving Trumpeter Crawford's life at Balaclava. A painting by Chevalier Desanges.

this when below the Kitspur. As discussed earlier, there were men at Inkerman who, if they did not actually take to their heels in panic-stricken flight, were able to make themselves unavailable due to the prevailing conditions. Most, however, seem to have stuck it out.

Keegan suggests one important motivating factor at Waterloo was 'group solidarity':[23] the sense of security afforded by the unit to which a man belonged, his loyalty to his comrades within it, his wish not to betray them and to earn their esteem. Keegan mentions a regiment's Colours as a powerful symbol of that loyalty, exemplified by the sacrifices made to preserve them. Not every regiment at Inkerman took its Colours into action, but examples have been seen in the battle showing that they remained an important focus for infantrymen's endeavours (and would continue to do so for nearly three decades). In the same vein was the regimental spirit, probably more highly developed in 1854 than in 1815, evinced by the 20th's 'Minden Yell' and the 57th's 'Remember Albuera',

with its appeal for solidarity, not merely with present comrades, often of long standing in the regiment, but also with those who had fought and died for it in the past. Every regiment, each a close-knit entity and particularly so on active service, was jealous of its honour in the sight of others. The two companies of the 46th, the only representatives then in the Crimea of a regiment which had attracted such adverse publicity before the war, would have been well aware how much their regiment's reputation depended on them as they charged alongside the 68th down the Kitspur. At Balaclava, the 13th Light Dragoons were exhorted to keep going, not so much to get at the Russian guns, but to avoid being outdistanced by the 17th Lancers. Even when men of different regiments became mixed up, as happened at Inkerman, each ad hoc group would have become a microcosm of inter-regimental rivalry, each man mindful of not betraying the numerals on his cap before the others. The regiment was, after all, for better or worse, the Victorian soldier's home, his family, and therefore not to be let down.

At Waterloo Keegan also rates highly 'individual leadership',[24] especially that of the regimental officers. They, he concludes, were motivated by their concept of honour: how their conduct as gentlemen, more than as officers, was perceived, not so much by their men, as by their brother officers. Of individual leadership being a prime motivator at Inkerman there can be no doubt: an obvious example being Acton and his 77th company. Though the tradition of the gentleman-officer remained in 1854, and though it was still important for him to stand well with his fellows, there was an added dimension. The mid-Victorian officer, particularly in the field, had a greater sense of obligation and attachment to his men than his Regency counterpart. He may not have yet acquired the close identification with every aspect of his soldiers' lives as, say, the subaltern of 1914, but he was closer to them in spirit. Keegan mentions how Waterloo officers in their recollections were often vague about their soldiers' names and identities.[25] Carmichael of the 95th, writing 40 years after Inkerman, remembered not only his soldier servant's Christian name, but also his regimental number, as well as the first names of other 95th men; he could even recall the name of an old soldier of the ambulance service who had asked

Loyalty to the regiment: the Grenadiers' fight to save their Colours on the Kitspur. After the painting by Edward Armitage.

to fall in with his company. Other officers' recollections mention the deeds of individual soldiers, sometimes giving their Christian names and almost always their ranks. There are countless references in Captain Wilson's book which reveal the admiration and respect he had for the ordinary Crimean soldier, not just his own Coldstreamers, but of the Line as well.[26] Strange Jocelyn of the Fusilier Guards wrote movingly of his sergeant, mortally wounded in the battle, whose widow he had confided to his sister-in-law's interest, and who was 'one of the noblest and finest fellows that ever breathed . . . his loss to me was as great almost as a brother's. I had great affection for that man and would do anything for his widow and children'.[27] In an otherwise highly critical 1855 report on Crimean operations, its authors singled out for praise the way officers 'had not only shared all the danger and exposure and most of the privations which the men had to undergo, but the evidence is full of incidental indications of their solicitude for the welfare of those under their command'.[28]

That their officers' regard was reciprocated by the men has been quoted in several soldiers' accounts: Private Evans for 'poor Mr Clutterbuck' of the 63rd; Sergeant Connor for Captain Nichol-son; Private Oliver for Sir Thomas Troubridge. Sergeant McMillan thought Captain Tower of the Coldstream 'as brave a young man as any on the field';[29] a completely spontaneous tribute, being written in his diary the evening of the battle, as were the others, all written to relations soon afterwards, not years later in the hope of gain from publication. The 1855 report, mentioned above, commented warmly on 'the community of feelings and interests that appeared everywhere to subsist between officers and their men'.[30]

Men will surely follow more willingly and wholeheartedly an officer who has earned their respect and esteem by his example and care for them, than merely obeying his orders for fear of the consequences if they did not. How else does one explain the actions, seemingly against all common sense and natural inclinations to self-preservation, of private soldiers like James Tyrell, George Bancroft and Anthony Palmer, in support of officers like Acton, Burnaby and Sir Charles

Russell? Perhaps they were exceptional and simply just very brave men. Even so each demonstrated a willingness to stand by a particular officer.

As remarked in Chapter 1, the Crimean officer's care for his men and his readiness to set an example can possibly be attributed in part to the Arnoldian ideal of 'the Christian gentleman'. Not all were paragons of virtue, nor did they exhibit the stifling, sometimes hypocritical respectability of much of the Victorian middle class, but most became imbued with a well-intentioned paternalism towards their men, inspired as much by their education as by the heroic endurance of their soldiers.

The times, too, witnessed a pervasive religious feeling, with the emphasis on personal conduct, among all classes in England, far stronger than 40 years earlier – though the Army, and particulary the rank and file, was probably less affected, having only seven chaplains in the whole service in 1854. Despite the popular appeal of Methodism in the early nineteenth century, John Keegan found little reference to prayer and religious observance at Waterloo.[31] To what extent religious faith sustained men at Inkerman is hard to say. There were truly devout men like Champion of the 95th, but he was atypical. Men who left memoirs of their service would not necessarily have mentioned what was essentially a private matter. In letters home, however, there are references to the Almighty, usually in the context of expressing thankfulness for deliverance after battle, by soldiers as well as officers, though of course they were the better educated and therefore a minority.

A more immediately sustaining factor to the majority before battle may have been their estimation of the enemy. Many Waterloo men were veterans of the Peninsular War, but Napoleon's reputation and the spectacle of his 1815 army still exerted a powerful, even intimidating impression.

The men of Inkerman had beaten their enemy at the Alma and more recently at Little Inkerman, they knew of their cavalry's exploits at Balaclava, and before their very eyes they could see how a few files with Miniés could cause havoc to an 800-strong Russian column.

The Waterloo soldiers were not short of John Bull-ish characteristics, but in 1854 Britain was a greater power than it had been in 1815, in wealth and the extent of its empire. Whatever their circumstances, its inhabitants were aware of this and, however poor, however little they may have benefited, when it came to dealing with foreigners, they were Englishmen (or Britons) first and foremost. The admonition, 'Remember you are born a true Englishman', which Sir Harry Smith received from his mother,[32] was typical of much parental or schoolmasterly advice in the nineteenth century. Bosquet caught a whiff of it from Brown and Cathcart. How it struck the Russians is apparent from Colonel Seaton's account of the war from Russian sources, in which he quotes how, during the periodic truces to recover casualties, the Russian troops fraternized easily with the French, but the English soldiers treated them as they treated all foreigners, 'with good-tempered condescension or amused contempt'. One Russian apparently found that some British infantrymen's idea of fraternization was to remove their coats and suggest 'a bout of fisticuffs'.[33]

Nowadays such manifestations of national superiority are deplored, indeed over the last three decades national guilt has been actively propagated in some influential quarters. But for the galloping, ex-stable-boy lancer staring a Russian gun in the muzzle, or the ploughman turned infantryman only yards from a thicket of out-thrust bayonets, to believe he was the better man may have just stiffened his resolve.

Noble Exertions

Three days after the battle, Raglan penned to the Secretary of State for War, the Duke of Newcastle, what he rightly called an 'imperfect description of this most severe battle'.[1] It cannot have been an easy task so soon afterwards; even with the benefit of hindsight many who have written of it have found its course and nature difficult to describe. What many found less excusable when his description was published was Raglan's sadly typical apportioning of praise.

In modern times a 'mention in dispatches' merits an oak-leaf upon the relevant campaign medal, and rates just below a decoration for gallantry or distinguished service. This was not the case in 1854, nevertheless a 'mention' implied recognition of valuable service rendered and could benefit a man's career. Yet in Raglan's dispatch on 'the Soldiers' Battle', only two officers below the rank of brigadier-general were singled out by name: Egerton of the 77th and Jeffries of the 88th; no Daubeney, Haines, Burnaby, Acton, Bellairs and many others of equal worth, not even Collingwood Dickson whose guns Raglan had himself summoned. On the other hand, Sir George Brown's 'admirable behaviour' was of course noted. Sir George Cathcart, allotted four paragraphs, might have derived some comfort, from the grave, at the omission of his disobedience, and even managed a wry smile at being described as 'an attached and faithful friend'. De Lacy Evans received 69 words for being present; Pennefather only a somewhat lukewarm 23 for the way 2nd Division 'gallantly maintained itself under the greatest difficulties'. His Royal Highness the Duke of Cambridge was

mentioned no less than three times and 'particularly distinguished himself'. The only regiments, other than the Guards Brigade, specifically mentioned were the 20th, 68th, 77th and 88th, and those little more than in passing; for the 21st, which had held the vital Barrier for so long, not a word. The ordinary soldiers, it almost goes without saying, featured merely as 'the troops', and not very often. But then Raglan neither knew them, nor they him.

When the officers of the Grenadiers first read it in the Crimea, Higginson recorded 'we are all frantic', while as for the custom of reading it out to the troops: 'I could not bring myself to do it, so shamefully are we treated'.[2] It was accompanied by news of Raglan's promotion to field-marshal. Calthorpe, Raglan's nephew and ADC, wrote: 'This, I need hardly say, gives general satisfaction'.[3] Captain Clifford's more jaundiced view of Raglan's new baton – 'He has more to thank the Army for, than it has him' – was mild compared with another's 'The Queen ought to break it over his head!'[4] Such sentiments were more common than Calthorpe's.

Raglan was not an inconsiderate man nor was he contemptuous of his juniors, like Menshikoff. He was indeed both kindly and courteous – some thought excessively so for his task – but he was remote, intensely undemonstrative, an aristocrat formed in an earlier age with an uncritical sense of hierarchy. After the Light Brigade's charge he had ridden through its camp without a word of sympathy or praise, not from indifference, but because he himself found dispensing commenda-

Three VCs in later life. From left: William Hewett, for 26 October and 5 November when a midshipman in the Royal Navy; Alexander Dunn, for 25 October when a lieutenant in the 11th Hussars; John Owens, for 26 October when a sergeant in the 49th Regiment.

tion as embarrassing as receiving it. So it was after Inkerman.

Yet if he could find no words for the men who had done the work, the same was not true of the Queen. Although her reply to the dispatch expressed her 'approbation' for all the senior men listed by Raglan, she began by declaring her 'gratitude for the noble exertions of the troops in a conflict which is unsurpassed in the annals of war for persevering valour and chivalrous devotion', and expressly made the point that 'let not any private soldier believe his conduct is unheeded. The Queen thanks him. His country honours him'.[5] In special recognition of the NCOs, she commanded that one sergeant in every regiment of cavalry and battalion of infantry be granted a cornetcy or ensigncy to be dated 5 November 1854. One so promoted, Colour-Sergeant John Sexton of the 95th, who had skilfully extricated a detachment from the depths of Quarry ravine, eventually rose to the rank of major-general.

The Queen also perceived that there existed 'no means of adequately rewarding the individual gallant services', either of officers of 'the lower grades' of the Navy and Army or of NCOs and men of both services. Thus was created the Victoria Cross, for services 'in the presence of the enemy' while performing 'some signal act of valour or devotion'.[6] By the time it was formally instituted in 1856, many men who might have deserved it were dead (posthumous awards were not initially permitted), nevertheless six were awarded for the Alma, nine for Balaclava, four for Little Inkerman, and 20 for the great battle of 5 November (including five Royal Navy and one Royal Marine).

Such recognition, however, was more than two years in the future and in any case would only benefit a tiny minority.* In the immediate aftermath of Inkerman, a Gunner officer saw no

exaltation of spirit which usually follows the gain of a great battle, for the stress of the conflict had been too prolonged and heavy to allow of quick reaction. The gloom of the November evening seemed to overspread the wearied occupants of the hardly-contested ground and descended on a field so laden with carnage that no aspect of the sky could deepen its horrors.[7]

Or, to put it more simply, as an officer wrote about the end of the Great War, 'the soldier was too tired

---

* Most were gazetted on 24 February 1857, but Lieutenant Miller, Royal Artillery, not until 6 May 1859.

The great gale of 14 November. From Dickinson's 'Officers' Portfolio'.

to be elated'.[8] Landing on 7 November with the rest of the 46th, Captain Shervinton found that the remains of their two companies, which had been in the battle, 'seem half ashamed to claim our acquaintance and indeed it is difficult to recognise in their haggard faces and ragged clothing the gay soldiers who left us the other day'.[9]

In the ensuing days, bewilderment, disillusion and anger were added to sadness and grief over lost comrades. For all the efforts and sacrifices by regimental officers and men to compensate for the higher command's failings, the campaign was no further forward, indeed it had been set back. There could now be no assault on Sebastopol, the grinding routine in trenches and on picquet returned, and all was made worse by incessant rain churning the ground into mud and rendering the only track to Balaclava impassable, so that rations could not reach the camps. Overshadowing everything was the now certain prospect of wintering on the heights. Three days after the battle, Raglan instructed his commissary-general to make the necessary administrative arrangements.

The Russian climate gave that unfortunate official six days' grace; then, as though in mockery of such belated planning, showed the teeth the Tsar's army had lacked. From six o'clock on the morning of 14 November a hurricane accompanied by deluging rain struck the camps. Tents, stores and equipment flew in all directions, along with the meagre scrub which provided the only fuel. The Guards' bearskin caps, which normally stood on short pegs outside their tents, were later found in a ravine a quarter of a mile away. Where the hospitals had been, the sick and wounded lay helpless and dying in the mud under torrents of rain. The trenches were flooded; men and horses blown over; officers' camp kit whirled through the air; wagons were overturned. Around midday it grew colder, the rain turned to sleet, followed by a snowstorm until soon all the mud and wreckage were covered by a layer of white. Late in the

The road from Balaclava (*left rear*) to the heights in the wet. Kadikioi church is beyond it. After W. Simpson.

afternoon the wind abated a little and attempts were made to re-erect the tents. But there was now an acute shortage of tent-poles and in any case the canvas, rotted by the summer sun and drenched by subsequent rains, leaked like a sieve. Worst of all, in Balaclava harbour 21 vessels were dashed to pieces, all containing badly needed stores of all kinds, clothing,* medical supplies, forage, tents and ammunition.

From this terrible day of harrowing misery began the Army's 'dire season of calamity'.[10] Balaclava was a shambles, its track to the heights a quagmire up which the few carts the commissariat possessed could not pass, while the baggage animals were starved for lack of forage and dying from overwork. Soon the transport system, inadequate at the start, had completely broken down, and the

only means of getting supplies and stores from the base to the heights – a round trip of 12 hours – was on the backs of undernourished infantrymen, already weak from exposure and exhausted by the never-ending trench work and picquets, or the cavalry and artillery horses which were in as pitiable condition as the baggage animals. By the end of November nearly 8,000 men were sick and their conveyance by these means from the camp to the harbour, for transmission to Scutari, was a nightmare experience of pain, cold and delirium from which many succumbed. The fighting troops who had given of their utmost, were being betrayed by the chaotic lack of logistic planning and foresight for the Crimean expedition – indeed the absence of any effective administrative and staff system in the Army as a whole. Regimental officers like Higginson marvelled at how 'the half-starved and scantily clothed British soldier dauntlessly persevered amid all this suffering, privation and heavy strain of physical endurance without a despondent word', but spoke for many like himself when he wrote home that 'we are by degrees getting roused, and suppressed indignation at the long-

---

* Ordinary replacement garments, not special winter kit, none of which arrived until after the year turned.

endured neglect which we have most patiently submitted to will at last burst all bonds and assert the truth'.[11]

The focus of their anger, not unnaturally, was Raglan, who, in Strange Jocelyn's bitter words, lived 'in a comfortable Farm House from which he never stirs, and knows but little of the misery his officers and men are living in'.[12] The diaries and letters of a more senior man like Windham, a highly professional and thoughtful officer, are full of concern for the desperate state of the army and indignation, mixed with contempt, about Raglan and his headquarters staff:

How any man who had served under the Duke of Wellington could ever have allowed such a state of affairs to arrive is incomprehensible. I am surprised that a man like him, so perfect a clerk, so continually calling for details, should have allowed his army to waste away from want of method and arrangement.

As for the staff,

they have every possible comfort: good beds, good fires and good dinners. If [their] farmhouse were only burnt down, we might get them possibly to move.[13]

Raglan's invisibility to his long-suffering troops stemmed not from idleness or lack of concern, but it was in the same vein as his inability to offer praise or inspiration. He spent hours labouring at paperwork from which a proper staff should have relieved him, while that staff, untrained for war, seem to have regarded their prime role as shielding their chief from unpalatable facts. All the hardships and deprivations of that terrible winter stemmed from the absence of measures that should have been pre-planned before its onset, for which the home authorities were as much to blame as Raglan. The Duke of Wellington, Raglan's mentor, neither loved, nor was loved by his men, but he always took great care that his army was well-found. He was also only 46 in 1815 and in his prime. Raglan, as Windham said, was without 'sufficient energy and far too old [66] for his post';[14] a clerk indeed, albeit an aristocratic one, rather than a commander.

Many officers, some with influential connections, wrote home about the sufferings and deteriorating health of their steadfast men and the incompetence and thoughtlessness of the staff: how

soldiers scrabbled for twigs and roots to make pathetic little smouldering fires, while a copse of trees sheltered the headquarters building; how a shipload of medical stores, urgently needed at Scutari, had first to sail on to Balaclava to offload the ordnance stacked on top before it could return to Scutari; how the 63rd, which had fought nobly at Inkerman, was reduced to only 20 effectives; how men spent every other night in the trenches, soaked through by rain or snow, and having no means to warm themselves and dry their clothing, now completely threadbare, in the brief times they had off duty, and all having such inflamed gums and rotting teeth that they could scarcely eat their paltry rations. The Government's announcement of a campaign medal for the Crimean Army drew from John Leach his famous *Punch* cartoon of two ragged, shivering Guardsmen: one saying, 'Well, Jack, here's good news from home. We're to have a medal', to which the other replies, 'That's very kind. Maybe one of these days we'll have a coat to stick it on'.[15] Such was the neglect of the men who had won Inkerman.

Not only were they fading away from cholera, scurvy, gangrene, frost-bite and dysentery, but more recent arrivals were suffering equally. By 6 December, a month after landing, the 46th had lost 160 dead, only a handful being killed by enemy action.

That something was eventually done was owed not so much to officers' lobbying but very largely to one man whom some officers regarded as 'a vulgar, low Irishman': *The Times* correspondent, William Howard Russell. He had covered the campaign from the start and from his descriptions of the battles people at home had acquired a pride and interest in their army which they had never displayed before. He had ruffled many feathers in the upper and staff ranks and been denied access to Raglan's headquarters. Clifford, who coined the above description, qualified it by saying Russell was 'looked upon by most in camp as a "Jolly Good Fellow"', and that he was 'rather an awkward Gentleman to be on bad terms with'.[16] Russell was aware that Raglan had accused him of providing the enemy with useful information through his dispatches (though actual publication of them was the responsibility of his powerful editor, J.P. Delane), but he maintained that the people of England had a right to know that 'the wretched

The plight of the infantry manning the trenches in the winter of 1854–55. A watercolour by Captain H.H. Clifford.

William Howard Russell, correspondent of *The Times*.

beggar who wandered about the streets of London in the rain led the life of a prince compared with the British soldiers who were fighting for their country'.[17]

The effect of Russell's graphic descriptions of the army's winter sufferings was summed up by Hamley as shaking

the nation with a universal tremor of anger and grief. It could not bear to think that the men of whom it had suddenly grown so proud should be perishing of want, while wealth and plenty reigned at home. The feeling found expression in two ways, very different. The one was an absorbing desire to afford immediate relief; the other a fretful craving to find scapegoats and make them atone for all this suffering.[18]

The latter, orchestrated by *The Times*, provoked a series of censuring letters to Raglan from the Duke of Newcastle, and a less hectoring, but nevertheless accusatory correspondence from the Queen. Raglan replied in detail to every criticism, manfully defending his staff. The attacks earned him some sympathy from formerly critical officers who considered the accusations reflected badly on the Crimean Army as a whole. However, as Clifford noted in January, 'the articles in "The Times" have had a wonderful effect. He [Raglan] rides about much more than he did, amongst the tents'.[19] Near the end of the month, with *The Times* setting its sights on the Government, Lord Aberdeen and Newcastle both resigned, being succeeded by Lords Palmerston and Panmure respectively, who immediately set up a commision under Sir John McNeill and Colonel Tulloch to enquire into the conduct of the Crimean operations. Their subsequent reports, while praising the behaviour of officers and men under appalling conditions, as mentioned in the last chapter, attributed blame to the commissary-general, Mr Filder, and Airey, the quartermaster-general, although the underlying cause was the inefficient and inadequate administrative system then pertaining in the Army. This was to be thoroughly reorganized after the war.

The more constructive response to *The Times* campaign resulted in a burst of industry to manufacture and send out all the tents, huts, warm clothing and supplies of all kinds which, if provided in November, would have saved countless lives. Some consignments of winter clothing reached Balaclava in January–February but, owing to the chronic transport difficulties, failed to reach many of the wretched troops on the upland. By the time most of the winter kits reached the infantry camps, spring was beginning and the photographer, Roger Fenton, was able to capture groups of men posing somewhat self-consciously in bright sunshine wearing sheepskin coats, fur caps and long boots. By then, however, many of the dauntless men of the Alma, Balaclava and Inkerman – Butler's 'old Greek gods' – were either dead, cripples or invalids.

New regiments arrived in the Crimea and fresh drafts for the old, but the latter were little more than recently enlisted, barely trained young recruits. The French, now greatly outnumbering the British, took over the 2nd Division's old area of responsibility and siege operations began again in earnest. Sardinia entered the war on the Allied side. In early June a bombardment, followed by an assault on part of the Sebastopol defences, had some success, but ten days later a joint Franco-British attack against the Malakoff and Redan redoubts failed with heavy casualties.

Among the latter was Raglan. Worn out by his exertions and the attacks upon him, he contracted diarrhoea and died, as much from depression as from physical weakness. Many of his severest critics regretted his passing. Florence Nightingale wrote: 'He was not a very great general, but he was a very good man'.[20] Sergeant Gowing thought 'we did not know, until he was taken from us, how deeply we loved him'.[21]

General Simpson took over, much against his will, and, after two more bombardments, a fresh assault against Sebastopol was made on 8 September. The French took the Malakoff, but the British failed at the Redan and again lost heavily. The burden fell once more on the over-used 2nd and Light Divisions, but their men were no longer of the previous year's calibre. That night the Russians evacuated Sebastopol and the siege was over. Some minor operations followed and just before Christmas destruction of all Russian naval and military installations commenced.

That winter, overtures were made to the King of Sweden with a view to bringing his country into the war on the Allied side and transferring operations from the Black Sea to the Baltic in 1856, but these resulted in no more than a defensive alliance. In the Crimea the fortunes of the Allied armies were reversed. The French, who had weathered the previous winter well, became smitten with disease and suffered as the old British army had the year before. The British, now 90,000 strong and under Codrington's command, well equipped and housed, prepared and trained for the spring.

But France had had enough. Austrian mediation secured an armistice and on 30 March 1856 the Peace of Paris was signed. The war had been primarily about the containment of Russian expansionism into the Near East at the expense of the Ottoman Empire. By the peace treaty, that empire's integrity was guaranteed by Britain, France and Austria, while the Black Sea and the Dardanelles were denied to all warships, with no naval installations being permitted on those shores.

This result was to hold good for 15 years. In 1871 Russia abrogated the treaty, refortified Sebastopol and rebuilt its Black Sea fleet. Her old ambitions resurfaced with another war against Turkey in 1877 and, although a replay of 1854 was averted by the Congress of Berlin, the British Army was again at war the following year, not directly against Russia, but to forestall her encroachment into Afghanistan,

Three of the 95th, typifying the men 'who held the ground they stood on as long as life was in them', in their new uniforms after returning home in 1856, their medals bearing clasps for 'Alma', 'Inkerman' and 'Sebastopol'.

the barrier to India. To win those two decade's respite from Russian aggression, 19,584 British officers and men had died – 80 per cent of them from disease and neglect.

By the time that the Crimean Army reached home, the events of the autumn of 1854, and of this book, were nearly two years old. Peace was declared; Russian pride and ambition brought low. But if the infantrymen and gunners of the old army had not stood their ground on that foggy November Sunday and denied the heights of Inkerman to Menshikoff's host, then that day would have spelled Britain's humiliation and could ultimately have given the Tsar mastery of the Dardanelles.

Britain owed those stalwart, patient, enduring men more than it gave them, more than a leaking tent, a shoddy greatcoat, raw coffee beans and death in a filthy Turkish barrack. But neither then nor since have they received full credit for their 'noble exertions'. Tennyson celebrated the deeds of both cavalry brigades, as have many others since in prose and art, even film. The names of the Light Brigade and Florence Nightingale are almost synonymous with the Crimean War. No one appreciated Miss Nightingale more than the wounded of Inkerman and the piteous sick of the winter camps, as she indeed did them. But no poet sang the praises of the men who fought 'the Soldiers' Battle' and saved their country's honour.

Let two who knew them pronounce their epitaph. Captain Shervinton of the 46th missed the battle by two days, yet what he saw and heard in the aftermath inspired him to write soon after his arrival:

We owe our existence to the pluck of the private soldiers. Surprised by immensely superior forces, without orders, without reserves, sometimes without ammunition when, after using that in the pouches of the dead and dying, they pelted the enemy with stones. Mixed up in strange groups away from the comrades they knew and the officers they trusted, the men held the ground they stood on as long as life was in them. Two mounds mark where hundreds of our dead have been packed away together – 'worthless refuse, what parents have cherished, friends esteemed, and women loved'.[22]

The last testimonial shall be W.H. Russell's, who tried to do in words what government and generals failed to do in deeds for the survivors of Inkerman:

If it is considered that the soldiers who met these furious columns of the Czar were the remnants of three British divisions, which scarcely numbered 8,500; that they were hungry and wet, and half-famished; that they were belonging to a force which was generally 'out of bed' four nights out of seven; which had been enfeebled by sickness, by severe toil, sometimes for twenty-four hours at a time without relief of any kind; that among them were men who had within a short time previously lain out for forty-eight hours in the trenches at a stretch – it will be readily admitted that never was a more extraordinary contest maintained by our army since it acquired a reputation in the world's history.[23]

Sixty years later, almost to the day, another extraordinary contest was fought by equally valiant soldiers – at Ypres, to deny the Kaiser mastery of the Channel ports. They became known to posterity as 'the Old Contemptibles'. Much of Russell's tribute could have been written for them, and 27 of their regiments possessed the battle honour, 'Inkerman'. It is perhaps too fanciful to suppose that some submerged memory of their forerunners' stand in November 1854 may have forged a spirit of emulation among the men who stood and died in the dark days of November 1914. Yet this, after all, is implicit in the traditions of Britain's unique regimental system which has proved its worth over so many years. Even today, after changes to that system and other, greater conflicts, there are officers and men who will set aside each 5 November, not for the pyrotechnics commonly associated with that date, but to commemorate those who won honour for their regiments and batteries on 'Inkerman Day'.

The Russians evacuating Sebastopol on the night of 8 September 1855. After W. Simpson.

Inkerman still remembered. A modern painting of the battle by
David Rowlands, showing the 20th Regiment, whose action is
commemorated annually by XX Lancashire Fusiliers' Inkerman
Dinner Club.

Appendix A
Order of Battle, the Army of the East, up to 5 November 1854, with later titles of regiments

(Later titles are as at 1900 and today; Royal Artillery batteries today only.)

CAVALRY DIVISION (Major-General Lord Lucan)

Heavy Brigade (Brigadier-General Scarlett)

4th Dragoon Guards	(same; 4th/7th Dragoon Guards)
5th Dragoon Guards	(same; 5th Royal Inniskilling Dragoon Guards)
1st Royal Dragoons	(same; Blues and Royals)
2nd Royal North British Dragoons	(Royal Scots Greys; Royal Scots Dragoon Guards)
6th (Inniskilling) Dragoons	(same; 5th Royal Inniskilling Dragoon Guards)

Light Brigade (Brigadier-General Lord Cardigan)

4th Light Dragoons	(4th Hussars; Queen's Royal Irish Hussars)
8th Hussars	(same; Queen's Royal Irish Hussars)
11th Hussars	(same; Royal Hussars)
13th Light Dragoons	(13th Hussars; 13th/18th Hussars)
17th Lancers	(same; 17th/21st Lancers)

Artillery

Maude's I Troop, Royal Horse Artillery	(O Battery [Rocket Troop], Royal Artillery)

FIRST DIVISION (Lieutenant-General HRH The Duke of Cambridge)

Guards Brigade (Brigadier-General Bentinck)

3rd Grenadier Guards	(same; same)
1st Coldstream Guards	(same; same)
1st Scots Fusilier Guards	(Scots Guards; same)

Highland Brigade (Brigadier-General Sir Colin Campbell)

42nd (Royal Highland)	(Black Watch; same)
79th (Cameron Highlanders)	(Cameron Highlanders; Queen's Own Highlanders)
93rd (Sutherland Highlanders)	(Argyll & Sutherland Highlanders; same)

Artillery

Paynter's A Battery, Royal Artillery	(94 [New Zealand] Battery, Royal Artillery)
Wodehouse's H Battery, Royal Artillery	(−)

SECOND DIVISION (Lieutenant-General Sir G. De Lacy Evans)

1st Brigade (Brigadier-General Pennefather)

30th (Cambridgeshire)	(East Lancashire; Queen's Lancashire)
55th (Westmoreland)	(Border; King's Own Border)
95th (Derbyshire)	(Sherwood Foresters; Worcestershire & Sherwood Foresters)

2nd Brigade (Brigadier-General Adams)

41st (The Welch)	(Welch; Royal Regiment of Wales)
47th (Lancashire)	(Loyal North Lancashire; Queen's Lancashire)
49th (Hertfordshire)	(Royal Berkshire; Duke of Edinburgh's Royal)

Artillery

Franklin's B Battery, Royal Artillery	(17 [Corunna] Battery, Royal Artillery)
Turner's G Battery, Royal Artillery	(49 [Inkerman] Battery, Royal Artillery)

THIRD DIVISION (Major-General Sir Richard England)

1st Brigade (Brigadier-General Sir J. Campbell)

1st (Royal)	(Royal Scots; same)
38th (1st Staffordshire)	(South Staffordshire; Staffordshire)
50th (Queen's Own)	(Royal West Kent; Queen's)

2nd Brigade (Brigadier-General Sir W. Eyre)

4th (King's Own Royal)	(King's Own [Royal Lancaster]; King's Own Border)
28th (North Gloucestershire)	(Gloucestershire; same)
44th (East Essex)	(Essex; Royal Anglian)

Artillery

Swinton's F Battery, Royal Artillery	(16 Battery [Sandham's Company], Royal Artillery)
Baker's W Battery, Royal Artillery	(–)

FOURTH DIVISION (Lieutenant-General Sir George Cathcart)

1st Brigade (Brigadier-General Goldie)

20th (East Devon)	(Lancashire Fusiliers; Royal Regiment of Fusiliers)
21st (Royal North British Fusiliers)	(Royal Scots Fusiliers; Royal Highland Fusiliers)
57th (West Middlesex)	(Middlesex; Queen's)

2nd Brigade (Brigadier-General Torrens)

46th (South Devon) (2 companies)	(Duke of Cornwall's Light Infantry; Light Infantry)
63rd (West Suffolk)	(Manchester; King's)
68th (Durham Light Infantry)	(Durham Light Infantry; Light Infantry)
1st Rifle Brigade	(same; Royal Green Jackets)

Artillery

Townshend's P Battery, Royal Artillery	(152 [Inkerman] Battery, Royal Artillery [suspended animation])

LIGHT DIVISION (Lieutenant-General Sir George Brown)

1st Brigade (Brigadier-General Codrington)

7th (Royal Fusiliers)	(Royal Fusiliers; Royal Regiment of Fusiliers)

23rd (Royal Welch Fusiliers)	(Royal Welch Fusiliers; same)	*Artillery*	
33rd (Duke of Wellington's)	(Duke of Wellington's; same)	Brandling's C Troop, Royal Horse Artillery	(C Battery, Royal Horse Artillery)
		Anderson's E Battery, Royal Artillery	(8 [Alma] Battery, Royal Artillery)

2nd Brigade (Brigadier-General Buller)

19th (1st York. North Riding)	(Princess of Wales's Own Yorkshire; Green Howards)
77th (East Middlesex)	(Middlesex; Queen's)
88th (Connaught Rangers)	(Connaught Rangers; disbanded 1922)
2nd Rifle Brigade	(same; Royal Green Jackets)

SIEGE TRAIN, 11th Battalion, Royal Artillery

6th Company	(–)
7th Company	(156 [Inkerman] Battery, Royal Artillery)

Appendix B
British Casualties – Inkerman
(Adjutant-General's Return, 22 November 1854)

The breakdown of each regiment's casualties are shown as follows:

Killed; Wounded; Missing. Inner bracketed figures represent number of officers in each total category.

Regiment	Total	% of actual strength
Staff: (5); (11); –	16	–
4th Light Dragoons: 2; 1; –	3	–
11th Hussars: 1; 2; –	3	–
17th Lancers: 2(1); 2; –	4	–
Royal Artillery: 18(2); 83(4); –	101	8
3rd Grenadier Guards: 79(3); 151(6); 2	232	46
1st Coldstream Guards: 70(8); 121(5); –	191	41
1st Scots Fusilier Guards: 50(1); 123(8); 4	177	45
1st: 1; –; –	1	0.2
7th: 8; 54(5); 6	68	18
19th: 2(1); 3; –	5	3
20th: 31(1); 137(8); 6	174	51
21st: 15(1); 97(6); 6	118	29
23rd: 7; 22(1); 13(1)	42	13
30th: 27(2); 100(5); –	127	31
33rd: 11(1); 52(2); 1	64	26
41st: 39(5); 97(6); –	136	23
46th: 11; 29(2); –	40	30
47th: 20; 48(2); 2	70	12
49th: 43(2); 107; –	150	31
50th: 13(1); 18(1); –	31	7
55th: 14; 73(5); 4	91	21
57th: 17(1); 73(3); 1	91	26
63rd: 16(3); 92(7); 4	112	24
68th: 13(2); 35(2); 8	56	21
77th: 20(1); 39; –	59	23
88th: 38; 83(3); –	121	31
95th: 28(1); 113(3); –	141	32
1st Rifle Brigade: 23(1); 83(3); 6	112	40
2nd Rifle Brigade: 9(1); 27(1); –	36	25
Ambulance: –; 1; –	1	–

Breakdown by ranks:

	Killed	Wounded	Missing	Total
Officers	43	100	1	144
Sergeants	37	112	4	153
Drummers	4	21	–	25
Rank & File	548	1645	58	2251
Totals	632	1878	63	2573

Sources

Published Books

Airlie, Mabel, Countess of, *With the Guards We Shall Go* (Letters of Col. Strange Jocelyn, 1854–55) (Hodder & Stoughton, London, 1933)

Allan, William, *My Early Soldiering Days* (The Edinburgh Press, Edinburgh, 1897)

Anglesey, Marquess of, *A History of the British Cavalry*, Vol. II, 1851–71 (Leo Cooper, London, 1975)

— (ed.), *Little Hodge: Letters and Diaries of Col. Edward Cooper Hodge, 1854–56* (Leo Cooper, London, 1971)

Barker, A.J., *The Vainglorious War, 1854–56* (Weidenfeld & Nicolson, London, 1970)

Barthorp, Michael, *Crimean Uniforms – British Infantry* (Historical Research Unit, London, 1974)

— *The British Army on Campaign, 1816–1902 (2): The Crimea* (Osprey, London, 1987)

Bell, Sir George, *Rough Notes of an Old Soldier* (1867), reprinted as *Soldier's Glory* (Bell, London, 1956)

Blackmore, Howard L., *British Military Firearms, 1650–1850* (Herbert Jenkins, London, 1961)

Brackenbury, George, *The Campaign in the Crimea* (Colnaghi, London, 1855)

Buchan, John, *History of the Royal Scots Fusiliers, 1678–1918* (Nelson, London and Edinburgh, 1925)

Butler, Sir William, *An Autobiography* (Constable, London, 1911)

Calthorpe, Lt.-Col. S.J. Gough, *Letters from Headquarters* (John Murray, London, 1856), reprinted as *Cadogan's Crimea* (Hamish Hamilton, London, 1979)

Clifford, Henry, *Letters and Sketches from the Crimea* (ed. C. Fitzherbert) (Michael Joseph, London, 1956)

Compton, Piers, *Colonel's Lady and Camp Follower* (Robert Hale, London, 1970)

— *Cardigan of Balaclava* (Robert Hale, London, 1972)

Curtiss, John Shelton, *Russia's Crimean War* (Duke University Press, Durham NC, USA, 1979)

Fortescue, Hon., J.W., *History of the British Army*, vol. XIII (Macmillan, London, 1930)

Gathorne-Hardy, Jonathan, *The Public School Phenomenon* (Hodder & Stoughton, London, 1977)

Gernsheim, Helmut & Alison, *Roger Fenton, Photographer of the Crimean War* (Secker & Warburg, London, 1954)

Gowing, T., *A Soldier's Experience: A Voice from the Ranks* (Thos. Forman, Nottingham, 1895)

Hamley, Gen. Sir Edward, *The War in the Crimea* (Seeley, London, 1896)

Harris, John, *The Gallant Six Hundred* (Hutchinson, London, 1973)

Hibbert, Christopher, *The Destruction of Lord Raglan* (Longman, London, 1961)

Higginson, Gen. Sir George, *Seventy-One Years of a Guardsman's Life* (John Murray, London, 1916)

James, Lawrence, *Crimea, 1854–56* (Van Nostrand Reinhold, New York, USA, 1981)

Jocelyn, Col. J.R.J., *The History of the Royal Artillery, Crimean Period* (John Murray, London, 1911)

Keegan, John, *The Face of Battle* (Penguin, Harmondsworth, 1978)

Kinglake, A.W., *The Invasion of the Crimea*, Vol. IV (1868), Vol. V (1875), Vol. VI (1880), Vol. VII

(Blackwood, Edinburgh and London, 1887)

Lawson, George, *Surgeon in the Crimea* (ed. Victor Bonham-Carter & Monica Lawson) (Constable, London, 1968)

Longford, Elizabeth, *Wellington, Pillar of State* (Panther, London, 1975)

Lummis, William & Wynn, Kenneth, *Honour the Light Brigade* (Hayward, London, 1973)

Lysons, Gen. Sir Daniel, *The Crimean War from First to Last* (John Murray, London, 1895)

McClellan, Maj.-Gen. G.B., *The Armies of Europe* (USA, 1861)

Mollo, John & Boris, *Uniforms and Equipment of the Light Brigade* (Historical Research Unit, London, 1968)

— *Military Fashion* (Barrie & Jenkins, London, 1972)

Paget, Lord George, *The Light Cavalry Brigade in the Crimea* (John Murray, London, 1881)

Palmer, Alan, *The Banner of Battle* (Weidenfeld & Nicolson, London, 1987)

Parry, D.H., *Britain's Roll of Glory* (Cassell, London, 1895)

Pemberton, W. Baring, *Battles of the Crimean War* (Batsford, London, 1962)

Priestley, J.B., *Victoria's Heyday* (Heinemann, London, 1972)

Rait, Robert S., *The Life of Field-Marshal Sir Frederick Haines* (Constable, London, 1911)

Ray, Cyril, *Regiment of the Line: XX Lancashire Fusiliers* (Batsford, London, 1963)

Regimental Officer, A (Col. C.T. Wilson) *Our Veterans of 1854* (Skeet, London, 1859)

Ross of Bladensburg, Lt.-Col., *The Coldstream Guards in the Crimea* (Innes, London, 1897)

Russell, W.H., *Despatches from the Crimea* (ed. Nicolas Bentley) (Panther, London, 1970)

Russian Account of the Battle of Inkerman (translated from German) (John Murray, London, 1856)

St Aubyn, Giles, *The Royal George: Life of the Duke of Cambridge* (Constable, London, 1963)

Seaton, Albert, *The Crimean War: A Russian Chronicle* (Batsford, London, 1977)

Selby, John, *The Thin Red Line of Balaclava* (Hamish Hamilton, London, 1970)

Small, E. (ed.), *Told from the Ranks* (Melrose, London, 1898)

Smith, George Loy, diaries published as *A Victorian RSM* (Costello, Tunbridge Wells, 1987)

Spiers, Edward M., *The Army and Society, 1815–1914* (Longman, London, 1980)

Steevens, Lt.-Col. N., *The Crimean Campaign with the Connaught Rangers* (Griffith & Farran, London, 1878)

Strachan, Hew, *Wellington's Legacy: Reform of the British Army, 1830–54* (Manchester University Press, Manchester, 1984)

— *From Waterloo to Balaclava: Tactics, Technology and the British Army, 1815–54* (Cambridge University Press, Cambridge, 1985)

Taylor, G. Cavendish, *Journal of Adventures with the British Army in the Crimea* (Hurst & Blackett, London, 1856)

Warner, Philip, *The Crimean War: A Reappraisal* (Arthur Barker, London, 1972)

— (ed.), *The Fields of War* (letters of Capt. Temple Godman) (John Murray, London, 1977)

Whinyates, Col. F.A., *From Corunna to Sevastopol: History of C Battery RHA* (W.H. Allen, London, 1884)

Ward, S.G.P., *Faithful: History of the Durham Light Infantry* (Nelson, Edinburgh & London, 1963)

Wilkinson-Latham, Robert, *Crimean Uniforms – British Artillery* (Historical Research Unit, London, 1973)

Windham, Lt.-Gen. Sir Charles Ash, *Crimean Diary and Letters* (ed. Maj. Hugh Pearse) (Kegan Paul, London, 1897)

Wood, FM Sir Evelyn, *The Crimea in 1854 and 1894* (Chapman & Hall, London, 1896)

— *From Midshipman to Field-Marshal*, Vol. I (Methuen, London, 1906)

Woodham-Smith, C., *The Reason Why* (Constable, London, 1954)

Woods, N.A., *The Past Campaign* (two volumes) (Longman, London, 1855)

Privately Printed

Bannatyne, Lt.-Col. N., *History of the 30th Regiment* (Liverpool, 1923)

Cavendish, Brig. A.E.J., *The 93rd (Sutherland) Highlanders* (1928)

Champion, Maj. J.G. (95th), *Sketch of the Life and Letters* (ed. anon) (1856)

Franks, Sgt.-Maj. Henry (5th DG), *Leaves from a Soldier's Notebook* (n.d.)

Hume, Maj.-Gen. J.R., *Reminiscences of the Crimean Campaign with the 55th Regiment* (1894)

Lomax, D.A.N., *History of the Services of the 41st Regiment* (Devonport, 1899)

Moore, Geoffrey, *Vincent of the 41st* (1979)

Neville, Hon. Henry & Hon. Grey, *Letters from Turkey and the Crimea* (1870)

Petre, F. Loraine, *History of the Royal Berkshire Regiment*, vol. I (Reading, 1925)

Slack, J., *History of the 63rd Regiment* (London, 1884)

Whitehorne, Maj. C.A., *The Welch Regiment, 1719–1914* (Cardiff, 1932)

Woollright, H., *History of the 57th Regiment* (1893)
— *Records of the 77th Regiment* (1909)

Wylly, Maj. H.C., *The 95th (Derbyshire) Regiment in the Crimea* (London, 1899)

Manuscripts

Armstrong, Lt.-Col. J.W., Testimonial re. Capt. Astley, 49th (Duke of Edinburgh's Royal Regiment Museum)

Carmichael, Lt.-Col. G.L. (95th), Notes on the Battle of Inkerman (National Army Museum, 6807–264–1)

Fisher, John (Rifle Brigade), Scraps from a Corporal's Notebook (National Army Museum, 7606–38, 39)

Haines, Maj.-Gen. F.P. (late 21st), Recollections of Inkerman (National Army Museum, 6807–146–2)

Heap, Shoeing-Smith Richard (RA), Letter, 14 December 1854 (P.J. Haythornthwaite Collection)

Image, Lt. J.G. (21st), Journal (Manitoba Museum)

Lee, 2nd Lt. Vaughan Hanning (21st), Letters, 22 August 1854–13 June 1856 (Maj. F. Myatt MC)

Leith Hay, Maj. A.S. (93rd), Letter, 27 October 1854 (Scottish Record Office, GD225/Box 42/14)

Macdonald, Lt. A. (95th), Letters, September 1854 and undated (Maj. P.J. Mercer)

Mollo, John (ed.), Various accounts, Heavy and Light Brigades (Mollo Collection)

95th Regiment, Record of Service (Sherwood Foresters Museum)

Shervinton, Capt. Richard (46th), Journal (Duke of Cornwall's Light Infantry Museum)

Smith, Sgt. Thomas (30th), Letter, 17 November 1854 (P.J. Haythornthwaite Collection)

Walters, Sgt. George (49th), Record of Service (Duke of Edinburgh's Royal Regiment Museum)

Periodicals

Durham Light Infantry Journal
Torrens, Capt. H.D. (23rd), Letter, 3 April 1856 (Vol. I, 150)

Guards Magazine (1987)
Diary, 3483 Sgt. William McMillan, Coldstream Guards, 4 March–8 November 1854

Illustrated London News (July–December 1854)

Journal of the Society for Army Historical Research
Letter, Pte. Alfred Oliver (7th), dated 20 November 1854 (Vol. XLVI, 116)

Barnsley, Maj.-Gen. R.E., 'Diaries of John Hall, Principal Medical Officer in the Crimea' (Vol. XLI, 3)

Jackman, S.W. (ed.), 'Crimean Experiences of Gnr. William Love RA' (Vol. LX, 103)

Lagden, A.A. (ed.), 'Letters, Lt.-Col. F.G. Ainslie, 21st' (Vol. LVIII, 6, 98)

Selby, J.M. (ed.), 'Lt. Anthony Morgan, 95th, 20 Sep–26 Oct 1854' (Vol. XLIV, 44)

Tylden, Maj. G., 'The Heavy Brigade at Balaclava' (Vol. XIX, 98)
— 'C Battery RHA and the Light Brigade at Balaclava' (Vol. XXII, 260)

Punch, Vols. XXV–XXVII (1853–54)

Tradition
Anon. Surgeon, Letter, 8 November 1854 (no. 31)

Connor, Sgt. J. (77th), Letter, 6 November 1854 (no. 28)

Corporal-Drummer (Scots Fusilier Guards), Letter, undated (no. 28)

Evans, Pte. George (63rd), Letter, 6 November 1854 (no. 28)

Gough, Cpl. T. (5th DG), Letter, 27 October 1854 (no. 28)

The War Correspondent (Crimean War Research Society)
Cliff, D., 'Russian Army at the Alma' (Vol. 5, 22)
McGuigan, R., 'British Generals in the Crimea' (Vol. 5, 15; Vol. 6, 21)
Nicasie, M.J., 'Organisation and Strength of the French Army' (Vol. 7, 31)

Manuals and Orders
Army List (1854, 1855)
Field Exercises and Evolutions of the Army (1833)
General Orders for the Army of the East, 20 Apr 1854–31 Dec 1855 (ed. Col. Alexander Gordon, 1856)
Infantry Manual (1854)
Orders, General, Divisional and Brigade, for the Crimea (PRO WO 28/47–107)
Regulations for the Instruction, Formation and Movements of Cavalry (1844, 1851)

Picture Credits

Argyll & Sutherland Highlanders: 42. Army Museums Ogilby Trust: 41, 48, 84-5. Author: 107. Captain J. Clover: 144. Coldstream Guards: 65. Duke of Edinburgh's Royal Regiment: 64. Durham Light Infantry: 99. N.J. Fitzherbert: 30, 72, 124 (top), 140 (top). Grenadier Guards: 92, 101. R.G. Harris: 52 *Illustrated London News*: 22. Imperial War Museum: 29, 50, 81, 126, 130, 131, 136 (left), 142. Manchester City Art Gallery: 55. Major P.J. Mercer: 21 (bottom, right), 59, 78. John Mollo: 25, 58, 73, 74, 86, 102, 117. Middlesex Regiment Museum: 89, 118. National Army Museum: 12, 17, 18, 21 (bottom left), 28 (bottom), 31, 33, 35, 36, 39 (both), 40, 43, 47, 51, 53, 61, 62, 66, 67, 68, 76, 77 (both), 82, 87, 90, 91, 104, 105, 110, 112 (both), 113 (right), 119, 120, 123, 125, 127, 129, 136 (centre, right), 137, 138, 140 (bottom), 143. *Naval & Military Magazine* (1884): 133. Parker Gallery: 11. Private collection: 97. *Punch*: 27, 71. Queen's Royal Irish Hussars: 20, 132. Royal Artillery Institution: 106. Royal Green Jackets: 28 (top). Royal Highland Fusiliers: 108, 113 (left), 114. Royal Hussars: 15. Royal Regiment of Wales: 95. Royal Scots Dragoon Guards: 46. Science Museum: 19, 21 (top). Staff College: 54. Worcestershire & Sherwood Foresters Regiment: 124 (bottom).

References

For the full title of each reference, see Sources.

1 Cheer, Boys, Cheer!
1 Higginson, p. 79.
2 Quoted Priestley, p. 145.
3 Quoted Woodham-Smith, p. 138.
4 Anglesey, *Little Hodge*, p. 8.
5 Regimental Officer, p. 21.
6 Quoted Strachan, *Wellington's Legacy*, p. 173.
7 Quoted Hibbert, p. 126.
8 Windham, p. 67.
9 Ibid., p. 72.
10 Quoted Longford, p. 460.
11 Quoted Strachan, *Wellington's Legacy*, p. 37.
12 Higginson, p. 76.
13 Steevens, p. 43.
14 Quoted Strachan, *Wellington's Legacy*, p. 42.
15 Fortescue, XIII, p. 42.
16 Regimental Officer, p. 351.
17 Ross of Bladensburg, p. 303.
18 Wylly, p. 118.
19 S/Sgt. Macmullen (13th), quoted Anglesey,
   British Cavalry, I, p. 115.
20 *Autobiography of a Working Man* (1848), p. 114.
21 Franks, p. 5.
22 Quoted Small, p. 61.
23 *United Service Magazine* (1898), p. 520.
24 Quoted Strachan, *Wellington's Legacy*, p. 111.
25 Kinglake, II, p. 353.
26 Woodham-Smith, pp. 53–99.
27 Quoted Strachan, *Wellington's Legacy*, p. 111.
28 Letter, 14 November 1854, to Lord
   Braybrooke, Neville, p. 153.
29 Higginson, pp. 205–206.
30 Capt. Sargent, quoted Wylly, p. 52.
31 Regimental Officer, p. 38.
32 Butler, pp. 41–2.

2 A Blow at Sebastopol
1 *Maud*, written in 1854.
2 Quoted Spiers, p. 98.
3 Higginson, p. 126.
4 Regimental Officer, p. 81.
5 Franks, pp. 56–60; Anglesey, *British Cavalry*, II,
   p. 41; Warner, *Fields of War*, p. 50.
6 Lysons, p. 61.
7 Quoted Palmer, p. 61.
8 See Hibbert, pp. 33–34; Kinglake, II, pp.
   107–125.
9 Kinglake, II, p. 139.
10 Quoted Small, p. 26.
11 Letter, quoted Hibbert, p. 51.
12 Quoted ibid., p. 93.
13 Gowing, p. 53.
14 Kinglake, II, p. 455.
15 Quoted Seaton, p. 101.
16 Kinglake, II, p. 337.
17 Clifford, p. 51.
18 Hon. H.A. Neville to his sister, 21 September
   1854, Neville, p. 124.
19 Quoted Small, p. 29.
20 Letter, 'Heights above River Alma, Septr 1854'.
21 Diary, published *Guards Magazine* 1987, 6.
22 Calthorpe, p. 46.
23 Regimental Officer, p. 201.
24 Ibid., p. 212.
25 C. Cattley, former British Consul, Crimea,
   quoted Hibbert, p. 128.
26 Hibbert, p. 131.

3 The Trumpet, the Gallop, the Charge
1 Tennyson, *The Charge of the Heavy Brigade*.
2 *Recollections*, Mollo MSS notes.
3 Diary, quoted Pemberton, p. 77.
4 Letter, Mollo MSS notes.

5 *Recollections*, Mollo MSS notes.

6 *Recollections of One of the Light Brigade*, quoted Mollo MSS notes.

7 Letter, 27 October 1854, Scottish Record Office, GD225/Box 42/14.

8 Russell, p. 122.

9 Quoted Cavendish, p. 100.

10 Ibid.

11 Ibid., p. 103.

12 Whinyates, pp. 128, 130, 131 (probably written by Lt. Fox-Strangways, C Troop; see *Journal of the Society for Army Historical Research*, XIX, p. 98.

13 Quoted Seaton, p. 147.

14 Warner, *Fields of War*, p. 75.

15 Franks, p. 70.

16 Letter, Mollo MSS notes.

17 Heavy Brigade staff-surgeon's letter, 23 December 1854, Neville, pp. 161–5.

18 Whinyates, p. 132.

19 Maj. Thornhill, quoted Anglesey, *Little Hodge*, p. 49.

20 Kinglake, IV, p. 208.

21 Whinyates, pp. 135–6.

22 Kinglake, IV, p 208.

23 Ibid., p. 236.

24 *Strand Magazine*, II, p. 348, quoted Mollo MSS notes.

25 Quoted Anglesey, *British Cavalry*, II, p. 93.

26 *Strand Magazine*, I, p. 287, quoted Mollo MSS notes.

27 Cornet Wombwell (17th), quoted Pemberton, p. 100.

28 Quoted ibid., p. 100.

29 Quoted Harris, p. 219; Selby, p. 154.

30 Mollo MSS notes. Nunnerly's narrative was written in the third person, but has been transposed here into the first for clarity.

31 Lt. Kubitovich, quoted Seaton, p. 150.

32 Loy Smith, pp. 131–3.

33 Quoted Small, pp. 66–7.

34 Quoted Loy Smith, p. 243.

35 Journal, 8th Royal Irish Hussars, Mollo MSS notes.

36 Quoted Anglesey, *British Cavalry*, II, p. 97; Pemberton, p. 104.

37 Paget, pp. 69–70.

38 Quoted Loy Smith, p. 244.

39 Quoted ibid., p. 238.

40 Ibid., pp. 134–9.

41 Quoted ibid., p. 243.

42 *Reflections*, p. 86, quoted ibid., p. 147.

43 Quoted Harris, p. 244.

44 Quoted Seaton, pp. 151, 153, 154.

45 Kinglake, IV, p. 356.

4 The Minié's Murderous Effect

1 Curtiss, p. 321; see also Seaton, pp. 137, 139, 142.

2 Hon. Strange Jocelyn (Scots Fusilier Guards), quoted Airlie, p. 95.

3 Ibid., p. 126.

4 1st Division Order, 16 October 1854, quoted Ross of Bladensburg, p. 120.

5 Field Exercises and Evolutions of the Army (1833), p. 310.

6 Lt. A. Morgan (95th), *Journal of the Society for Army Historical Research*, XLIV, p. 47.

7 Hume, p. 57.

8 Cavendish Taylor, p. 49.

9 Ibid., p. 49.

10 Kinglake, V, p. 8.

11 Dispatch, 27 October 1854, to Brig.-Gen. Pennefather, Champion, p. 58.

12 Kinglake, V, p. 11.

13 Champion, pp. 54–6.

14 Morgan, op. cit., p. 48.

15 Wood, Evelyn, I, p. 50.

16 Hume, p. 58.

17 Quoted Wylly, p. 26.

18 Quoted Bannatyne, p. 412.

19 Letter, 20 November 1854, *Journal of the Society for Army Historical Research*, XLVI, p. 117.

20 Cavendish Taylor, p. 49.

21 Regimental Officer, p. 267.

22 Ibid., p. 266.

23 Champion, p. 54.

24 Morgan, op. cit., p. 48.

5 The English Shall Be Attacked

1 Regimental Officer, p. 141; Warner, *Fields of War*, p. 83.

2 Kinglake, II, p. 267.

3 Bell, p. 251.

4 Quoted Seaton, p. 59.

5 Regimental Officer, p. 309.

6 Quoted Pemberton, p. 48.

7 Regimental Officer, p. 292.

8 Quoted Mollo, *Military Fashion*, p. 136.

9 Regimental Officer, p. 288.

10 Quoted James, p. 28.
11 Quoted Blackmore, p. 204.
12 Curtiss, p. 307.
13 Quoted Kinglake, V, p. 109.
14 Champion, p. 65.
15 Calthorpe, p. 86.
16 Wylly, p. 10.
17 Hume, p. 60.
18 Carmichael MSS, p. 3.
19 Cavendish Taylor, p. 72.
20 Carmichael MSS, p. 6.
21 Woods, II, p. 115.
22 Hume, p. 63.

6 Facing Fearful Odds
1 Hume, p. 61.
2 Carmichael MSS, p. 7.
3 Lieut. A. MacDonald, letter to Capt. Sargent.
4 Quoted Whitehorne, p. 91.
5 Hume, p. 66.
6 Lieut. Elton, letter to his father, quoted
  Pemberton, p. 128.
7 Cavendish Taylor, p. 76.
8 Carmichael MSS, pp. 9, 10.
9 Kinglake, V, p. 216.
10 Ibid., p. 130.
11 Ibid., p. 131.
12 Steevens, p. 123.
13 Kinglake, V, p. 141.
14 Letter, 6 November 1854, Clifford, pp. 88–9.
15 Woolwright, *Records of the 77th Regiment*, p. 84.
16 Ibid., p. 85.
17 Letter, 7 November 1854, quoted *Tradition*, no.
  28, p. 28.
18 Letter, 23 August 1854, quoted *The War
  Correspondent*, vol. 7, no. 2, p. 15.
19 Quoted Hibbert, p. 173.

7 Load, Fire and Charge!
1 *Illustrated London News*, 16 December 1854.
2 Quoted Small, p. 34.
3 Sgt. Ford's statement, quoted Lomax p. 226.
4 Higginson, p. 197.
5 Diary, *Guards Magazine*, 1987, 7.
6 Regimental Officer, p. 288.
7 Woods, II, p. 143; Hume, p. 80.
8 Capt. Tower Diary, quoted Ross of Bladensburg,
  pp. 167–9.
9 Regimental Officer, p. 288.
10 Captain Tower Diary, quoted Ross of

Bladensburg, pp. 167–9.
11 Regimental Officer, p. 288.
12 Kinglake, V, pp. 210–11.
13 Carmichael MSS, p. 10.
14 Fisher MSS, pp. 62, 63.
15 Kinglake, V, p. 242.
16 Windham, p. 71.
17 Letter, 3 April 1856, *Durham Light Infantry
  Journal*, vol. I, p. 150.
18 Sgt. Campbell, quoted Ray, p. 102.
19 Letter to his mother, quoted *VC Gallery
  Catalogue*, 1900.
20 Bancroft's account, quoted *Army Diary*, 5
  November 1971.
21 Champion, p. 66.
22 Carmichael MSS, p. 16.
23 Quoted Windham, p. 63.
24 Ibid., p. 65.
25 Diary, *Guards Magazine*, 1987, 7.
26 Quoted Ray, p. 103.
27 Carmichael MSS, p. 16.
28 Quoted Ward, p. 166.
29 Quoted Ray, p. 103.
30 Higginson, p. 200.
31 Pte. Archer, quoted Kinglake, V, p. 281.
32 Quoted Kinglake, V, p. 282.
33 Diary, *Guards Magazine*, 1987, 7.
34 Kinglake, V, p. 308.
35 Haines MSS, 5, quoting Todleben.
36 Letter, 6 November 1854, *Tradition*, no. 28, p.
  28.
37 Hume, p. 73
38 Letter, 10 November 1854.
39 Letter, 6 November 1854, *Tradition*, no. 28, p.
  28.
40 Haines MSS, p. 4.
41 Woods, II, p. 150.

8 A Hell of a Towelling
1 Collingwood Dickson, quoted Hume, p. 71.
2 Kinglake, V, p. 375.
3 Vaughan Lee letter, 18 November 1854.
4 Letter, 16 October 1854, *Journal of the Society for
  Army Historical Research*, vol. LVIII, p. 101.
5 Haines MSS, p. 6.
6 Letter, 10 November 1854.
7 Ibid.
8 Haines MSS, p. 8.
9 Letter, 10 November 1854.
10 Quoted Pemberton, p. 161.

11 Haines MSS, p. 8.
12 Carmichael MSS, pp. 17–20.
13 Lawson, p. 99.
14 Quoted Bannatyne, p. 419.
15 Regimental Officer, p. 291.
16 Calthorpe, p. 100.
17 Ibid.
18 Fisher MSS, pp. 66, 67.
19 Quoted Small, p. 144.
20 Haines MSS, p. 8.
21 Kinglake, V, p. 425.
22 Letter, 20 November 1854, *Journal of the Society for Army Historical Research*, vol. XLVI, pp. 117–18.
23 Ibid.
24 Capt. Hugh Hibbert, quoted Pemberton, p. 162.
25 Quoted Seaton, p. 176.
26 Quoted ibid., p. 82.
27 Quoted Ray, p. 105.
28 Quoted Pemberton, p. 160.
29 Regimental Officer, pp. 300, 308.
30 Patullo, quoted Pemberton, p. 163.
31 Quoted ibid., p. 164.

9 The Reckoning
1 Bell, p. 248.
2 *Journal of the Society for Army Historical Research*, vol. LX, p. 110.
3 Woods, II, pp. 142–3.
4 Regimental Officer, p. 317.
5 Woods, II, p. 145.
6 Regimental Officer, pp. 316, 317.
7 Ibid., p. 319.
8 Letter, undated, *Tradition*, no. 28, p. 26.
9 Letter dated 8 November 1854, *Tradition*, no. 31, p. 10.
10 Regimental Officer, p. 314.
11 Letter dated 6 November 1854, *Tradition*, no. 28, p. 30.
12 Quoted Small, p. 145.
13 Ibid., p. 36.
14 *Tradition*, no. 28, p. 27.
15 Quoted Compton, *Colonel's Lady and Camp Follower*, p. 103.
16 Taylor, I, p. 129.
17 Gowing, pp. 94–5.
18 Menshikoff's orders, quoted Kinglake, V, p. 491.
19 Sgt. McMillan, *Guards Magazine*, 1987, 8.

20 *Tradition*, no. 28, p. 27.
21 Regimental Officer, p. 112.
22 Keegan, p. 135.
23 Ibid., pp. 46, 185–8.
24 Ibid., pp. 185, 188–194.
25 Ibid., p. 189.
26 Regimental Officer, *Our Veterans of 1854* (1859).
27 Quoted Airlie, p. 176.
28 McNeill and Tulloch Report, June 1855, quoted Strachan, *Wellington's Legacy*, p. 109.
29 *Guards Magazine*, 1987, 7.
30 McNeill and Tulloch, op. cit.
31 Keegan, pp. 137–8.
32 Lehmann, Joseph, *Remember You are an Englishman* (Jonathan Cape, 1977), p. 3.
33 Seaton, p. 136.

10 Noble Exertions
1 Lord Raglan to the Duke of Newcastle, 8 November 1854.
2 Higginson, p. 215.
3 Calthorpe, p. 123.
4 Clifford, p. 120; quoted Hibbert, p. 199.
5 Quoted Gowing, pp. 88–89.
6 Royal Warrant, 5 February 1856.
7 Hamley, p. 157.
8 Dowie, Charles, *The Weary Road* (1929, reprinted 1988), p. 16.
9 MSS Journal, November 1854.
10 Hamley, p. 167.
11 Higginson, pp. 211, 212, 215.
12 Quoted Airlie, p. 147.
13 Windham, pp. 85, 101, 87, 71.
14 Ibid., p. 88.
15 *Punch*, vol. XXVII, p. 64.
16 Clifford, p. 146.
17 Russell, p. 150.
18 Hamley, p. 174.
19 Clifford, p. 155.
20 Quoted Hibbert, p. 296.
21 Gowing, p. 139.
22 MSS Journal, November 1854.
23 Russell, p. 140.

Index